Social Network Analysis in Telecommunications

Wiley & SAS Business Series

The Wiley & SAS Business Series presents books that help senior-level managers with their critical management decisions.

Titles in the Wiley and SAS Business Series include:

Activity-Based Management for Financial Institutions: Driving Bottom-Line Results by Brent Bahnub

Branded! How Retailers Engage Consumers with Social Media and Mobility by Bernie Brennan and Lori Schafer

Business Analytics for Customer Intelligence by Gert Laursen

Business Analytics for Managers: Taking Business Intelligence beyond Reporting by Gert Laursen and Jesper Thorlund

Business Intelligence Competency Centers: A Team Approach to Maximizing Competitive Advantage by Gloria J. Miller, Dagmar Brautigam, and Stefanie Gerlach

Business Intelligence Success Factors: Tools for Aligning Your Business in the Global Economy by Olivia Parr Rud

Case Studies in Performance Management: A Guide from the Experts by Tony C. Adkins

CIO Best Practices: Enabling Strategic Value with Information Technology, Second Edition by Joe Stenzel

Credit Risk Assessment: The New Lending System for Borrowers, Lenders, and Investors by Clark Abrahams and Mingyuan Zhang

Credit Risk Scorecards: Developing and Implementing Intelligent Credit Scoring by Naeem Siddiqi

Customer Data Integration: Reaching a Single Version of the Truth, by Jill Dyche and Evan Levy

Demand-Driven Forecasting: A Structured Approach to Forecasting by Charles Chase

Enterprise Risk Management: A Methodology for Achieving Strategic Objectives by Gregory Monahan

Executive's Guide to Solvency II by David Buckham, Jason Wahl, and Stuart Rose

Fair Lending Compliance: Intelligence and Implications for Credit Risk Management by Clark R. Abrahams and Mingyuan Zhang

Foreign Currency Financial Reporting from Euros to Yen to Yuan: A Guide to Fundamental Concepts and Practical Applications by Robert Rowan

Information Revolution: Using the Information Evolution Model to Grow Your Business by Jim Davis, Gloria J. Miller, and Allan Russell

Manufacturing Best Practices: Optimizing Productivity and Product Quality by Bobby Hull

Marketing Automation: Practical Steps to More Effective Direct Marketing by Jeff LeSueur

Mastering Organizational Knowledge Flow: How to Mae Knowledge Sharing Work by Frank Leistner

Performance Management: Finding the Missing Pieces (to Close the Intelligence Gap) by Gary Cokins

Performance Management: Integrating Strategy Execution, Methodologies, Risk, and Analytics by Gary Cokins

The Business Forecasting Deal: Exposing Bad Practices and Providing Practical Solutions by Michael Gilliland

The Data Asset: How Smart Companies Govern Their Data for Business Success by Tony Fisher

The Executive's Guide to Enterprise Social Media Strategy: How Social Networks Are Radically Transforming Your Business by David Thomas and Mike Barlow

The New Know: Innovation Powered by Analytics by Thornton May

Visual Six Sigma: Making Data Analysis Lean by Ian Cox, Marie A. Gaudard, Philip J. Ramsey, Mia L. Stephens, and Leo Wright

For more information on any of the above titles, please visit **www.wiley.com**.

Social Network Analysis in Telecommunications

Carlos Andre Reis Pinheiro

WILEY

John Wiley & Sons, Inc.

For general information on our other products and services or for technical support, please contact our Customer Care Department within the United States at (800) 762-2974, outside the United States at (317) 572-3993 or fax (317) 572-4002.

Wiley also publishes its books in a variety of electronic formats. Some content that appears in print may not be available in electronic books. For more information about Wiley products, visit our web site at www.wiley.com.

Library of Congress Cataloging-in-Publication Data:

Reis Pinheiro, Carlos Andre, 1940-
  Social network analysis in telecommunications / Carlos Andre Reis Pinheiro.
    p. cm. – (Wiley and SAS business series)
  Includes index.
  ISBN 978-0-470-64754-7 (hardback); 978-1-118-01077-8 (ebk); 978-1-118-01094-5 (ebk); 978-1-118-01095-2 (ebk)
    1. Telecommunication–Customer services.   2. Social networks.
    3. Customer relations–Technological innovations.   I. Title.
  HE7631.R45 2011
  384.068'8–dc22
                                          2010039895

Printed in the United States of America

10 9 8 7 6 5 4 3 2 1

This book is dedicated to my small but crucial social network, which supports me unconditionally. This small social network has been serving as my inspiration to do everything in my life. This book is dedicated to my wife Daniele, my son Lucas, and my daughter Maitê.

Contents

Foreword   ix

Preface   xv

Acknowledgments   xix

Part I: Foundation of Social Network Analysis 1

Chapter 1:   An Introduction to Social Network Analysis 3

Chapter 2:   Formal Methods for Network Analysis 27

Chapter 3:   Theoretical Foundation 41

Chapter 4:   Measures of Power and Influence 65

Part II: Social Network Analysis Case Study 83

Chapter 5:   Telecommunications Environment 85

Chapter 6:   Social Network Modeling 107

Chapter 7:   Assessing the Social Network Model 139

Chapter 8:   Evaluating the Business Results 165

Chapter 9:   Final Remarks for the Case Study 205

Part III: SAS Capabilities for Social Network Analysis 219

Chapter 10: Basic Statistics 221

Chapter 11: Overview of the Link Analysis Node 241

Chapter 12: Visualization Capabilities for Social Network Analysis..255

Chapter 13: A Note about OPTGRAPH..263

Bibliography   273

About the Author   277

Index   279

Foreword

SOME PEOPLE ARE SPECIAL

Large communications service providers lose some customers every month and they work hard to keep this number as low as possible. In fact, most have become quite good at understanding the causes of customer churn and improving customer service to minimize the things that make customers leave. Of course, the competition has also improved at creating offers to attract your customers away. This healthy competition is good for consumers and is the source of great innovations, but it forces even the best service providers to constantly ask, "How can we do better?"

One way to do better is to pay attention to special people–connectors. So who are these connectors and what makes them so special?

THE CONNECTOR WHO CHANGED THE COURSE OF HISTORY

Tensions ran high between American colonists and British soldiers in the spring of 1775. On the morning of April 19th, a few hundred British soldiers set off from Boston to capture a cache of arms and arrest rebel leaders. Marching north into the small towns of Lexington and Concord, the British were astonished to encounter fierce and well organized resistance. Soundly beaten, they beat a hasty retreat back to Boston under constant harassment from colonial militia. The nascent rebellion was given a huge boost in confidence. Thus began the war for American Independence from Great Brittan.

How the colonial militia was notified in time and able to assemble ahead of the advancing British troops is a story well known to American schoolchildren, many of whom have read or perhaps even memorized the Henry Wadsworth Longfellow poem called "The Midnight Ride of Paul Revere," Revere rode his horse through the night alerting militia men of the approaching army. Hundreds quickly turned up ready to fight the heavily armed British troops.

A young man named William Dawes also rode out of Boston the same night with the same message. Starting earlier than Revere, and riding through more populous towns along a more westerly route, Dawes could have been expected to arouse even more rebels. He didn't. The few militia men who responded to Dawes turned up too late to be of much use.

Paul Revere is an essential figure in American History. William Dawes is but a footnote. Both men carried the same message into towns where the people had equal motivations. One started a word-of-mouth epidemic, the other was mostly ignored. But why? Malcolm Gladwell proposes an answer to this question in his 1999 book *The Tipping Point: How Little Things Can Make a Big Difference*. According to Gladwell, Paul Revere was a special type of person—a connector.

William Dawes was a shoemaker—age 26. He rode through towns knocking on random doors and shouting that the British were coming. But people in these towns didn't know who he was, didn't have confidence that his message represented an immediate threat. They didn't see their neighbors doing anything so they went back to bed, figuring they would check it out in the morning. Paul Revere on the other hand was well known. He was a successful businessman who at age 40, had been at the center of events in and around Boston for years. When Paul Revere rode into a town he didn't knock on a random door but went straight to the local militia commanders. Opening their doors in the middle of the night and recognizing Paul Revere on the doorstep, they sprung into action, alerted their neighbors, and spread the word. Revere alerted enough of the right people, so the alarm reached the tipping point.

COMMUNICATIONS SERVICE PROVIDERS AND THE TIPPING POINT

This story is a classic example of how connectors are essential to get an idea to tip. But what can this history lesson from 235 years ago tell us about today's fast-moving high-technology marketplace? Instead of riding around on horses shouting to each other, we use mobile phones, e-mail, and social network sites. But these special people, the connectors, are still with us. The technology may have changed but connectors still influence our behavior and they are worth paying attention to.

Connectors know lots of people, many times the number of people the average person knows. But, they also know essential facts about people. Chances are you know someone like this, someone that seems to know everyone and stops to talk wherever they go, but it isn't all small talk. Connectors know what to talk about with the people they meet. If you tell a connector about your hobby they can give you the names of several people who share that interest. Tell them about a problem you have and they will give you the names of people who can be helpful. Tell them about a great new product and a connector will spread the word. Research has shown that most people have at one time or another found a job because a connector put them in contact with someone they did not know who helped them get the job. Connectors play a vital role in our social networks.

The impact of connectors to a small neighborhood business is quite obvious. A local restaurant owner would obviously want to give his best table to a customer who is very influential in the neighborhood while the lone traveling businessman will likely find himself seated near the kitchen. I bet tavern owners in colonial Boston bent over backward to make sure Paul Revere had a good table, a well-prepared meal, and excellent service. The smart tavern owner would realize that he had more customers on nights when Paul Revere stopped in, he observed other customers saying hello to Paul and asking him to please join them. People stayed longer and spent more money when Paul was around. Then as now, owning a tavern is high risk business venture and the presence of one man like Paul Revere can determine if the business will tip toward profitability.

A communications service provider is not a local tavern. The managers can't personally know 10 million customers. Yet the impact of connectors can be vital clues to what others will be doing in the future. Lose a connector to a competitor and next quarter your churn numbers may shoot up. Entice a connector away from your competitor and others may follow. Have a new service, get the word to a connector and see how fast it spreads.

But how does a communications service provider know that someone is a connector? You can't just put a check box on the service application that says, "Are you a connector, yes or no?" Connector is not a binary status like gender. Sure connectors could be expected to be heavy service users, but just adding up call minutes and numbers of messages is not a good indicator, because these calls and messages may be only a small number of people. Looking at the number of people someone calls won't help either. A taxi driver may speak with hundreds of people a month, but if he's just arranging pick-ups, he's not a connector.

THE ROLE OF MAVENS IN SOCIAL NETWORKS

The ideas connectors spread are not always their own. Paul Revere didn't see the British troops on the move before setting off to spread the word. A stable boy overheard a conversation between British officers. Other people saw an unusual amount of activity on British ships and around their barracks. They knew exactly where to go with this news, to the home of Paul Revere. Connectors don't just indiscriminately spread the word, they consolidate ideas, filter the important from the trivial, and think about who would want to know that idea.

I attended a wireless industry conference last year and met a man named Michael Gartenberg. To say that Michael is talkative would be an understatement. He has a lot to say, but he is not interested in small talk or talking about himself. He asked me a lot of questions to find out what I was interested in. As he learned more about me he started offering me all kinds of suggestions. Easily switching between his three handsets, he showed me dozens of applications and could talk in depth about how they worked on different platforms. Michael is a geek, no doubt about it, but a special kind of geek—a maven. Mavens, Malcolm Gladwell says, are one of the other types of people who contribute to tipping points.

Michael Gartenberg is very smart and loves to play with his gadgets. He knows a lot about the industry and has a widely read blog.

He makes his living as a consultant, but never asked me about getting consulting business from SAS. From my perspective, his motivation seemed to be more about helping me than impressing me. According to Gladwell mavens combine intense curiosity with a passion to spread their knowledge in a way that is helpful.

By paying attention to mavens we can spot new ideas. Mavens share those ideas with connectors, and by watching connectors we can see which ideas become trends and spread through a social network. If you have a new product or service, show it first to a maven who will help you improve it. If a maven likes it, he will pass it along to connectors and this new idea may be one of the few that reach the tipping point.

The author of this book is a maven. I have had the pleasure of meeting Dr. Pinheiro at several SAS events and he is a classic example of Gladwell's definition. By leading analytic projects in a broad range of subjects, including customer segmentation, churn prediction, payment risk, customer profitability, and revenue assurance, Dr. Pinheiro has become one of the world's top experts in telecommunications data and analytical models. His willingness to share his knowledge has benefitted many SAS® users. Dr. Pinheiro's presentation at SAS forums are always well attended and highly rated.

Among our telecommunications industry customers, social network analysis is one of the most frequently discussed topics. A recent survey of telecommunications service providers by industry analyst firm The Yankee Group validates that social network analysis is one of their top areas for new investment.

It is with great pleasure that I am able to introduce this book, which will guide SAS users on every aspect of social network analysis, from theory to practice. By applying the principles and examples laid out by Dr. Pinheiro, your attempts to increase profitability will reach a tipping point.

Ken King, Product Manager, SAS Institute Inc.

Preface

Traditional methods and techniques for identifying patterns in business data—such as K-means, self-organizing maps of Kohonen, and others—can achieve good results. However, they are usually focused on identifying individuals' behaviors. They are based on a set of information about individuals and are clustered according to similar characteristics. All behaviors are placed in one of those cluster groups, so presumably individuals included in each group have similar characteristics and behaviors. However, as with any analytical model, it is an approximation of similar behaviors. Each group holds a particular average behavior. Each observation inside the group holds its own behavior. Some observations have behavior similar to the average group, some do not. By being aware that a clustering model is an approximation, any practical action should consider, for instance, the closest observations to the center of each cluster, assuring that these observations hold behavior similar to the cluster. Some particular clusters exhibit an average behavior. Some observations (customers) are close to this behavior, some are not. This is the approximation. The closer to the cluster's center the observations are, the closer their individual behavior will be to the average cluster.

Social network analysis is also an approximation, but about the group rather than about the individual. The characteristics that are taken into consideration are not ones assigned to the individuals, but rather to the groups' behaviors and the connections' attributes. The main objective is to gather knowledge, not about the individuals, but about the group in which these individuals are set. More important than the individual's characteristics is the group behavior, how the individuals inside a group relate to each other. In most cases the relationships among the individuals are the key to recognizing the group's behavior. The individuals' attributes are nothing more than additional information about the nodes inside a network. The links assigned to the network reveal the group's behavior and the features of the community.

Attributes in relation to nodes and links depict the network structure and the knowledge of communities inside the entire network. This approach allows companies to understand beyond the customers, recognizing the relationships, and, hence, identifying the influential nodes, the ones that marketing campaigns should target.

The first part of this book describes the theory of social network analysis, presenting a sociological perspective, where this methodology started, but most important, the mathematical foundations that allow us to create metrics and compute measures to analyze the network in practice. Distinct network measurements and methods of calculation are discussed in this first part. The majority of the theoretical foundations presented in this book are based on the work of professors Robert A. Hanneman and Mark Riddle, of the Department of Sociology at the University of California, Riverside.

This first part also covers the concept of social network analysis, drawn from sociological studies. A theoretical foundation, based primarily on the graph theory, is presented in order to establish a base for the concept of social networks, the possible measures, and the structures assigned to the social networks in general. Formal methods used for the presentation and analysis of social networks are covered in Part II. Methods used to measure social networks are presented, depicting the algorithms and the methods used to compute the most relevant measures of centrality and power.

Part II of this book presents a case study, in which the concepts covered in Part I, through the use of SAS® capabilities, were used to distinguish results in terms of business challenges. The methodology used for social network analysis was applied to a telecommunications company in order to understand the customers' relationship, and, hence, to identify influential customers from the perspective of distinct businesses. Two different business issues were addressed by using social network analysis to prove the value of this approach to telecommunications. The first issue dealt with the recognition of influential customers in terms of churn events, and, therefore, identification of the crucial customers who should be retained. The second approach dealt with bundle diffusion, identifying the central customers who should be targeted by marketing campaigns in order to spread the bundle quickly and effectively through the network.

This case study was elaborated, developed, and deployed during postdoctoral research at Dublin City University. This research was accomplished inside the Business Informatics Group at the School of Computing, under the direction of Dr. Markus Helfert.

Part III of this book presents the SAS capabilities used to address the challenge of social network analysis. Different modules of SAS solutions can be deployed to analyze social networks, compute measurements, calculate scores, identify communities, and draw the network structure. SAS® Enterprise Miner™ features the Link Analysis node, which provides a wide range of functionality to create and analyze the relationship among the nodes according to their links. Macros related to the Link Analysis node will be described in an isolated way, presenting a distinct approach to SAS capabilities when used to analyze social networks. Multidimensional scaling, used to establish coordinates based on the distance among the nodes will be shown as well, as an alternative method of identifying clusters of nodes based on the strength of their relationships. Some additional features to plot a network structure will be presented, such as using the macro %ds2const, which draws different types of networks.

In Part III, basic statistics are presented as a complementary way to analyze social networks. Statistical processes used to sort, create frequencies, identify extreme values, compute coordinates based on multidimensional scale and clustering nodes, and link connected components and communities are also presented at the end of Part III. The basic task of social network analysis is computing network measures. A more complex task is to analyze the network measures upon a particular business perspective. The measurements of nodes and links should be compared according to a particular target, highlighting the influential nodes, the strong links, the leaders of the network, as well as the followers. The analysis of the network measurements reveals the main characteristics of the social network and makes it possible to understand it from a business point of view.

Acknowledgments

I would like to thank everyone who assisted me in the production of this book. The actions of many people from all over the world were instrumental to the success of this project, especially the support of my family, discussions with my colleagues, and kindness from my friends.

A special thanks to my supervisor Dr. Markus Helfert, who led me through eighteen months of research during a postdoctoral term at Dublin City University. Dr. Markus leads the Business Informatics Group at the School of Computing where a tremendous amount of research in data management and analytics takes place. Thanks also to all members of the Business Informatics Group for sharing ideas and discussing projects and applications with no objections.

Many thanks to James Davey, Gavin Kiernan, and Brian Buckley for making available all telecommunications data that supported this research, and, most important, for sharing such valuable knowledge during this study.

Also thanks to my colleagues from SAS Ireland, John Farrelly, Eamonn McQuaid, Eoin Byrne, John Curran, Karl Langan, Sarunas Tankeliavicius, Kielty Hughes, Alan Gormley, David Ferguson, Martin Duffy, Turlough Fitzpatrick, Paul Power, John Lyons, Julianne Purcell, and Linda Moran. Special thanks to John Curran, Karl, and Eoin, who shared their very good knowledge of analytics.

Very special thanks to SAS Press, particularly to Stacey Hamilton and Shelley Sessoms, for helping me in this endeavor. This book would not have been possible without the unique involvement of Stacey. Thanks also to Stacey Rivera from Wiley for conducting such a rigorous review process.

Thanks to Ken King for his knowledge of telecommunications, analytics, SAS® software, and many other things. Also thanks for the great foreword and the amazing story.

Over these 18 months of research at Dublin City University, my family and I had the privilege of sharing great moments with our extended family and friends. We realized that in terms of a social network, the following group of people became very important to build our own. I really appreciate the kindness and friendship from all our "visitors." We certainly have built the best social network ever. Thus, many thanks to my mother Suely; to Alex and Irma; to my sister Joseanne and my brother-in-law Gustavo; to my father-in-law Ivan and my mother-in-law Ana; to my "brother" Andre Brugger; to Rita and Sonia; to Claudio and Daniela; to Marco Aurelio and Rosane; to Marcelo and Patricia; to Michele and Daniel; and finally to Graziela and Eduardo. This is the sort of social network that never ends.

PART I

Foundation of Social Network Analysis

The first part of this book presents the basic theories of social network analysis. Chapter 1 introduces the foundation of this social science and the approaches to analyze social relations. Chapter 2 presents the formal theory and the most important concepts of social network analysis. Chapter 3 describes the formal methods to analyze social networks. Finally, Chapter 4 presents the most relevant measurements of social network analysis, such as degree, power, and influence.

An Introduction to Social Network Analysis

This chapter introduces the origins of social network analysis as a social science. A basic approach of studying social relations comes from the 1950s, when it was an important tool in understanding relationships among people within some particular social groups. How this approach evolved during the years is also briefly described, as well as how mathematical concepts, such as graph theory, were introduced to create a formal method to analyze and provide relevant information about social groups.

Therefore, Chapter 1 presents the evolution of social network analysis, from its appearance as a social science until its development into a more formal method based on mathematical concepts.

EVOLUTION OF SOCIAL NETWORK ANALYSIS

Social network analysis takes into consideration the fact that social life is relations among individuals. Behaviors within a network are critical to understanding social connections, and—more important—the

3

implications that they create inside a community. The most relevant implication is how particular people inside a social network can influence others to perform similar events. In terms of business, what makes an individual a leader or follower? What is the impact when a telecommunications company loses an influential customer within a social network? Are companies able to lead other customers afterward? Are companies able to lead other customers to purchase new products and bundles or to consume new services? Understanding the consequences from the new perspective of social relations can allow companies to predict new business events and to focus the customer relationship management more accurately.

The study of social networks is formally defined as a set of *nodes*, which consist of *network members*. Those nodes are connected by different types of relations, which are formally defined as *links*. Network analysis study takes all those connections as the primary building blocks of the social world. It does not collect just unique types of data, but traditional analysis takes into consideration individual attributes. Social network analysis also considers the attributes of relations from a fundamentally different perspective than that adopted by individualist or attribute-based social science. Traditional methods of data analysis usually consider individual attributes from all observations in order to analyze the information available. What is the average characteristic from a particular population of companies, employees, customers, or markets? Particularly in telecommunications, it is quite common to analyze the individual data to understand customer behavior, such as the average billing, type of payment, frequency and amount of service usage, and so on. Besides the individual attributes, social network analysis considers all information about the relationships among the network members (nodes). As a matter of fact, the information about the relations among the individuals within a social network is usually more relevant than the individual attributes of the individuals. The relations among the individuals can tell more about customers than their individual attributes. This is the basic difference between data analysis and social network analysis. What you are is not as important as how you behave and connect with others.

Alexandra Marin and Barry Wellman published a survey describing some case studies about social relations. According to them,

A conventional approach to understanding high-innovation regions such as Silicon Valley would focus on the high levels of education and expertise common in the local labor market. Education and expertise are characteristics of the relevant actors. In contrast, a network analytic approach to understanding the same phenomenon would draw attention to the ways in which mobility between educational institutions and multiple employers has created connections between organizations. Thus, people moving from one organization to another bring their ideas, expertise, and tacit knowledge with them. They also bring with them the connections they have made to coworkers, some of whom have moved on to new organizations themselves. This pattern of connections between organizations, in which each organization is tied through its employees to multiple other organizations, allows each to draw on diverse sources of knowledge. Since combining previously disconnected ideas is the heart of innovation and a useful problem-solving strategy, this pattern of connections—not just the human capital of individual actors—leads to accelerating rates of innovation in the sectors and regions where it occurs.[1]

The most relevant fact of analysis here is not the individual attributes or characteristics. Certainly, all the information about the individual is quite important—the level of education, papers published, conferences attended, researches conducted, and so on. However, from a perspective of innovation and how data evolves over time, the relationship among the individuals and the institutions with which they are associated are more important than the attributes of the individuals. The way individuals share their ideas, compile their works, and how their institutions collaborate their resources is more influential than individual skills, talents, and initiatives.

A social network is basically comprised of a set of nodes connected by one or more links, which represent distinct types of relationships. For instance, in telecommunications, the nodes are usually assigned to the customers; landlines, broadband, mobiles, or whatever other type of communication device. The links, especially in the mobile environment, are assigned to the calls, the texts, the messages, e-mail, and any sort of communication's connections that can be collected somehow.

The conception of nodes and links can change according to the subject of interest or the business area which is under consideration. In the financial or banking industry, the nodes can be not only the customers but the accounts, and links can be represented by transactions, policies, claims, mortgages, payments, and so on.

One of the most important stages in this sort of exploratory analysis, particularly involving social networks, is to properly define the role of the nodes and the links. This phase is certainly crucial to find applications in relation to business issues. If you do not define roles of nodes and links, you will be able to build and analyze a social network, but it will not lead to applications for business.

The task of choosing which kind of available data to use, based on different sort of problems that are particular to different kinds of businesses, constitutes the work of the network analysts. As a matter of fact, for the same industry, but considering different problems, the same data can be used differently. For example, consider the telecommunications environment. Telephone numbers are usually thought of as nodes and calls are thought of as links. However, if the subject matter is fraud, and the identification of the perpetrators of fraud is the focus, the telephone number could be viewed as a link that connects two distinct individuals. In this way, the telephone number can be used to compose a node for a particular problem and can be used to compose a link for another one.

Indeed, the first endeavor in a social network analysis approach is to properly define what the nodes are supposed to be and what the links are supposed to be. In telecommunications, it is quite straightforward to define customers as nodes and calls as links, especially in mobile operations, even though there is more than one type of link in mobile operations, such as calls, text messages, multimedia messages, e-mail, and even Internet access. In the case of Internet access, what is the destination node? Is it a Web site? Even in a straightforward scenario such as telecommunications, we can visualize more than one type of node and more than one type of link. Thinking about landlines, where the relationship between the device and customer is not one to one, nodes can be defined in different ways. For instance, the nodes can be defined as the residents in a household, splitting the links among them, or as the household itself, aggregating the links into the telephone number.

In some industries more complex than telecommunications, such as insurance and banks, it is possible to identify distinct types of nodes and links, according to the sort of business problem to be addressed.

Also, when there is more than one type of node to be considered and more than one type of link to connect nodes, it is possible to include different weights for nodes and links as a way to distinguish them based on some particular rule.

Laumann identified three distinct approaches to select nodes and links according to the specification of the edge of the social network.[2] The first approach is based on position, considering the members of a particular organization or community as the nodes within the network. The second approach is based on event, considering the nodes with their positions well defined within an organization or community as members of the network. The third approach is based on the relation, considering the members of an organization or community based on a set of nodes that clearly present strong relationships within a particular network.

All these approaches can occur simultaneously and can also be applied at the same time for some different types of networks. In this way you define not just the nodes and links but also the boundaries of the network, which then helps to define nodes and links to be included in the study of communities.

In telecommunications, for instance, customers can be considered as a position-based approach, where any type of customer can be considered as a particular node. Also, in most cases, companies affect their own customers, and, therefore, the boundary of their network analysis could be considered to be their own network. However, considering the high migration of customers among telecommunications companies, especially the number portability in mobile operations, some specific mobile numbers could be accepted as members of the inside network. These external nodes could be quite relevant for understanding churn and customer acquisition, and thus they can be included in the internal network analysis process. Finally, the consideration of the population of interest is crucial for network analysis. By considering any telephone as a customer and then as a node, some telephone numbers should be discarded from the network, such as emergency numbers, customer care numbers, some particular services based on automatic response units, and so on. Those types of numbers do not represent a node in the social perspective. In addition, when analyzing the individual customers in terms of relationships, it is possible to consider all links and all nodes, but in order to compare usage among the customers, perhaps some kinds of customers should be excluded from the entire population, such as private companies and special individuals playing professional roles.

Because the process of identifying nodes and links is not straightforward at all, considerable time and effort should be spent in this stage. This recognition process is a key factor in whether social network analysis succeeds or not.

When social networks are considered, the relations between the nodes should be considered rather than their isolated attributes. In this way, the individuals hold a set of attributes that must be analyzed when the network is built. In order to study the effects of attributes such as average revenue, billing, payment history, active products and services, and so on, they should be sorted to reveal their relevance in the network environment.

A particular method to consider the impact of some attributes in social network analysis is presented in the case study presented in Part II. The effect of business attributes in relation to the social network analysis over time can reveal the average individual behavior assigned to some business events. For instance, when analyzing product and service acquisition, it is possible to correlate influential customers, the ones who lead other customers to purchase the same type of product or service, and then highlight the average values of some particular business attributes for those leaders. By doing this, companies are able to identify the leaders for particular business events; in addition, companies can identify their average behavior in terms of usage and characteristics.

It is important to note that, when attributes are taken separately, individuals with common attributes can produce the same outcome or be considered to have the same value of corporate importance. This isolated attribute analysis can link individuals with same average values for those business variables, even if they have completely distinct behavior in terms of usage or relationship.

Conversely, when examining a social network and its behavior, individuals are analyzed by their relationships (strength, frequency, importance, etc.). This distinct approach might lead the analysis in a completely different direction: evaluating individuals with common attributes in distinctive ways, hence producing totally different outcomes. In contrast to the evaluation of individual attributes, the network analysis can put together nodes with similar behavior in terms of relationships even though they hold completely different values in their individual attributes. The key to grouping similar nodes is the relationship rather than the attributes.

The relevant message here is that individuals with common characteristics can behave in completely distinctive ways. Using traditional clustering techniques, these individuals might be considered similar because of their attributes and would probably fit in the same group. However, based on social network analysis, those same individuals would fit into distinct groups or communities. Even though individuals with common attributes can behave in similar ways, in social network analysis, the most relevant analysis is the relationship with the neighbor nodes instead of their own characteristics.

By analyzing the behavior embedded in social networks, it is possible to exploit different levels of patterns. The results are especially useful for marketing, especially in diffusing processes related to product and services acquisition. Similar behaviors can lead a business to purchase new types of products and services, or even churn.

In most industries, especially in telecommunications, churn and product and service acquisition can be understood as a chain of events. In other words, some key customers, the leaders, can lead other customers to leave after they churn or they can lead other customers to acquire similar products and services after them. For this reason, it is crucial to target the right subset of customers in a particular campaign, whether it is in relation to customer retention or to product acquisition. The right set of customers can diffuse products or services within the telecommunications network.

Also, analyzing social networks requires looking at individuals not as a group but, instead, as a *community*. A group is comprised of individuals with similar characteristics, whereas a community is grouped together by their similar behavior.

Social network analysis should also take into consideration business strategy, which indicates different weights of importance to be used in the network analysis of nodes and links. In telecommunications, for instance, you might consider different weights according to distinct types of links, such as calls, text messages, multimedia messages, e-mails, and so on. In order to increase a specific text message service, for example, social network analysis should consider the weight of the links established based on text messages as highly relevant in the network relationship, rather than the calls themselves. Similarly, in order to increase a particular roaming package, all roaming calls should be considered more important than other calls. Although all distinct types of communications or relationships should be considered in the analyses—such as local calls, national calls, international, texts, multimedia, and so on—the specific roaming calls should hold a higher weight than other calls in order to highlight the relevance of roaming in the particular study.

BUILDING SOCIAL NETWORKS BASED ON NODES AND LINKS

Social networks analysis is not really a brand-new discipline even though it has been gaining popularity in academia. In terms of academic approach, researchers have published experiments to describe the connections among people in distinct types of environments. In addition to the experiments, several theories in relation to social network analysis, and with respect to algorithms to calculate network measures have been published. One of the oldest articles about social network analysis is the one known as the Small World Experiment.[3] It is still fairly well known, and it is about the length of the path in a particular social network.

Stanley Milgram conducted some experiments in order to examine the average length of the path for some particular networks. The main objective of these experiments was to suggest that the human communities were not too big, where one individual could reach any other one by some maximum number of steps, or, in other words, by a certain number of intermediate individuals between them. The research outcomes have, indeed, suggested that the networks were characterized by short paths among the nodes considering the number of those intermediate steps. One particular experiment was associated with the famous phrase "six degrees of separation." However, Milgram himself had never used this term to refer to his experiment.

Milgram coauthored the experiment called the Small World Problem, which created a great deal of publicity. This publicity was mostly supported by several studies conducted simultaneously and focusing on the concept that the world was becoming highly interconnected. Bear in mind that this particular experiment took place in 1967. It is not difficult to imagine now the impact this concept had, viewing the possible types of relationships people could establish, with the use of different devices, technologies, and geographies.

Milgram's experiment intended to highlight the likelihood that two randomly selected people would know each other, regardless of the length of the path or, in other words, the number of steps (nodes and links) between them. This is certainly one way to solve the problem. A straight method to solve the Small World Problem is by calculating the average length of path connecting any two distinct nodes inside the network. Milgram's experiment ultimately created an algorithm to calculate the average number of links that connected any two nodes.

The procedure in relation to the Small World Problem was established in the paper by Jeffrey Travers and Stanley Milgram called "An Experimental Study of the Small World Problem."

> The procedure may be summarized as follows: an arbitrary target person and a group of starting persons were selected, and an attempt was made to generate an acquaintance chain from each starter to the target. Each starter was provided a document and asked to begin moving it by mail toward the target. The document described the study, named the target, and asked the recipient to become a participant by sending the document on. It was stipulated that the document could be sent only to a first-name acquaintance of the sender. The sender was urged to choose the recipient in such a way as to advance the progress of the document toward the target; several times of information about the target were provided to guide each new sender in his choice of recipient. Thus, each document made its way along the

acquaintance chain of indefinite length, a chain which would end only when it reached the target or when someone along the way declined to participate. Certain basic information, such as age, sex and occupation, was collected for each participant.

PARTICIPANTS. Starting Population. The starting population for the study was comprised of 296 volunteers. Of these, 196 were residents of the state of Nebraska, solicited by mail. Within this group, 100 were systematically chosen owners of blue-chip stocks; these will be designated by Nebraska stockholders throughout this paper. The rest were chosen from the population at large; these will be termed the Nebraska random group. In addition to the two Nebraska groups, 100 volunteers were solicited through an advertisement in a Boston newspaper (the Boston random group). Each member of the starting population became the first link in a chain of acquaintances directed at the target person.

INTERMEDIARIES. The remaining participants in the study, who numbered 453 in all, were in effect solicited by other participants; they were acquaintances selected by previous participants as people likely to extend the chain toward the target. Participation was voluntary. Participants were not paid, nor was money or other reward offered as incentive for completion of chains.[4]

Travers and Milgram had also defined the *rules of participation* for this particular study, which described how the participants should include personal information and forward the document ahead. The rules also defined the *target person* as a stockholder who lives in Boston, Massachusetts; the *roster*, who was the person to avoid looping; and the *tracer cards*, which were business cards that requested a reply and contained information about the participant and the person who sent the card.

INFLUENCE

The idea behind finding out the number of degrees that separate people in a network has triggered further concepts about how people behave inside the network rather than the number of connections they have. In terms of business, it is more important to know how each individual behaves inside the network than it is to know how many connections there are among people—that is, of prime importance is their correlated nodes through their connected links.

Considering that case of six degrees of separation between any two nodes in a network, the important thing to be analyzed is the role of each one of those six nodes inside the network: how they connect the other nodes, how strong their links are, how central they are in the network, how many short paths they belong to, and so on. These answers drive the network analysis to identify the influential nodes, the leaders, the followers, and also the isolated or irrelevant nodes.

According to Simmel, social ties are primarily based on viewing components as isolated units. However, those components are better understood as being at the intersection of particular relations and as deriving their defining characteristics from the intersection of these relations. He argues that society itself is nothing more than a web of relations. He wrote:

> The significance of these interactions among men lies in the fact that it is because of them that the individuals, in whom these driving impulses and purposes are lodged, form a unity, that is, a society. For unity in the empirical sense of the word is nothing but the interaction of elements. An organic body is a unity because its organs maintain a more intimate exchange of their energies with each other than with any other organism; a state is a unity because its citizens show similar mutual effects.[5]

This statement is an argument against the premise that a society is just a bunch of individuals who react individually and independently to particular circumstances according to their personal desires. Based on his belief that the social world is found in interactions rather than in an aggregation of individuals, Simmel argued that the primary work of sociologists is to study patterns among these interactions rather than to study the individual motives.

Simmel wrote in the same study:

> A collection of human beings does not become a society because each of them has an objectively determined or subjectively impelling life-content. It becomes a society

only when the vitality of these contents attains the form
of reciprocal influence; only when one individual has an
effect, immediate or mediate, upon another, is mere
spatial aggregation or temporal succession transformed
into society.[6]

There also are some formal theories that are focused on the
study of the effects of relationships among the individuals rather
than on the attributes that describe the individuals themselves. For
instance, if communities within social networks are densely connected, you can expect to find short paths linking most pairs of
nodes.

By using these theories, mathematical models and computer simulations can be built to analyze social networks describing the patterns
inside the entire network and also in several smaller communities
within the network. The study of internal communities, whether
densely or sparsely connected, is quite relevant to analyze some business actions over time, such as churn, diffusion, and even fraud
events. Dense communities tie their members to each other and,
therefore, are often targeted in retention and sales campaigns. Sparse
communities are useful in analyzing patterns of behavior of the
overall network.

Community analysis is quite relevant for business purposes and
can reveal distinctive patterns inside networks that can be used to
target particular marketing campaigns. In telecommunications, for
instance, where the entire network is huge and sparse, the identifications of smaller internal communities comprising tight connections
can be used to create specific bundles of products and services directed
toward particular patterns of behavior. Highly dense communities
inside sparse networks can be viewed as a single unit, and, therefore,
individual churn from this unit (or a product acquisition from it) can
represent cascading events; that is, one churn or one purchase can
trigger a chain of churns or purchases.

The average behavior in a very tight community is usually well
distributed throughout the members of this community, which means
that the values assigned to the individual members are similar to the
average values of the entire community. Because of this, it is easy to
establish bundles of products and packet of services for the entire

community when the average behavior is well distributed among the members.

STRUCTURES OF SOCIAL NETWORKS

According to the type of social network and its structure, the outcomes in terms of metrics and measurement can be quite different, indicating distinct approaches to exploit the networks.

Based on the study of Borgatti,[7] there are four main categories to classify networks according to their arguments. The *argument transmission* represents networks in which connections are widely distributed by their nodes. *Argument adaptation* represents two nodes with similar network positions that are likely to follow similar behaviors when faced with similar circumstances. *Argument binding* represents two subnetworks bound to each other so that they act as a single network. Finally, *argument exclusion* represents a particular link that, because of its presence, excludes another link within the network.

The transmission argument in telecommunications is quite relevant. As long as some types of communications, such as text messages, remain popular, the connections inside the network can spread faster and wider than before. Considering particular massive marketing campaigns and spam messages, this transmission argument can be very relevant to analyze network structure and behavior.

The adaption argument has two distinct aspects, occurring simultaneously or sequentially. When two nodes perform the same event at the same time, and they do not hold any kind of connection, we can consider that similar positions inside subnetworks or similar constraints and circumstances could take in place. However, if they do hold some sort of connection or, even more important, if they hold a strong relationship, we can consider that they have exerted some influence on each other. They may have previously decided to follow the same event at the same time. In the first case, the adaptation argument is more about the environment and scenario, but in the second case, this argument is more about influence.

The binding argument can be closely associated to a concept called articulation point. The articulation point is the node that links two connected components. Connected components are a set of nodes that can reach each other, no matter what path they take to do it. Nodes that play the articulation point role usually are central nodes, connecting small groups, subnetworks, or even communities. All nodes as articulation points can be targets for further analysis.

The exclusion argument is not so applicable in telecommunications. For example, in social networks based on employer and employees, if two persons are married, they cannot work in the same company. In this way, the married link excludes the workmate link. However, in telecommunications, it is possible to have several types of links at the same time, such as calls, texts, media, e-mail, and so on.

ANALYSES APPROACH FOR SOCIAL NETWORKS

All data in relation to networks are critical to performing any sort of exploratory analysis. This includes information about the nodes and the links, as well as the types and weights assigned to the nodes and links.[8]

One of the most important analyses in relation to social networks is the comparison among distinct behaviors. These behaviors are assigned to the nodes as well as to the links. Most often, the links' behaviors—their frequency, relevance, regency, and so on—can change the importance of the node assigned to the links. Thinking about telecommunications networks, customers who hold several links to very important nodes also become important. It is possible to include, in the social network analysis, individual attributes, such as customer segmentation, customer value (a corporate score for each customer), average billing, and then use them in the network analysis. In the same way, it is possible to include individual attributes for the links, such as the price of the call, the duration, the time, the frequency, among others, and then use these attributes in the network analysis. Those distinct attributes can create different weights for nodes and links, and thus completely change the network analysis. Once again, nodes comprising high value links become more important, and links connecting high–value nodes also become important.

Several measures can be calculated to represent the properties or characteristics of the network, as well as the subnetworks or subgraphs within it. Metrics in relation to networks include the number of connections a particular node has. This particular metric can be split into two distinct measures, describing the number of incoming connections and the number of outgoing connections. This is quite relevant in the telecommunications industry, representing the value of the outgoing and incoming calls among customers. Other network metrics include the path through the network, such as the length of the paths connecting nodes, the distance among them, how central the nodes are within the network, and so on.

Also, the distance of these relations can show some relevant features about the network's structure. The strength of the links is very important to establish the relationship behavior among the nodes. A particular link between two nodes can be very central to the entire network. Therefore, not only can the nodes be valued in terms of closeness but also the links can be measured in terms of how they connect nodes within the network.

In addition, when a network analysis takes place, the properties of the entire network should be calculated. Properties such as the number of degrees for each node, incoming and outgoing links, centrality, closeness, betweenness, and influence over the other nodes should all be calculated as well and compared to each other. This comparison analysis enhances the pattern of behavior for the entire network but especially of the individual behavior for each node and link inside the network, revealing the high-value nodes in terms of network measures.

Networks can also be analyzed by dividing the entire population into small connected communities. Similar to the comparison analysis for nodes and links, a comparison evaluation based on the small internal communities can reveal how the network is clustered and which communities are more important in terms of network metrics. In this way, it is possible to see that the average network metrics for the communities' nodes are also the network metrics for the communities themselves.

Community analysis can describe the network behavior, but, mostly, it is useful to highlight unexpected clusters within the network in terms of behavior. When considering usage, unusual groups of nodes—in telecommunications, for instance—can represent a possible set of customers committing suspect or fraudulent events.

Even if these customers are not committing fraud but are just high-usage customers of telecommunications services, this particular group of nodes should be handled in a distinct way by the company, protecting them from competitors.

GRAPH THEORY AND SOCIAL NETWORK ANALYSIS

Social network analysis can be explored and explained by two distinct approaches: by social sciences, as described so far in this chapter, and also by mathematical science, described briefly at the end of this chapter and later in the book (Part II).

The mathematical science that describes and explains the social network analysis is graph theory. Several concepts and measures in relation to social network analysis come from graph theory. A great advantage of graph theory is the mathematical formulas that can be applied in computing and, therefore, in business problems.

Graphs can be considered mathematical structures used to model pairs of relations between distinct objects. The study of graphs should consider a set of vertices or nodes and a set of edges or links, which connect pairs of vertices or nodes. Basically, these are the same explanations that the social sciences make, but now the explanations use mathematical formalism. Based on formal formulas, it is possible to implement algorithms and hence apply social network analysis to practical problems. Social sciences usually involve small networks, comprising a reasonable number of nodes and links. However, for business problems in some industries, such as telecommunications, banking, and credit-card companies, the social network can be huge, with a really large number of nodes and links. Considering, for instance, a medium-size telecommunications company, with 10 million customers, a regular network can reach these 10 million nodes with 1 billion links. Efficient algorithms, based on formal methods, are, therefore, completely mandatory in order to address business issues in those types of industries.

A graph may be undirected or directed. *Undirected links* mean that there is no distinction between the two vertices associated with each edge; in other words, there is no direction in relation to the link that connects two nodes. Node A relates to node B the same way as node B relates to node A. This concept is well understood when thinking about friendship: Andre is a friend of Bruno the same way Bruno is a friend of Andre. There is no differentiation between the links that connect the nodes. *Direct links* mean that there is a direction in relation to the connection between two distinct nodes. In that case, node A may relate to node B in a different way than node B relates to node A. In telecommunications, traditional graphs are always directed: Node A calls to node B or node B calls to node A. Analogously, if Andre calls to Bruno 100 times and Bruno calls back to Andre just 10 times, this differentiation should be clear in the network. The way to make it clear is by establishing a direction for the links. There are two possible approaches to represent this scenario. The first one is creating 100 links (arrows) from Andre to Bruno and an additional 10 links (arrows) from Bruno to Andre. The second approach is to create one link (arrow) from Andre to Bruno and another link (arrow) from Bruno to Andre. In this case, the link from Andre to Bruno should be 10 times thicker than the link from Bruno to Andre.

One of the first people to use graph theory was probably Leonhard Euler in 1736, when he proposed the solution for the problem about the Seven Bridges of Königsberg, presented in the book authored by Barabási.[9] Figure 1.1 shows the question of the seven bridges, a historical problem in mathematics. As many cities in Europe evolved near rivers, Königsberg was set on both sides of the Pregel River. The city included two large islands connected to the mainland by seven bridges. The problem was formulated to find a way to walk through the city crossing each bridge only once. The islands could not be reached by any route but the bridges.

Euler indicated that the only important characteristic in this particular problem was the sequence of the bridges to be crossed. Therefore, it is possible to discard any sort of characteristic except the list of bridges connecting two landmasses. This problem is a foundation of graph theory. Extrapolating this concept to social network analysis, each landmass is a node, and each bridge is a link. The mathematical structure assigned to this problem is known as a graph, and in terms of social science, components constitute a network.

In this sort of problem, only the connection information is relevant. The graph can be represented in different shapes without

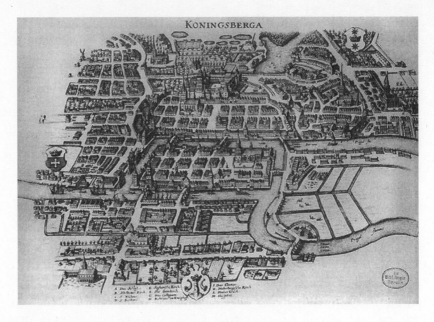

Figure 1.1 Problem of the Seven Bridges of Königsberg

changing the graph itself. The existence or absence of a link between a pair of nodes represents everything in terms of social network analysis. Even when calculating individual network metrics for the nodes, the links are taken into consideration to perform it. For instance, the degree of a particular node is the number of related nodes it has. The related nodes are established by the link between a pair of nodes, the original one and the related one. Then the node's measure degree is computed by counting the number of links it has. Social network analysis is the study of the relationship among the nodes, and the relationship is defined in this context by the links.

Turning back to the bridge problem, Euler observed that whenever a walker gets a link and reaches a vertex by a bridge, he leaves the vertex by a bridge. In practical terms, during any walk through the city, the number of times a walker enters a bridge is equal to the number of times he leaves a bridge.

In a mathematical formalism, Euler said that the existence of a path in a particular graph depends on the nodes' degrees. The degree of a node is the number of links it has, regardless of whether the link

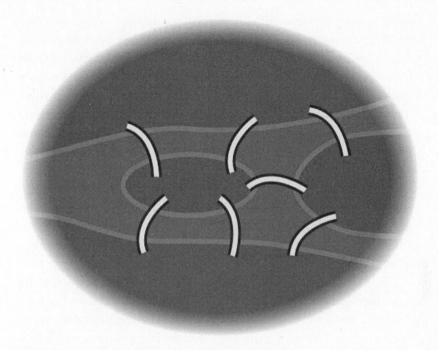

Figure 1.2 Euler Circuit for the Seven Bridges' Problem
Source: Creative Commons Attribution ShareAlike 3.0.

is arriving to or departing from it. The importance is the number of links that are touching this particular node. Then, by Euler's observation, a necessary condition for a particular walk-through is that the graph be connected and have zero or two nodes with odd degrees.

An alternative formulation for the bridge problem is to discover a path by which all bridges are crossed and the starting and ending points are the same. This walk-through is known as Eulerian Circuit. This walk-through exists only if the graph is connected and there are no nodes with degrees having odd values. If this circuit crosses over all seven bridges just once, the Eulerian Circuit is called an Eulerian Path. Figure 1.2 shows the Seven Bridges' problem.

Nowadays, graph theory is regularly used for finding communities in networks. Algorithms regarding community detection have been increasing every day, making it possible for more real-world and business problems to be addressed by this sort of methodology. By detecting not just the small networks, communities, or subgraphs, but also their structures—hierarchical, circular, and others—it is possible to apply social network analysis to several distinct types of problems, such as cross-selling and up-selling in marketing and fraud and money laundering in revenue assurance. By understanding the small communities and their structures, it is possible to understand the network's behavior and also the way these networks diffuse over the time, even allowing some predictions.

The types of real applications of social network analysis have been increasing. It will be possible to address more and more kinds of problems in the future by using this methodology. Different kinds of industries, of different sizes, will be able to target their business problems, especially those related to customer behavior and relationships, by using social network analysis technique.

The case study in this book (see Part II) presents two distinct approaches for the use of social network analysis in telecommunications. The first one is the use of social network analysis for churn, which involves identifying the most influential customers who could possibly lead other customers to leave the company. The second example is the use of social network analysis for purchasing, identifying once again the influential customers who can possibly lead other customers to purchase similar products in the future. These influential customers are identified based on their relationships inside the network. Their network's measures in relation to degrees, distances, and paths will define their ability as leaders and how effective their influence can be over other customers.

STATISTICS AND SOCIAL NETWORK ANALYSIS

Social network analysis started as a social science, and, therefore, it can be considered a branch of mathematical sociology more than it can be considered statistical or quantitative analysis.

However, the boundary between the social science approach and the statistical one is not so well defined and easy to understand. The mathematical methodology often handles the social network analysis in terms of a deterministic study, gauging the network data based on algorithms that compute the relationships among nodes and their respective strength, frequency, recency, direction, and so on. Contextualized in a mathematical model, social network analysis tends to consider all observations about a particular population, according to a specific subject of interest.

Statistical methodology often considers stochastic events about the relationship strengths in terms of distribution. Statistical analysis also considers particular subsets of the network as samples of a larger population. In the mathematical approach, a subset of a particular network is considered definite and encompasses the subject of interest of some sort of study. In the statistical approach, a subset of a particular network is considered a sample; because of this, the concern is to keep the results consistent and reproducible for similar samples from the same population.

This book, and mainly the case study presented in Part II, is more concerned with the mathematical approach. The network considered in the case study, for instance, is a subset of a particular subject of interest, considering a subset of the entire population. According to the statistical approach, the results from a network analysis about a subset of a particular population, which is a sample at the end, should be reproducible when similar analysis is applied to similar samples from the same population. This can be true in some environments or scenarios, but not in all.

In the case study, for example, the social network analysis was performed on the residential customers for a particular telecommunications company. Suppose this particular case study had taken a subset of the residential customers—for instance, a segment of them in terms of market. That social network analysis would have reached different outcomes if applied over a different sample, even though using the same residential-customer population. Thus, the mathematical methodology does not consider the subset of the network as a sample but as a definite population. The entire population could be considered all customers, including the wholesale, government, corporate companies, and so on. However, in that particular case, the subset is residential customers only.

Although the mathematical approach was put in place in order to analyze the social network of that particular telecommunications company, a statistical methodology was not ignored. Some specific statistical procedures, such as multivariate analysis, principal component analysis, clustering, and others, aimed at analyzing outcomes of social network analysis were applied to describe the results accomplished by network computation, which are depicted by several network metrics, such as degrees, centralities, closeness, betweenness, influence, and others.

Finally, a different sort of statistical approach, based on data mining techniques, can also be applied to understand some patterns of behavior for a particular social network being studied. For temporal analysis—that is, looking at the social network over time—predictive methods such as regression, decision tree, and artificial neural networks can be implemented in order to define some possible scenarios of evolution for the social network.

At the end, both mathematical and statistical approaches are put in place in order to analyze social networks, and each one is useful in some particular stage of the process. The mathematical approach is often used to compute the network measures and to establish the overall topology of the network. The statistical approach is often applied to analyze the outcomes from the network analysis, describing some relevant characteristics and particularities of the network, its distribution, outliers, communities, clusters, and so on.

SUMMARY

This chapter introduced social network analysis from different perspectives. The first perspective was its basis as a social science, by analyzing the relationships among real social groups, such as authors, employees, students, and so on. This perspective was used to understand how people relate to one another and the impact of their actions over the social network. This perspective can be used to identify who the leaders are and who the followers are. The mathematical foundations were not so strong even though, for small networks, comprised of a reasonable number of nodes and links, it is possible to evaluate and analyze the social interactions over the network based on the social science theory.

Graph theory is a mathematical formulation that explains and depicts the social network analysis in terms of formulas and geometric concepts. These formulas can be translated into algorithms and then applied to business problems that involve huge social networks. Social networks in business occur in telecommunications, insurance, banking, and credit card operations. By creating social networks based on customers and calls, for instance, a huge network can be established, and efficient algorithms should be deployed in order to achieve useful and practical results.

Chapters 2, 3, and 4 present more concepts and foundations in relation to social network analysis. These foundations are more mathematical and, therefore, are basically built on the graph theory briefly presented here. Chapter 2 presents the theoretical foundation based on mathematical concepts in respect to social network analysis. Chapter 3 presents formal methods to create, describe, and evaluate social networks. Finally, Chapter 4 presents the measures in relation to social network analysis—metrics assigned to influence, power, and centrality. These metrics describe how influential and central the nodes are and how important they are in the social network for problem solving.

NOTES

1. Alexandra Marin and Barry Wellman, "Social Network Analysis: An Introduction," June 2009. Available at http://www.hsph.harvard.edu/massconect/files/social_network_analysis._an_introduction.pdf (accessed October 26, 2010).

2. Edward O. Laumann, Peter V. Marsden, and David Prensky, "The Boundary Specification Problem in Network Analysis," in *Research Methods in Social Network Analysis* (Piscataway, NJ: Transaction Publishers, 1992), 61–87.

3. Jeffrey Travers and Stanley Milgram, "An Experiment Study of the Small World Problem," *Sociometry* 32 (4) (December 1969): 425–443.

4. Ibid.

5. Georg Simmel, Donald N. Levine, and Morris Janowitz, *Georg Simmel on Individuality and Social Forms: Selected Writings* (Chicago: University of Chicago Press, 1972).

6. Ibid.

7. Stephen P. Borgatti, Ajay Mehra, Daniel J. Brass, and Guiseppe Labianca, "Network Analysis in the Social Sciences," *Science* 323 (5916) (2009): 892–895.

8. For the following discussion, I am indebted to Marin and Wellman, "Social Network Analysis: An Introduction."

9. Albert-László Barabási, *Linked: The New Science of Networks* (New York: Basic Books, 2002).

CHAPTER 2

Formal Methods for Network Analysis

T he main idea behind social network analysis is not so difficult. A social network is a set of nodes. These nodes may have relationships, or links, with one another. Social networks can be comprised of many or few nodes, connected by one or several types of relationships. In order to create useful information about a particular social network, a complete and rigorous description of the measurements assigned to nodes, links, and patterns of behavior should be applied. Ideally, some knowledge about all the relationships between each pair of nodes will arise.

Often the amount of data used to describe social networks is huge, even for so-called small networks. In the case study presented in this book, involving the telecommunications market, the amount of information can be an impediment. In order to understand the social network and its structure, pattern, behavior, and member characteristics, an elaborate manipulation of the data is required. This can be a complex and time-consuming process. Effective computer algorithms are crucial to compute the relevant network measures that describe the network structure and topology. Analysis of these network measures is the real social network analysis. In other words, the very first step is data preparation, as in any analytical process. In social network analysis, this step is much more important than in other analytical processes, because the identification of nodes and links is made in this phase. The second step is network measurement calculation. This step computes all measurements assigned to the nodes, links, communities, connected components, and so on. The network structure and topology is revealed in this phase. However, information from the social network analysis is really extracted from evaluation of the network measures computed in the previous step. Who are the leaders? Who are the followers? Who are in the boundaries? Who are the outliers? How many communities are in the network? How many connected components are in the network? What do these communities and connected components look like? All these questions are answered by statistical analyses of the network measurements.

This chapter describes the formal method of social network analysis. The first, and most intuitive, approach is based on graphs. A graph can reveal the social structure, the relationships among the nodes, the strength of these relations, how the nodes are concentrated or dispersed, and many other indicators of social interactions. By visualizing social networks as graphs composed of nodes and links, it is possible to understand the overall network shape and how the members of this particular community interacts with one another, and also to highlight relevant nodes and relations pertaining to a particular business perspective.

Graphs can reveal a lot of information about social interactions and, therefore, the features of communities, groups of people, or even individuals. Graph theory can also support the measures and methods of computation of social network analysis. A wide range of network measures depicts the nodes and links, or the structure and individual components of the network. In addition, each network measure can be calculated by more than one algorithm, which brings further complexity to the social network analysis. The measures used to describe the network and also the algorithms used to compute these measures are a matter of the business problems to be solved.

Although the use of graphs to describe the characteristics and structure of the network and their individual components, such as nodes and links, is quite straightforward and intuitive, larger networks become far more difficult to analyze in this manner.

Imagine a social network created by researchers who are authors. This author and coauthorship network is often small, involving a long timeline and a large number of journals. By focusing on a particular subject or a specific discipline, this network can reach, at most, hundreds of nodes and thousands of links. A social network like that can easily be described by using graphs that highlight the influential nodes, the central nodes, or the strongest relationships among them.

However, consider a small telecommunications company as presented in the case study used in this book. A network like that can easily reach millions of nodes and hundreds of millions of links. A graph to describe this sort of network can reveal very little useful information about the nodes and links. Certainly, the task of analyzing millions of nodes and hundreds of millions of links is not easy or straightforward. Identifying influential nodes, leaders, followers, or strong links is difficult or impossible through the use of graph analysis. Although useful information about individual nodes and links is quite unlikely to be achieved, the recognition of relevant communities or groups is possible by using this technique.

In this way, measures for nodes and links are analyzed simply by values comparison due to the size of the network. Community detection and cluster recognition can be performed by visual methods, but, depending on the network size, even these tasks are difficult to accomplish. For huge social networks, community detection and cluster recognition should be performed by analyzing the networks as well as individual measurements.

A GRAPHICAL APPROACH FOR SOCIAL NETWORK ANALYSIS

Mathematical and graphical techniques are often used to represent the descriptions of the social network in a systematic way. Also, mathematical techniques are usually converted into computer algorithms that can be applied to massive amounts of data. As a matter of fact, computer algorithms are used not just for massive processing but also for accurate calculations of network measurements and individual metrics of relationships.

For small networks, such as students in a school, professors in a university, or employees in a company, it is possible to describe the pattern of relationships inside the network by using words. However, for a complete description of the relationships among nodes, a long list would be required. This list should record all possible pairs of nodes connected within the network and also describe each type of relationship linking a pair of nodes. Using words, this task could be tedious, time consuming, and—most important—susceptible to a significant number of errors. Even for small networks, such as those mentioned earlier, this process can take a very long time and incur important mistakes that can have ramifications for future analyses.

For this reason, a formal representation assures that all information required to describe a particular social network is properly presented in a straightforward manner. A formal representation also assigns rules and roles to the nodes and links, which are much more effective than lists of words.

Hanneman described some gains from using formal methods to represent a social network:

> A related reason for using (particularly mathematical) formal methods for representing social networks is that mathematical representations allow us to apply computers to the analysis of network data. Why this is important will become clearer as we learn more about how structural analysis of social networks occurs. Suppose, for a simple example, we had information about trade-flows of 50 different commodities (e.g., coffee, sugar, tea, copper, bauxite) among the 170 or so nations of the world system in a given year. Here, the 170 nations can be thought of as actors or notes, and the amount of each commodity exported from each nation to each of the other 169 can be thought of as the strength of a directed tie from the focal nation to the other. A social scientist might be interested in whether the "structures" of trade in mineral products are more similar to one another than the structure of trade in mineral products are to vegetable products. To answer this fairly simple (but also pretty important) question, a huge amount of manipulation of the data is necessary. It could take, literally, years to do by hand; it can be done by a computer in a few minutes.[1]

Table 2.1: Social Network Represented by Matrix

	John	Karl	Eoin	Eamonn
John	—	1	1	1
Karl	0	—	0	1
Eoin	1	1	—	0
Eamonn	1	0	0	—

Graphing Social Relations

In a small social network composed of four members, or nodes, based on friendship, it is possible to define a matrix describing the relations within this particular network.[2] Consider the friendship of John, Karl, Eoin, and Eamonn. Suppose that John likes Karl, Eoin, and Eamonn. Karl likes Eamonn, Eoin likes John, and Eamonn likes John and Eoin. This particular social network is easily described by words, and it can be easily represented by a simple matrix, as presented in Table 2.1.

Looking at the matrix, it is easily observed that John likes more people than anyone else. Also, it is possible to see that Eoin likes more people than Karl and Eamonn, just by counting the numbers of zeros and ones in the lines of the table. In this particular case, the direction of the action is quite relevant. The fact that Eoin likes John doesn't necessarily mean that John likes Eoin. This method of counting is made easier by using a matrix rather than words. Furthermore, if we had more information about the members of the network, such as age, salary, or address, it would be possible to recognize more patterns from the matrix, such as young people have more friends than older generations, or those who earn high salaries like fewer people than those who earn less money, or people who live close to each other have more propensity to like each other.

By using a matrix to represent the relationships among the members of a particular social network, it is possible to find patterns about the communities that these social networks represent. Descriptions with words are not rich enough to highlight patterns within a group of data records, especially patterns about relations among nodes.

As long as the amount of data increases, either in terms of the number of attributes or in terms of the amount of records, descriptions using words become even less accurate. However, descriptions using formal methods such as matrices, based on a mathematical approach, are able to explain the data in a straightforward manner way, no matter the number of attributes or the number of records.

In addition, formal representation of relations among members within a social network makes it possible to compute measures by algorithms, which is crucial for large datasets. A computational process is mandatory when analyzing large social communities. Calculations of the network measures are possible only by using computer algorithms.

As Hanneman noticed, there are three principal benefits from using graphs and matrices to represent social networks. Graphs and matrices can be summarized in a set of information about the relations within a social network, highlighting relevant patterns about nodes, links, and communities inside networks. Graphs and matrices can also make it possible to apply computer algorithms to calculate network measures about nodes, links, and communities inside social networks. The process to calculate these types of measures is iterative and hence completely assigned to computer operations. Finally, graphs and matrices consist of rules that help to clarify what the nodes and links are referring to. Once again, the graph representation drives the interpretation of the data toward knowledge acquisition, providing useful information about the set of row data available.

In terms of telecommunications, the second reason is the most relevant due to the size of the network. Telecommunications networks, even for small companies, are too large to calculate by hand. Any sort of analysis should be performed by computers. It is totally impossible to perform any network measure calculation by hand.

As a matter of fact, the graphical approach provides more benefit when performed on particular subnetworks inside the entire network. These subgraphs can highlight the relationships that matter for a particular subject, such as fraud or credit risk. Other than the relationships, and probably more important, is the possibility of highlighting the correlated nodes, which can reveal groups of people involved in the event being studied. Therefore, by graphically analyzing a particular subnetwork, it is possible to identify the perpetrator of fraud and all people involved in the act of fraud.

Using Graphs to Analyze Social Relationships

Graphs and matrices represent two distinct approaches used to describe social relations within communities. Graphs are more closely related to mathematical formalism, and for this reason this book will focus on them in more detail.

Regardless of which type of representation is used to depict social relations, these two approaches—graphs and matrices—make it possible to understand most of the connections inside a network and also to calculate some general measures. Both techniques contain features of visual analyses and can assist the process of gathering useful knowledge about some particular social network. Graphs can certainly be more intuitive than matrices in order to visually understand the structure and relations of the social network. Despite this fact, matrices remain a strong analytical tool, a better option than written data analysis.

The various graphs used to represent social networks are very simple, consisting basically of points that represent nodes and lines or arrows that represent links. In most cases lines represent relations with no direction, such as friendship, and arrows represent relations in which the direction is important, such as calls in the telecommunications industry. The points often used to represent nodes can be modified to squares, triangles, or any other shape, distinguishing different types of nodes. It is quite common to use different shapes simultaneously in order to differentiate nodes with distinct characteristics, such as marketing segmentation, customer value, and social range, among others.

An important aspect of social network representation, particularly graphic representation, is to identify the nodes and links. By taking the example previously presented about John, Karl, Eoin, and Eamonn, Figure 2.1 shows a graph with four labeled nodes but no connections.

The data that describes the social network among John, Karl, Eoin, and Eamonn is a directed graph. John nominated Karl, Eoin, and Eamonn as friends. Karl nominated Eamonn as a friend, Eoin

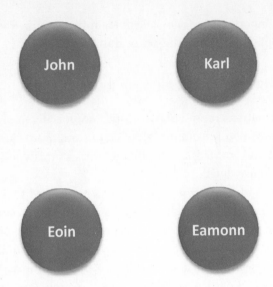

Figure 2.1 Nodes for a Simple Graph

nominated John and Karl as friends, and Eamonn nominated John as a friend. If there were no nominations in relation to the friendship—that is, if John is a friend of Karl and Karl is a friend of John—there would be lines instead of arrows in that particular graph. However, considering the nomination process, the arrows represent who nominates whom. This information is showed in Figure 2.2.

The relationship between John and Eoin in this directed graph is bidirectional; John nominated Eoin as a friend and Eoin also nominated John as a friend. This relationship is represented by two arrows, but in order to make the graph cleaner and easier to understand, a double–headed arrow was used. This type of arrow is used to represent reciprocal relationships.

LEVELS OF MEASUREMENT FOR SOCIAL RELATIONS

The description of who nominated whom as friend can also describe how close one person is to another. Instead of merely describing that John is a friend of Karl, it is possible to describe how close they are.

For instance, a graph such as Figure 2.2 could describe how close to each other John and Karl are: if they are just friends, if they are

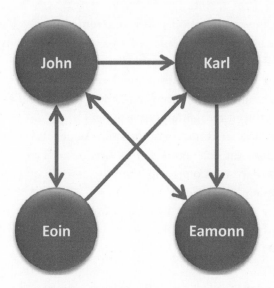

Figure 2.2 A Directed Graph of Friendship Ties

very close friends, or if they are best friends. The level of friendship—just friends, very close friends, and best friends—could also be represented by 1, 2, and 3, respectively, in the matrix, and by arrows of different thicknesses in the graph. The higher the level of friendship, the thicker the arrow will be. This type of description is of additional benefit to the formal method of network representation such as graphs.

In the same way, the type of relationship can be described according to different aspects. For instance, John and Karl can be friends, or brothers, or workmates. Each type of relationship can have distinct weights and different thicknesses in the graph representation. Workmates could be, by some definitions, less important than friends, and friends can be less important than brothers. These different types of relationships, represented by distinct levels of representation, can lead the computation of the network measures in different directions, and thus the analysis of the social network would be distinct.

In relation to the telecommunications industry, different levels of measurement can be used to rank calls among the customers. Local calls, for instance, hold less value financially than long-distance calls. Also, long-distance calls have less value than international calls. When considering international calls only, different countries have different rates. All these rates can be used to evaluate the calls inside the network and, therefore, distinguish the relationships among the customers. The number of international calls between two particular customers can indicate a stronger relation than a higher number of local calls between two different customers.

Additionally, the duration of the calls can also be used to rank the relations among the customers. Long-duration calls indicate a stronger relationship than short ones and, therefore, would be used to valuate the links among the nodes.

Finally, a combination of rate and duration can be used to rank calls inside the network and, hence, evaluate the relationships among the customers.

Directed and Undirected Links in Graphs

For the three examples presented—friendship, level of friendship, and type of relationship—the information required to build the social graphs could be extracted by questions. John could be asked to nominate his friends, his level of friendships among a list of members, and finally the type of his relationships from a list of members. The type of question points to the sort of links that will be used in the formal representation of the graph. The links within the graphs should represent the types of relationships among the social network. If the links show distinct thicknesses, they represent different strengths of relationships, such as the level of friendship—just friend, very close friend, and best friend—or the type of relation—friend, sibling, or workmate.

It is useful to describe social networks as being composed of directed links, as in the telecommunications industry. These directed links can represent different values, types, frequencies, and so on. These links describe not just the relationships involved in the social structure but also the relevance of these connections.

Indeed, most social processes comprise sequences of directed actions, as shown in the case study presented in this book. For example, suppose that person A directs a comment to B, and B directs a comment back to A, and so on. It may not be possible to know the order in which actions occurred or, in other words, who started the conversation. In this example, we may merely want to know that A and B are having a conversation. In this case, the relation that represents the conversation necessarily involves both nodes A and B. Both A and B are participating in the relationship of having a conversation. Also, it may be possible to describe the situation as one of the social institutions of a conversation, which by definition involves two or more nodes bonded in an interaction.

Directed links in social networks use the convention of connecting nodes by arrows. These arrows can be directional, indicating which node is directing the connection, or multidirectional, indicating that both nodes in that particular link are directing the connection. Each type was presented in the examples shown earlier.

A simple connection between a pair of nodes, where the direction is not relevant, is represented by a single line, indicating that there is no direction regarding the relationship. A to B means exactly the same thing as B to A.

The distinction between these two types of links, directed and undirected, can be subtle, but it is an important aspect of social network analyses. This is what makes it possible to analyze the interactions inside the networks and study how relationships affect network behavior, especially when the analysis takes place over time, highlighting how the network has been evolving.

Social network analysis in telecommunications always takes into consideration the direction of the link. In order to represent who calls whom or who texts whom, the directed links should be used. If Bob calls Ted 100 times and Ted calls back Bob just a dozen times, this difference in the direction of the relationship should be highlighted. Some network measures should be the same, due to the method of computing, such as in-degree and out-degree. However, some other measures, such as eigenvector and influence, should be different considering the strength or the weight of the relationships, like 100 calls against one dozen.

Simple and Multiple Relations in Graphs

Very often the nodes within a network are connected by more than one link and, usually, by more than one type of link. In that case, the graphs are called multiple or multiplex graphs. The examples presented previously, about the friendship network, are called simple or simplex graphs, in which the nodes are connected by a single type of link.

It is also possible to combine the information from multiple links into a single, aggregated link. Aggregated links can use different thicknesses, colors, and even symbols to represent all information about the relationships among the nodes that they are connecting.

Considering the size of telecommunications networks, multiplex relations are quite straightforward. Distinct types of connections, such as calls, text messages, multimedia messages, e-mail, and so on, can be represented by distinct types of links in the analysis, holding different values of importance. Calls can be more important than text messages, and e-mails can be more important than multimedia messages. All definitions of what is more important are just a matter of the business rules involved in the subject of study. The same types of relations could hold different values in distinctive social network analyses. For instance, in an analysis designed to improve Internet usage, all relations based on e-mail connections should have more value than any other.

SUMMARY

This chapter has covered a few basic concepts in relation to social network analysis, presenting the formal methods used to describe social networks, such as graphical and matrix-based approaches, and the levels of measurement. The use of graphs to represent the social relations is emphasized in this book due to its mathematical approach. In addition, graphical representation seems to be more intuitive in terms of visual analysis than any other methodology.

Finally, levels of measurement were presented mostly to establish the distinct ways of collecting and presenting the relations within the. Directed or undirected links and single or multiple relations are essential in order to depict the social network as accurately as possible. Particularly in telecommunications, networks, the direction of the link, and the multiple types of relations are crucial in order to describe the social network properly.

NOTES

1. Robert A. Hanneman and Mark Riddle, *Introduction to Social Network Methods* (Riverside, CA: University of California, 2005). Available at http://faculty.ucr.edu/~hanneman/nettext/Introduction_to_Social_Network_Methods.pdf (accessed November 3, 2010).

2. I am indebted to Hanneman, "Introduction to Social Network Methods," for the following discussion.

CHAPTER 3

Theoretical Foundation

hapter 2 presented a brief theoretical foundation about social network analysis, including concepts about nodes, relations, network structures, types and levels of analyses, scales of measurements, and finally a rough explanation of network analysis on a statistical basis.

The theoretical foundation is quite important in order to understand network structure and the measurements related to it. It is also important to visualize the entire network in terms of the business, such as marketing, sales, finance, and optimization. The concepts of social network analysis describe characteristics of nodes and links, which are important in business applications. Mr. Ken King wrote the foreword for this book, which describes the amazing story of Paul Revere. This story reveals how important some particular nodes inside the social network are. The type of links and the kind of nodes reveal much about the entire social network, how it behaves, and the implications of some events inside it.

William Dawes and Paul Revere performed basically the same kind of tasks, spreading some particular message. However, the outcomes of their actions were completely different. As an influential node inside the social network, Paul Revere broadcast his message more effectively than William Dawes. Also, the links used by Paul Revere were better chosen than the ones chosen by William Dawes. Revere selected the militia in order to start the diffusion of the message instead of knocking door to door as Dawes did. By doing this, Revere was able to diffuse his message faster and wider than Dawes.

The concepts[1] of social networks presented in this chapter and on depict networks in terms of who the influential nodes are, who the leaders are, who the followers are, and, also, which links are relevant. Links among influential nodes become relevant as well. This is particularly recognized when thinking about distinguished networks, such as networks of politicians or big corporations. Links among executives are usually more important than connections among regular employees. In addition, links among executives from distinguished corporations are even more important than the relations among regular employees from distinguished companies. Those links can represent prospective business, mergers and acquisitions, or a fusion process among companies. Connections among regular employees from distinguished companies can represent just regular relationships among people.

TYPE OF DATA FOR SOCIAL NETWORK ANALYSIS

The type of data involved in social network analysis is slightly different from the data of other analytical models, such as clustering models (unsupervised) and classification models (supervised). Social network analysis contains data about the observations, as in those kinds of models mentioned earlier, as well as data that describe the relationship among these observations. These types of observations are the nodes or vertices, and the relationships among them can be understood as the links or edges. Probably the most distinct data in terms of the network are those that contain information about the connections among the nodes or vertices. These sorts of data differentiate network data from the other models' data. The information about the connections—the links or edges—reveals a brand-new possibility to increase knowledge about not just the customer's behaviors but also the customers' relationship behaviors. It can certainly turn into a new approach to model how and when customers behave and (most important) what the implications are of that behavior.

Essentially, the data about links—their frequency, strength, relevance—describe the most important attributes about the network, and enable fundamental analysis about communities and the entire network. The data about the nodes—their attributes, weights, and some additional personal or corporate information—reveal the importance of the nodes inside the network and provide an overall analysis of customers. Although the individual information about customers is quite relevant, and very often is used to describe their characteristics, the most relevant data about the network are assigned to the links. Information about the links describes how the nodes relate to one another, and this sort of information is crucial for the analysis of the network. The information about the links also describes the strength of the connections of the nodes, what the frequency is, and, in terms of the entire network, how far and fast a particular sort of information can be spread over the network in future business events.

Thinking in terms of business events, it is possible to see how fast a marketing campaign could flow through the network—for example, a customer retention ad or bundle diffusion. As an outcome of the network analysis, a list of network measures is computed. The most important measures in relation to the network are assigned to the nodes. However, these measures are usually computed based on the links that connect those nodes. The links reveal the number of connections of each node, how central each is, and the path that each holds in terms of the network. By choosing the right nodes that comprise the best links or paths, it is possible to eventually identify the best and fastest nodes that will spread some message throughout the internal communities within the network.

It is also possible to observe how fast a particular business event can spread inside the network or subnetwork as well as the direction of that flow in terms of geographic localities. Is a churning event heading to some particular virtual location, such as a particular small community, or geographic position, such as a neighbor? Is product or service acquisition heading to some particular direction? By looking at the network and analyzing the sequence of events inside it, it is possible to predict the next step in terms of business events. A social network over time plays like a movie—a sequence of snapshots. Analyzing each snapshot is certainly a good approach to predict the next one. For this reason, even though social network analysis can be considered an unsupervised model, if there is no target or premise, it is possible to use this sort of approach to predict certain types of events. Based on some isolated actions, or some previous business events, it is important to know which direction the network could take in terms of diffusion. Will this particular business event tend to increase through the social network; will it decrease and stop somehow? Social network analysis over time can help us answer these kinds of questions.

Although the language used to describe the set of nodes and links and the way they relate to one another may be new, there is nothing new about social network data. The information to describe the set of nodes can still be set down in terms of a single table, comprising data about name, age, gender, salary, revenue, and other business attributes in relation to the particular company. Similarly, the information to describe the set of links can also be set down in terms of tables, such as the operational transactions that connect one node to another.

In telecommunications, a table containing personal and usage information about customers can be easily used to provide the set of nodes, and a table containing the call-details records can easily be used to build the set of links.

Although the same type of data can be used in distinct ways to build different social networks, the correlation between conventional and network data to create graphic relationships among the nodes is still true. For instance, in the insurance industry, the data from claims can be used to connect different nodes (participants) or to represent a particular node, and the data from the claims are still provided by easily accessed tables.

As a conventional approach to represent data, traditional statistical methods can be applied to analyze data and depict the information about a particular point of interest. Such straightforward correlations between conventional data to describe social networks and traditional analytical methods to evaluate the characteristics of these data make it easy to study particular business issues by using an innovative method of analysis.

Conventional data for statistical analysis are received in an array of measurements, and information about social networks is received that way as well. The array of measurements is arranged in tabular format: in a set of rows, which are observations about some particular business interest, such as customers, and a set of columns, which are the attributes about each observation in the array, such as name, age, gender, marital status, and so on. Each cell of that array describes a particular observation (e.g., a customer) and a specific attribute (e.g., the salary).

In some cases, additional dimensions are included, such as time, in order to enrich the data available about a particular point of interest and thereby enhance the possible data analysis.

Table 3.1 contains information about some observations: name, sex, age, and the number of directed incoming connections. This sort of measure is called "in-degree" in terms of social network analysis, and it is a measure of a network's distance, representing the number of links a particular node receives.

The data structure presented in Table 3.1 leads the statistical analyst to compare the nodes in terms of similarities. How are these nodes similar in terms of gender, age, and number of connections they have? It is straightforward analysis, performed by comparing the rows and the columns in the table.

Table 3.1: Table about the Observations

Name	Sex	Age	In-Degree	Out-Degree
Carlos	Male	42	2	4
Dani	Female	36	1	3
Bruno	Male	44	1	2
Ivan	Male	61	3	1

We can easily see that Ivan is the node in this network who receives more links, whereas Dani and Bruno are the nodes who receive fewer links. Similarly, Carlos is the node who generates more links, and Ivan is the node who generates fewer links. In term of telecommunications, Ivan is the customer who receives more calls in this particular social network, and he is named "call receiver," whereas Carlos is the customer who makes more calls, and he is named "call maker." Also, by analyzing the table, we see that although Ivan is the call receiver, generating perhaps a great amount of revenue in terms of interconnection rates, he is simultaneously the customer who makes the fewest number of calls, hence generating irrelevant revenue in terms of call rate.

The traditional approach to analyze data based on tabulated information is quite straightforward and suitable for statistical assessment. It is suitable for comparing observations and highlighting particular information. However, social network analysis also considers the data structure in a holistic way.

Based on the example presented in Chapter 2, a regular analysis might reveal a greater number of ones than zeros, which could suggest that this small social network is highly connected. John and Eoin have degree equal to three, Eamonn to two, and Karl to one. The information about the degree, or the level of connection, is straight from Table 3.2.

Table 3.2: Cross-Tabulate Information about the Relationship

Friendship links			
	Chosen		
Chooser	John	Karl	Eoin	Eamonn
John	—	1	1	1
Karl	0	—	0	1
Eoin	1	1	—	1
Eamonn	1	0	1	—

This kind of visualization is similar to the multidimensional scaling described in Part III, where the SAS® capabilities for social network analysis are presented. In order to produce the virtual coordinates based on some particular similarity (or dissimilarity), it is necessary to create this sort of square matrix. The problem is the missing values between some pairs of nodes create a very sparse square matrix. Consider, for example, a telecommunications network consisting of 1,000 customers. In order to produce this sort of table to analyze the network data or to calculate the virtual coordinates, the square matrix reaches 1 million cells, many of which are lacking information.

It is possible to observe all rows as a listing of cases, as in conventional data. Also, it is possible to see all columns as attributes of each node, similar to the approach of traditional statistical data. By doing this, the relations with other nodes can be viewed as attributes of each node. Indeed, many techniques used by network analysis, such as calculating correlations and distances among the nodes, are applied exactly in the same way to network data as they would be to conventional data.

Network data could be considered as just a distinct form of the traditional statistical data, and the network analysis might take this sort of information as a fundamental approach for pattern recognition, predicting modeling, and exploratory analysis. Social network analysis considers how nodes relate each other by seeing the structure of connections that comprise the node. Nodes are described by their relations rather than by their attributes.

The major difference between conventional and network data is that conventional data focus on observations and attributes, whereas network data focus on observations and relations. In terms of telecommunications, for instance, conventional data describe the average characteristics of customers—who they are—whereas network data describe the average behaviors of the customers—how they play. Naturally, network data, depicting the overall customers' behavior, describe who they are in addition to how they play. In a corporate perspective, who they are might be nothing more than just a potential capacity for consuming. However, by knowing how they behave, you can understand the actual scope of their current consumption, consuming, which may lead to new boundaries of sales and relationships.

IDENTIFYING NODES AND LINKS WITHIN SOCIAL NETWORKS

Network data are basically defined by information about nodes and links. Nodes are usually the part of the network data that represent the observations, people, companies, or any sort of institutions that have some kind of relationship internally. There is not much difference between conventional data and network data, except in the way network data are collected, formatted, and studied. Network analysis focuses on the relations among nodes and not about a particular node and its attributes. This means that the nodes are usually not sampled independently, as in many other kinds of studies. Take a study about the friendship ties, for example. John has been selected to be part of the sample. When John is analyzed in terms of social networks, he has seven friends. Hence, he needs to be tracked for each of those seven friends, and their friendship ties should be analyzed as well. The seven friends should be in the sample because John is. In this way the elements inside the sample are no longer independent.

The nodes that are included in some particular study that are not related to social networks tend to be the result of independent probability sampling. Social network studies generally include all the nodes that occur within some boundary of a particular social structure. More often, network studies do not use samples at all, at least in the conventional sense of statistics, which is the traditional collection of a small subset of the entire data available. Rather, these studies include all the nodes in some population or populations. The populations that are included within some particular network study might be considered as a sample of some larger set of populations.[2]

As stated previously, if John is within some particular sample of network analysis, all links in relation to him should be within this sample as well. As a consequence, all nodes related to these links should also be included into that sample. In order to respect the starting scenario, if all of John's related nodes are within the sample, all links of these nodes should be included as well as all correlated nodes.

Because of this cascade method of selecting or defining the sample, very often the entire population is considered in a network analysis. It is not possible to compare all calls made by John against some of the calls made by Peter. The outcome of this comparison is not realistic.

In terms of business problems, particularly considering the telecommunications environment, social network analysis could be a real challenge. Think of a regular telecommunications company with 10 million customers. By using a very low average number of two calls per day, a social network analysis for this particular company should consider 10 million customers and 60 million calls during three months of average behavior.

Because network methods focus on relations among nodes, these nodes can't be sampled independently in order to be included as observations inside some particular sample. If one node happens to be selected, then all other nodes which hold some particular relationship with that node should be included in the sample as well. As a result, social network analysis approaches tend to study whole populations by means of census rather than by independent samples.

The populations that network analysis usually take into consideration are remarkably diverse. Hanneman stated in his book:

> At one extreme, they might consist of symbols in texts or sounds in verbalizations; at the other extreme, nations in the world system of states might constitute the population of nodes. Perhaps most common, of course, are populations of individual persons. In each case, however, the elements of the population to be studied are defined by falling within some boundary.[3]

The boundaries mentioned by Hanneman are basically identified by two distinct approaches. The first one is based on the nodes within a social network, such as all members who take part in a community, like a group of friends, a corporation, a college, or the customers of a particular company. This is probably the most common approach to establish the boundary of some social network analysis.

The second approach is based on some geographic or demographic edge, such as all observations in some particular region that match some specific criteria. This approach is less common, although it might be applied for several business problems.

In terms of telecommunications, for instance, the first approach could take into consideration all customers from a particular operator. The second approach could consider all customers for a particular region of service, such as a specific county, city, or state.

MODALITY AND LEVELS OF ANALYSIS

Social network analysis tends to visualize individuals within networks. The idea of studying individuals based on their relationships is the motif of the social network analysis.

Different communities hold distinct levels of connection, according to the average degrees of connection among members. Family is a social network in which the members are very close, and hence, their individual degrees are quite high. Companies are social networks in which their members might have close relations or not. Also, these relations are involuntary. The employees must relate to each other somehow. Some employees might associate with other employees outside of work, in their leisure time, but this type of social network is distinct from the ones within the companies. In summary, there are different types of social networks, with distinct kinds of roles, which hold completely different modalities and levels of degrees.

Network data are described by the nodes and the relations among them, given a particular boundary of relationship. Friends, workmates, and mates are the level of the network analysis, which, depending on the type of relationship, might be strong or weak. Friends very often have stronger connections than employees or even than workmates. The level of relationship drives the social network analysis in different ways, producing distinct outcomes.

In terms of telecommunications, the network can be extrapolated at different levels of analysis, such as customers, households, neighborhoods, local areas, counties, cities, provinces, and so on. Most often, the customer network level is the subject of marketing campaigns, sales activities, and loyalty programs. However, many studies may take into consideration the household level, analyzing the relationships among them. For broadband or fixed-line purposes, for instance, the household should be part of the analysis rather than individual customers. However, for analysis of traffic and capacity of delivery and demand, neighborhood, counties, or cities might be part of the analysis as a node level, allowing the study of the network in terms of the relationships among the levels of those nodes.

In addition to the network structure, level, or modality, it is possible to employ distinct types of analysis according to the network used. For distinct analysis of networks according to the customer segmentation, it is possible to create different networks based on residential customers only, or business customers only, and so on. However, there is more than one way to build the network for this purpose. For the residential customers' network, for instance, there are at least two possible ways to build the network: consider all calls, regardless of the destination—residential or business numbers—or consider just the calls to and from residential numbers. These two distinct residential networks would produce different outcomes, highlighting different customers as influential, for example.

Another type of analysis involves splitting the network's outcomes into distinct groups. For instance, it is possible to build a telecommunications network that considers the entire scope of calls, whether they are coming from or going to residential or business numbers. Based on this entire network, all nodes and links measures are calculated, such as degree, closeness, betweenness, influence, and others. Although the measures are calculated based on the entire network, the analysis could be split in terms of customer segmentation. The network outcomes can be split into residential and business nodes. Therefore, just for analysis purposes, the residential nodes' measures are compared. The same approach could be deployed for the business nodes. The comparison among the residential nodes only can highlight the influential residential nodes. Similarly, the comparison among the business nodes only can highlight the influential business nodes.

In summary, according to the business problems to be addressed, there is more than one way to build the network and also more than one way to analyze the network. Perhaps more than one approach should be taken in order to cover all business options.

CORRELATING NODES WITHIN THE NETWORK

The other half of the design of network data has to do with what links or relations are to be measured for the selected nodes. There are two main issues to be discussed here. In many network studies, all the links of a given type among all the selected nodes are studied. In this way, a census is conducted. However, sometimes different approaches can use samples of the available links. This often happens because the links are less expensive or because of a need to generalize the network's relations. There is also a second kind of sampling of links that always occurs in network data. Any set of nodes might be connected by many different kinds of relations. For instance, neighbors in a particular neighborhood might like or dislike each other, they might spend time together or not, they might lunch or dine together, and so on. When the network data are collected, usually a selection or sampling process is performed from among a set of relations that were measured.

Given a set of nodes, there are some strategies to decide the proper direction of relationship collection for the individuals and, ultimately, how to calculate the network measures. It is possible to consider all relations available within the network. This approach produces the maximum amount of information, but it comes at a high cost. It is also difficult to generalize the network relations because of the number of distinct possible types of links.

Or we could consider just a subset of the possible types of relationships. This approach produces considerably less information for social network analysis. However, it is often less costly, and usually allows easier generalization about the individuals and their relations.

As usual, there is no one right method for all research questions in analytics. The best method, technique, methodology, or approach depends on the type of the data and, most important, the sort of problem to be solved.

Methods for social network analysis that consider all possible types of links require the collection of all information about each node and its links with all other nodes. In essence, this approach takes a census of the nodes' relationships rather than just a sample. For instance, it is possible to consider all different types of links among customers in a telecommunications environment, such as calls, short messages, multimedia messages, e-mails, data access, and so on. Any sort of relation among the customers is significant, because any possible types of links can drive the inclusion of the related nodes into the social network.

As the information about the links among the nodes is collected from the data, a full social network can be built, giving an overall picture about the entire population being studied. Because of the cost of this method, some intermediate approaches can be considered to collect as much relevant information as possible and to decrease as much as possible the cost of the whole process. Most of the social network analyses discussed in this book, particularly in the case study presented in Part II, were developed to be used with full network data, but with some particular boundary. For instance, in the case study, all residential customers were considered to take part into the social network rather than all types of customers.

Full network data are necessary to properly define and measure many of the structural concepts of network analysis, such as measures of distance among the nodes (i.e., closeness and betweenness). Full network data allow descriptions about the social structure and the network behavior with a considerable level of details. However, as mentioned earlier, full network data can be very expensive in terms of computational processes and also can be very difficult to collect. For large groups, such as the telecommunications industry, this task is even more challenging.

As Hanneman noted in his study,[4] most persons, groups, and organizations tend to have limited numbers of links and, most important, a limited number of possible kinds of links. This is probably due to individuals within the social networks having limited resources, such as time, money, energy, and capacity to maintain strong links for long periods. Also, most groups or communities are able to develop some sort of relationship among their members based on a few links.

In terms of business problems in telecommunications, particularly considering the huge volume of nodes and links, there are some distinct approaches to collecting the relationships among the customers.

The first and simplest approach is to consider and collect all links in relation to the network, in other words, to collect all calls, texts, and media messages exchanged among customers. Although this approach retrieves all information in the network, it is quite expensive in terms of computation. Sometimes the effort to compute measures based on all links is not only very high, it is also worthless.

For specific business purposes, some links can be irrelevant. Calls and text messages between residential customers and call centers, for instance, hold absolutely no value in terms of social network analysis. Those links can lead the analyses toward customers preferences or the relationships among particular customers and some private companies. However, in terms of how these customers relate with other customers, those links can contribute very little information.

For this reason, some specific calls and messages inside the network can be discarded when the network is being built. If it is possible to identify the number assigned to the call centers, for instance, all links to them would be discarded. Also, all links among customers and support, contact, and information numbers can be discarded. These links can highlight how satisfied customers are with their providers, but they do not raise any relevant or useful information about social relations.

Therefore, very often, some links assigned to calls and messages among customers and particular number providers are discarded in order to build the network and to calculate the measures.

Egocentric Networks

Egocentric method focuses on social analysis of groups based on a particular node. This method considers the individual rather than the structure of the entire network. This particular node is referred to as the *ego*. All of its connections are analyzed in order to identify the related nodes and, therefore, their neighborhood or their particular community. The analysis of the connections in relation to a particular node is important to highlight how the community affects the ego node over time and how this node can affect the entire community through a process known as cascade diffusion. This method considers a particular node, the ego, as the focal point of analysis.

Sometimes this approach is not possible or even necessary, especially when the network has a large number of nodes and links. For this type of network, tracking down the focal nodes, the egos, and all their links may be very time-consuming and require difficult data analysis. An alternative approach is to begin with a particular selection of focal nodes, the egos, and then identify the nodes to which they are connected. Once again, this process can be difficult. This alternative approach can be very effective for collecting data from surveys or interviews, in which case the focal nodes can be arbitrated and, therefore, analyses of their links can be performed afterward. This cascade process can speed the analysis of the social network for a particular community, such as relationships within schools, colleges, or companies, but it is not as effective for large social networks.

In egocentric networks, the links connecting the ego to all other related nodes within the network are called *alters*. In this case, if information about egos and alters is collected but no further information about the connections among alters is available, this type of data is not assigned to a social network at all. However, it is related to a particular subnetwork, considered a subset of selected nodes, the egos. This means that these data cannot be represented as a square actor-by-actor array of ties. In other words, with this sort of data, the only information available concerns a single node, the ego, and the links that connect it to other nodes; no information is available about the nodes connected to the ego and the links connecting them.

Despite the fact that this information does not represent an entire social network, egocentric data can still have value for network analysis. This approach is quite useful for understanding a particular structure of the social network and, therefore, the egos. This sort of analysis can indicate how egos influence their own subnetworks and how subnetworks affect egos over time. It is quite important to understand how those particular nodes behave within social structures. Analysis of the egos can also reveal particular trends in relation to their behavior, predicting eventual events within their social structure.

Once again, in terms of business problems in telecommunications, the analyses of egocentric networks are quite limited and specific. For general purposes such as churn, sales, and marketing, egocentric networks can contribute very little in terms of business outcomes. However, for particular applications such as financial risk and fraud, egocentric networks can be very interesting. Imagine an act of fraud in which the perpetrator was identified. The perpetrator's particular egocentric network can reveal all connections in relation to that particular node and, therefore, highlight some other suspicious nodes assigned to the act of fraud. A similar approach can be applied to credit risk. An egocentric network can be built to analyze the relationships of a specific insolvency node and thereafter highlight those relationships, particularly those that represent a credit risk.

Egocentric networks reveal very little useful information about the entire social network, especially in terms of business. However, the network assigned to a particular node comprised of characteristics such as insolvency, fraud, or risk can certainly reveal the correlated relationships with other nodes, which in turn can indicate a wider scope of usability.

Multiple Relations

Social network analysis relies on nodes and links. Nodes are individual observations described by one or more attributes. In the same way, these attributes can appear in many nodes simultaneously. Links are events that connect nodes to each other. However, links are usually described by a single attribute, even though different links might be described by different attributes.

In telecommunications, for instance, the nodes can be described by the customers' attributes, such as marketing segmentation, average revenue, types of products, services usage, and so on. The links can be described by different types of business transactions, such as calls, short messages, multimedia messages, e-mails, and so on. A combination of the customers' attributes might uniquely describe the nodes within the social network. Conversely, each business transaction should describe a particular link. For example, a call between two customers is a link. A short message between two customers is a new link, distinct from the first. In that particular case, distinct types of communication among the customers will reveal a specific type of link. The conventional social network analysis approach is interested in multiple attributes to describe nodes as well as multiple types of links connecting the nodes within the social network in distinct ways.

Positions in one set of relations may reinforce or contradict positions in another. Nodes may be linked together closely in one relational network but be quite distant from one another in a different relational network. The context of the social structure matters significantly. This fact will be explored in detail in the practical business case study presented in Part II of this book. The customer influence factor for churning is different from the factor for bundle diffusion, taking into account that the relations held by a node in terms of churning have values or weights distinct from the relations held by the same node regarding bundle diffusion. The locations of actors in multirelational networks and the structure of networks composed of multiple relations are some of the most interesting areas of social network analysis.

When social network data are collected, they usually contain particular types of relations among the nodes. Very often, these types of relations are different from each other, revealing distinct types of links. In a sense, this represents a possible way to define social structure when considering an entire population, comprised of several possible relations and distinct types. Usually the subject of interest indicates which type of relations among the nodes would be most relevant for a particular analysis, and, therefore, a selection of relations is performed, rather than a simple sample.

If there is no clear indication about what kind of relations should be considered in a particular study, a number of conceptual approaches might be of assistance. As Hanneman noted in his study, there are basically two domains for the examination of relationships: material and informational,

> Material things are conserved in the sense that they can only be located at one node of the network at a time.

> Movements of people between organizations, money
> between people, automobiles between cities, and the like
> are all examples of material things which move between
> nodes—and hence establish a network of material
> relations. Informational things, to the systems theorist,
> are "non-conserved" in the sense that they can be in
> more than one place at the same time. If I know
> something and share it with you, we both now know it.
> In a sense, the commonality that is shared by the
> exchange of information may also be said to establish a
> tie between two nodes.[5]

In terms of telecommunications, if one customer knows another customer, but they have never called each other (perhaps because they are neighbors), they share a link based on information that can be considered as bidirectional. For example, John knows Mary (one link) and Mary knows John (another link). However, as there are no calls connecting them, in terms of telecommunication networks, there is no link between those two nodes. If eventually John calls Mary, a link has been established. These two distinct theoretical concepts are dependent on the type of business problems to be solved.

Finally, when translating those concepts to the telecommunications environment, it is possible to confuse material and informational links. If the geographic location of a customer is known, links based on information can be established. If customer A lives in the same building as customer B, an informational link is created. If these two customers call each other, a physical connection has been created between them, establishing a material link. The crucial point here is to define the proper weight of those links once each one holds some particular relevance for the social network.

SCALES OF MEASUREMENT

As stated before, nodes can be described by a set of attributes, and links can be described by single events, in which different types of events reveal distinct types of links. The social data collected about the network structure, especially in relation to the links that connect the nodes, can be measured by different levels. In other words, it is possible to assign scores to all observations, either in terms of nodes or links. These different levels of measurement are important because they limit the types of questions that can be answered by social network analysis. By using different scales of measurement, it is possible to apply distinct algorithms to compute network measures, based on different mathematical properties.

It is conventional to distinguish nominal, ordinal, and interval levels of measurement. The ratio level can, for all practical purposes, be grouped with the interval level. It is useful, however, to further divide nominal measurement into binary and multicategory variations. It is also useful to distinguish between full-rank ordinal measures and grouped ordinal measures. Explanations about those types will be presented later.

Binary Measures of Relations

The most common method used to define scores for social network measures, particularly in terms of links, is simply to establish the presence of a connection between a pair of nodes. When connections are present, code zero (0) could be applied. If no connection exists, code one (1) could be designated. The example presented in Chapter 2, considering the network of friendships, is a good example. If two people are friends (e.g., John and Karl), code one (1) may be applied; if not, code zero (0) may be applied instead. This is a binary scale, the most common type of measurement.

Several real-world applications based on graph theory, and a substantial number of algorithms that are used to calculate the network measures concerning nodes and links are based on the binary method of measurement. Binary measurement is very common because of its ability to establish the presence or absence of a particular type of relation, assigning one (1) for the presence of a connection and zero (0) for its absence.

In telecommunications, the presence or absence of calls are coded one (1) and zero (0), respectively. If there is a call between two customers, the relation is coded one (1), and it would be counted in the network measures. Otherwise, if there are no calls between two customers, there is nothing to be counted.

Nominal Measures of Relations

Based on social network data, which contains information about nodes and links, a scale of measurement can be established to differentiate the relations among observations within a social structure. As presented in the previous section, binary levels of measurement are quite common for social networks, particularly relating to the presence or absence of connections among nodes.

Nodes are described by a set of attributes, and links by events, even though different types of events can reveal distinct types of links. Different types of links are usually observed in distinct ways, indicating that some types of links are quite different from others regarding a particular social structure. For instance, consider a social network based on personal relations. Kinship would be one type of friendship, relationships among coworkers another, and so on.

This scale of measurement is considered nominal or qualitative, as different types of attributes or events reveal distinct types of links. The subject indicates how different each type of link within the network is. This means that the same type of data could hold different levels, or differentiation, within the social structure, according to the network studied. This type of approach assigns nominal values for the links rather than strength. Note that the strength could be associated with the frequency or value of the connection between a pair of nodes, no matter how different the particular type of link is. Nominal measures of relations are intended to differentiate all types of links within a particular network, designating no importance or relevance between them at all.

Consider the telecommunications industry, for instance. It is possible to define multiple types of relationships such as calls, text messages, multimedia messages, e-mails, and so on. All of these types of links can be used to compute the network measures equally. Also, due to the peculiarities of telecommunications, it is possible for two customers to hold different types of links according to the types of connections established between them, such as calls and text messages. Notice that regardless of the frequency or duration of those types of connections among the customers, the strength of a particular link would not be weighted by the nominal level of measurement for this particular link. A link based on 120 minutes of calls between two particular customers is stronger than a link based on 40 minutes of calls between another pair of customers inside the same social network. The same concept can be applied to a link based on 30 calls against another based on 10 calls. The frequency here indicates which link is stronger than the other. However, there is no weight, rank, or order in relation to different types of links, such as calls and text messages. This means it is not possible to define which links are more important, those based on 30 calls or those based on 30 messages.

Ordinal Measures of Relations

Another method used to define the relevance or importance of the links among nodes within a social network is to establish an ordinal level of measurement for the connections or relationships. Ordinal measures for relations within social networks might be created by ranking the links in order of their importance to a particular piece of information, a combination of attributes, or a set of events, for example.

A ranking system using ordinal measures of relations can organize the links based on a particular factor of relevance to the social network analysis, such as minus one (−1) for links ranked as less important, zero (0) for links ranked as important, and plus one (+1) for links ranked as highly important.

Ordinal measures of relation are often used to designate distinct quantitative aspects of the links among nodes inside a network. In addition, some network analyses are concentrated to depict the strength of the links connecting the nodes. This strength can be calculated based on different approaches, including those based on frequency, proximity in time, or any other value assigned to intensity.

Ordinal scales of measurement consider more information than nominal scales. Based on network data containing information about nodes and links, a scale of measurement can be established in order to differentiate the relations among nodes given a particular weight. The binary level of measurement is commonly used to indicate the presence or absence of connections among nodes. The nominal level of measurement is often used to differentiate the distinct types of connections among nodes. And the ordinal level of measurement is used to rank the different types of connections among nodes.

The links within a social structure might be described by events or attributes. This information can be extremely relevant for social network analysis. For instance, considering the same types of personal relations described earlier, kinship would be more important than friendship, which could be more important than relationships among coworkers.

Once again, based on examples from the telecommunications industry, it is possible to define multiple types of relationships, such as calls, text messages, multimedia messages, e-mails, and so on, as presented before. However, in a distinct approach used to compute the network measures based on relations, those links can hold different weights in terms of social network analysis. Calls could be valued at three units (3), text messages as two units (2), and multimedia messages as one unit (1). In addition, the links and their weights would be considered separately or as a whole, adding the number of links and their respective values.

According to the previous example, a particular link based on 10 calls would be valued higher than a link based on 30 messages, because of the type of links. This level of measurement attaches value to the type of link, giving calls more value than text messages or e-mails.

Interval Measures of Relations

The final basic method used to measure links is based on interval values. In this approach, the level of measurement describes how important or relevant the links connecting the nodes within a social structure are. For instance, one particular type of link can be twice as valuable as another.

In this method of measurement, as in previous examples, the subject of interest dictates which type of link is more important than another and how much more important it is. Consider the telecommunications industry once again. Based on the revenue generated by different types of links, such as calls, text messages, multimedia messages, and so on, is possible to establish distinct values for all of them.

For instance, all links based on calls are valued five times more (5x) than links based on text messages. Also, multimedia messages are valued three times more (3x) than the text messages. Calls are assigned five times more value than text messages due to the revenue associated with this type of link.

Using intervals to measure the relations within a social network allows distinct statistical analyses to be applied to the outcomes. This approach makes it possible to create a wide range of values to be analyzed throughout the network, measuring for nodes and links, distribution of links, outliers, clustering, and so on.

In addition, there are numerous possibilities in terms of how you define interval measures in telecommunications networks. Calls among distinct classes of customers, distinct segments of marketing, distinct levels of financial groups, distinct ranges of risk, among others, could be used to establish the interval based on distinct scales of relations. For instance, a link between a node from class A and a node from class B could hold the same interval scale as a link between a node from class D and a node from class E.

SUMMARY

This chapter has introduced the major concepts of social network analysis, such as nodes and links. The most important foundation is based solely on the concepts of nodes and links. In the telecommunications industry, customers and phone numbers are the nodes and the calls and different types of messages are the links in the social network. The basic theory can be associated to landlines and mobiles, considering the one-to-one relationship between customers and phone numbers. In both cases the nodes are well defined because of the phone numbers. Calls, text messages, multimedia messages, e-mails, and other sorts of connections are well defined as links. The combination of nodes and links is, in essence, the network to be analyzed. These types of data, based on nodes (attributes) and links (relations), are the major characteristic of network data, and distinguish network data from other types of data used for common analyses.

One of the most important parts of social network analysis is the definition of the network itself. You must consider the population to be included in the analysis, the boundary of this population, and if the analysis should consider a sample or the entire network. This definition is crucial not just for the type of analysis to be performed but also for the outcomes that you hope to achieve.

The distinct types of relations were also covered in this chapter, presenting the different approaches used to define the relationships among nodes and, therefore, the different kinds of analysis that can be applied to social networks. Because different types of relations exist, network measures are computed in distinct ways, thus achieving different results. Networks can have different types of structures, including egocentric and multiple. All types produce distinct outcomes at the end.

Finally, the levels of measurement were presented in this chapter as a way to clarify the computing process of network measures. Depending on the scale of measurement adopted, the same network measures can reach completely different results. Binary relations can lead the calculation of network measures in a particular direction, depending on the network structure established for the analysis. In the same manner, distinct results may be reached by using nominal, ordinal, or interval relations.

In short, the network structure, boundary and population selected, and type of relations considered substantially affect the computation of network measures and thus the outcomes achieved through network analysis.

NOTES

1. I am indebted to Robert A. Hanneman and Mark Riddle, *Introduction to Social Network Methods* (Riverside, CA: University of California, Riverside, 2005), for the following discussion. Available at http://faculty.ucr.edu/~hanneman/nettext/Introduction_to_Social_Network _Methods.pdf (accessed November 3, 2010).

2. Ibid.

3. Ibid.

4. Ibid.

5. Ibid.

CHAPTER **4**

Measures of Power and Influence

O ne of the most common objectives of social network analysis
is understanding the relationships within a social structure
composed of customers, employees, students, or any other
group of people, and identifying how members of the network influence one another. Influence is a form of power, suggestion, or domi-
nation. Depending on the type of social structure, influence can take
different shapes and have different strengths.

For corporate purposes, influence is the capacity of one particular
customer to induce others to follow him or her in a specific business
event. In social structures such as universities and schools, influence
can take many forms. In these networks, power is often the strongest
form of influence. One particular member is able to induce others in
several distinct ways, about opinions or actions, depending on the type
of subject.

However, in business scenarios, influence is more often recognized
in the context of particular events. One group of customers can exert
influence over another for a specific business event, such as churn,
but not for purchasing. Customers can exert influence over others
when they acquire a product or service, leading related customers to

acquire something similar. Naturally, an intersection between these customers might exist, where a subset of influential customers can induce other customers regarding churning and purchasing. However, most often the influence is correlated to a particular business event.

The case study presented in Part II concerns social network analysis in the context of the telecommunications industry. The case study considers two distinct business events over time, churn and bundle diffusion. The list of influential customers for those events changed over time. Some customers were influential in terms of churn, leading others to leave after they quit. Some customers showed themselves to be influential in terms of bundle diffusion, leading others to acquire a bundle similar to what they had purchased. Some customers presented both influential characteristics over time, leading other customers to acquire a particular bundle and to leave the company afterward. But when considering multiple business events, the list of influential customers was quite short.

This chapter summarizes this theory in relation to the measure of power and influence in social network analysis. The measure of power is closely related to graph theory. Power is calculated by a particular node's connections, the strength of its links, and the length of its path to the other nodes within the network, among other factors. The measure of power is a network metric that indicates which nodes hold high values in relation to their social structure. There is no apparent correlation to a particular business event, for instance, when considering a social structure assigned to customers.

Influence, however, is the act of one person or group inducing another to do something. The behavior that a group is being influenced to perform must be well defined, and it is crucial to highlight in what manner group members are being influenced. Often influence is observed over time, describing the behavior of an individual customer and how that customer induces other related customers to behave in a similar manner.

Once again, in the case study presented in Part II, influence was calculated based on the historic occurrences of churn and bundle acquisition, driving the network metrics to be computed in a way that takes these occurrences into account.

TYPES OF NETWORKS

In terms of social network analysis, power and influence are measured by analyzing the social structures. Power is a property of social structures, and hence it relies on the shape of the structure being analyzed. There are distinct types of social networks, and, therefore, there are variations in the process and concept of computing power.

All social structures are based on relationships. Therefore, the measure of power is highly correlated to the relationships within the social network. A particular member of the social structure, or a node inside the social network, has power solely because of its relationships within the network.

The types of relationships that make up the network are related to the method used to calculate power. Different social structures have distinct methods of calculating power. Social structure usually refers to how nodes are settled within the network, how far they are from related nodes and how many nodes they are connected with. For business purposes, the connections of a particular node and how close it is to related nodes are crucial in order to calculate the measure of power. For instance, nodes with a high number of connections and with short paths to related nodes usually have more power than others. In terms of business opportunities, the number of connections and the length of the paths determine how many customers might be influenced and how quickly influence can spread.

This concept is demonstrated in the case study presented in Part II, in which a customer with strong influence can lead related customers to perform similar business actions—in that particular case, to leave the company or to acquire a bundle of services. Specifically, influential customers who decide to leave the company can induce related customers to leave as well. In the same way, influential customers who decide to buy some particular bundle can lead similar customers to acquire a similar bundle.

Influential customers inside the telecommunications network would be in a strong position in relation to the social structure being analyzed, both in terms of their number of connections and the length of their path to other customers.

To understand the approaches that social network analysis uses to study power and influence, it is useful to first consider some very simple systems.

Hanneman described three distinct types of social structures in his book.[1]

Figure 4.1 shows a social structure shaped as a star.

Upon first glance at the figure, it is apparent that node A occupies a strong position in this particular network. The star structure, consisting of a central node and several satellite nodes, bestows a favorable position on the central figure. In this case, node A is connected to nodes B, C, D, E, F, and G. Node A has six connections whereas all other nodes have just one. It is easy to observe that node A is well positioned in this social structure, or at least in a better position than the others. In this particular social structure, node A is just one step away from the other nodes it is connected to and has a high number of connections relative to the other members.

If node A is a customer, he is able to influence six other customers, regardless of the business event involved, and probably in a quick way, due to the short length of his connections. Any sort of information or

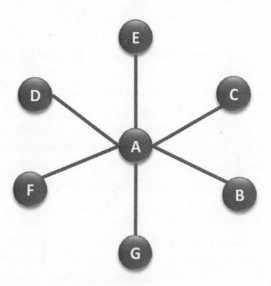

Figure 4.1 Star Network

Figure 4.2 Line Network

message can flow widely and quickly throughout this particular social structure if it is triggered by node A.

Figure 4.2 shows a network shaped as a line.

Consider node A in the social structure shown in this figure, configured in a line. Here node A is at the end or edge of the network. In this particular social structure, node A is certainly not in a position within the network to influence other nodes, regardless of the event involved.

Nodes B, C, D, E, and F have two connections, whereas nodes A and G have just one. The number of connections indicates that nodes B, C, D, E, and F have the same power within the network. However, node D is in the center of this particular social structure, one step away from nodes C and E, two steps from nodes B and F, and three steps from nodes A and G. Adding all of the steps needed to reach the other nodes in the network, node D is 12 steps away from every other node. Nodes C and E are 13 steps from the rest of the nodes, nodes B and F are 16 steps, and nodes A and G are 21 steps away. According to the number of connections, but also taking into account the average length of the paths between nodes within the network, node D is the most powerful node in this social structure.

Figure 4.3 shows a network shaped as a circle.

In this particular social structure, shaped as a circle, all nodes have two connections, one with each of their neighbors. This would indicate they are equally powerful in terms of the number of related nodes. As observed in Figure 4.2, not merely the number of connections should be taken into consideration in order to compute the power or influence of the nodes. Their position within the network is also important. However, in the circular network, all nodes are 12 steps away from the rest of the nodes in the network. All the nodes in the circular network have the same number of connections and the same average path length; therefore, they all have an equal amount of power.

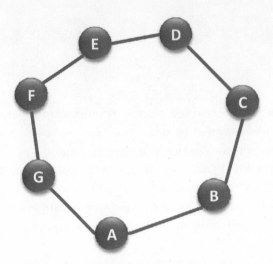

Figure 4.3 Circle Network

MEASURING POWER BY DEGREE CENTRALITY

Figure 4.1 presented a social structure based on a star network. In that network, node A clearly displayed more opportunities to reach the rest of the network and, importantly, reached the nodes faster. In that particular structure, node A has six straight connections, and, hence, it could reach six other nodes directly. All other nodes have just one straight connection. However, these nodes are able to reach all of the others, but only by going through node A. This means that node A is one step away from each node within the network, and the other nodes can reach the rest of the nodes within the social structure in two steps. This makes node A a logical place to trigger a message inside the network, as it can spread the message widely and quickly.

Imagine that node A is deleted from this social structure. The other nodes within the network will no longer be able to reach each other. Node A, in this particular social structure, acts as a hub.

As demonstrated in the case study discussed in this book, the more connections a customer has, considering his calls, text messages, multimedia messages, and so on, the greater his opportunity to diffuse his opinion. Power can also be thought of as information that is able to flow inside the network more efficiently because of nodes with many connections.

In that example, node A has more options (six related nodes) to diffuse a particular product more quickly and efficiently (one step away from any other node within the network).

Conceptually, node A has a degree of centrality of 6, and all other nodes, B, C, D, E, F, and G, have a degree of centrality of 1.

Consider now the social structure presented in Figure 4.2. Nodes B, C, D, E, and F have two related nodes, and nodes A and G have just one related node. In this particular social structure, all nodes in the first group (B, C, D, E, and F) have a degree of centrality of 2, and the nodes in the second group (A and G) have a degree of centrality of 1. Despite the fact that nodes B, C, D, E, and F have the same degree of centrality, node D has, on average, the shortest path to the rest of the social structure, making it a good choice for diffusion because it is able to move information throughout the network more efficiently.

Figure 4.3 shows a social structure based on a circular network. In that case, all nodes have the same opportunity to move information through the network as well as the same average length of path to move it. All nodes in that social structure have a degree of centrality of 2, because each one of them is directly connected to two other nodes. Also, the average distance for one node to reach any other node within the network is the same for all: one step to the directly connected node, two steps to the node with two degrees of separation, and three steps to the node with three degrees of separation.

Finally, in the circular social structure, any node would be a good choice to start a diffusion process within the network, because they all have the same measure of power. In a real-world business scenario, additional information about the customers should be taken into consideration in order to target the best set of customers.

In a telecommunications network, the degree of centrality is equal to the number of customers who make or receive calls to or from a particular customer. For instance, if John is a customer and makes calls to 5 friends, and receives calls from another 5 friends, he has a degree of centrality of 10. The number of calls he makes or receives is not important to this network measure; what matters is how many other customers he is connected to within the network.

The direction of the link is not important when calculating a customer's global degree of centrality. If John makes 10 calls to Karl and receives 5 calls from Karl, then both Karl and John have a degree of centrality of 1. The strength of the connections will be counted for another network measure presented later.

Taking this previous example, if John makes calls to Karl, Eoin, and Edward and receives calls from Edward, Julianne, and Linda, he has an out-degree of centrality of 3, an in-degree of centrality of 3, but an overall degree of centrality of 5, because Edward contributed to both measurements.

In summary, all connections coming into a particular node represent the in-degree of centrality, and all connections going out from a node represent the out-degree of centrality. Once again, in telecommunications, all customers who make calls to a particular customer represent his in-degree of centrality, and all customers who receive calls from that particular customer represent his out-degree of centrality.

In the telecommunications industry, directed graphs should be used to represent the customers and their relationships. Customers who make calls to several other customers can be viewed as potential leaders, and customers who receive calls from leaders can be viewed as potential followers. The term *potential* is used here to emphasize that different interpretations can be made. If you consider only the inside network, this may be true. However, if you also take the outside network into account, the understanding of the leader and the follower may be different. A customer who receives a call from outside the network can be an anchor to capture new customers or, in terms of revenue, can collect a substantial amount of interconnection rates from other operators. A customer who makes a call outside the network can be a high-risk customer in terms of churn if the majority of his connections are outside. He may eventually decide to move to another operator. The usage of network measures is a good way to establish customer value in terms of the relationships among the social structure in study. Additional network measures should be taken into consideration to accurately define leaders and followers within a network, as should historical information about a particular business event.

ADDITIONAL LEVELS FOR THE DEGREE OF CENTRALITY

The network measure that relates to the degree of centrality presented so far is always assigned to the first level of connection or relationship. When the degree of centrality, the in-degree, and the out-degree are computed, they are always based on the first and most direct link from and to the related nodes.

However, for marketing purposes, particularly when considering the concept of viral marketing, in which information should flow within the network, other levels of connections are also important. These additional levels of relationships are in fact what make the information flows inside the social structure possible.

The diffusion process, in a very straightforward way of thinking, is related to the degree of centrality. For instance, a particular node A has straight connection to nodes B and C. However, node B might connects to nodes D, E, and F, and node C might connect to node G. The degree of centrality, consisting of several distinct pairs of nodes, is the process that diffuses the information throughout the network. In this particular case, the first degree of centrality for node A is 2 (nodes B and C) and the second degree of centrality is 4 (nodes D, E, F, and G).

However, in order to highlight the nodes that have a better chance of diffusing information by cascading it through the social structure through their connections, it is crucial to recognize which nodes within the network have a high first degree of centrality with a good sequence of nodes in their connection paths. In other words, how far could the information spread inside the network through the connections of the original connections?

Figure 4.4 shows the same nodes A, B, C, D, E, F, and G, but now in a slightly more complex shape.

In this social structure, node A, according to the concepts presented previously, has a degree of centrality of 2, because it is connected to nodes B and C. Regardless of the direction of these connections, incoming or outgoing, the degree of centrality for node A is 2. However, the degree of centrality for node B is 3, once it is connected to nodes D, E, and F. Similarly, the degree of centrality for node C is 1, once it is connected to node G. Considering the

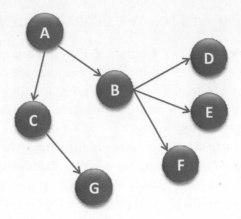

Figure 4.4 Social Structure for First- and Second-Degree Centralities

degree of centrality for nodes B and C, directly connected to node A, the total number of connections is 4, indicating that there are four nodes connected to nodes B and C. Thus, it is possible to say that the second degree of centrality for node A is 4, because the nodes connected to it (B and C) have four relationships (D, E, F, and G).

These network measures are also referred to as first-order centrality and second-order centrality, respectively. These metrics are very useful as a way to understand the possibilities of the diffusion or cascade process in which the information should flow throughout the social structure. In this way, the first-order centrality for node A is 2 (B and C), and the second-order centrality for node A is 4 (D, E, F, and G). First-order centrality can be expressed by the question, "How many friends do I have?" Second-order centrality can be expressed as, "How many friends do my friends have?"

Now consider the social structure shown in Figure 4.5.

In this social structure, the first-order centrality of node A is 3, larger than the previous network (Figure 4.4). The second-order centrality of node A is 2, fewer than in Figure 4.4. When analyzing a diffusion process in which information should flow inside the network, the number of nodes that can be connected is quite important. Despite the fact that the first-order centrality for node A in Figure 4.5 is greater than in Figure 4.4, node A can reach more nodes in Figure 4.4 because

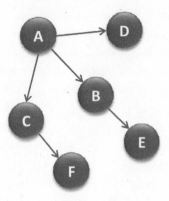

Figure 4.5 Social Structure for First- and Second-Degree Centralities in a Diffusion Process

its second-order centrality is greater than in Figure 4.5. Considering these two social structures, node A can reach six nodes in Figure 4.4, whereas it can reach only five in Figure 4.5. For diffusion purposes, second-order centrality is often quite important.

In telecommunications, well-connected customers are usually considered to be important and influential. Customers who are connected to other well-connected customers can represent low risk for churn but high potential for diffusion of products and services. In this case, a customer can decide to leave the company and not affect others directly because he has a small social network with other customers. But he could represent a high potential for diffusion because the information can spread throughout the network very quickly.

MEASURING POWER BY CLOSENESS CENTRALITY

Consider the social structure presented in Figure 4.1, the star-shaped network. Node A was shown to have the most influence, or power, in that particular social network. It is powerful because of its number of connections, or related nodes, but also because of the short average length of the path among the related nodes, B, C, D, E, F, and G.

In spite of the number of nodes connected, node A is closer to the other nodes than are any of the other nodes in that social structure.

All other nodes must go through node A to reach any other node within the network. Hence, all nodes except node A are two steps away from any other node. The average distance for nodes B, C, D, E, F, and G to reach any other nodes within the network is 1.83 steps (one step to reach A and two steps to reach any other). The average distance for node A to reach any other node is 1 step (one step to reach any other).

It is easy to observe that node A is the most important node in the social structure displayed in Figure 4.1. However, in Figure 4.2, based on the line network, it is more difficult to determine the most powerful node. Nodes B, C, D, E, and F are all linked to two nodes. Their degree of centrality is 2. However, node D seems to be the central node, the most important one in that particular social network. It is not difficult to prove that node D is closer to the other nodes than are any other nodes in the network. The average distance for nodes A and G to the other nodes is 3.5. (Using node A as an example, it is one step to node B, two to node C, three to node D, four to node E, five to node F, and six to node G.) The average distance for nodes B and F is 2.66. (Using node B as an example, it is one step to nodes A and C, two steps to node D, three to node E, four to node F, and five to node G.) The average distance for nodes C and E is 2.16. (Using node C as an example, it is one step to nodes B and D, two steps to nodes A and E, three steps to node F, and four steps to node G.) Finally, the average distance for node D to reach any other node within the network is 2 (one step away to nodes C and E, two steps to nodes B and F, and three steps to nodes A and G). This makes node D the most central node in this particular social structure. It is the most important, relevant, and powerful node in this social network, according to the network measure of power based on the degree of closeness centrality. It is important to note that this measure of power is based solely on the network metrics, not on past behavior.

EIGENVECTOR

The measure of power based on the degree of closeness centrality described to this point is relatively easy to understand in the social structures shown in Figures 4.1, 4.2, and 4.3. However, in more complex networks, this network metric of distance can represent a real challenge.

Consider two customers of a telecommunications operator, John and Karl. John makes and receives calls to and from several other customers on a regular basis. Therefore, he is part of a small social network, in comparison to the entire telecommunications network of this particular operator. His links are thicker because he has several calls assigned to him, both incoming and outgoing. John has also a small average distance between his connected customers, his relationships within the social network.

Karl, however, is connected to many customers in the network. Some of his links are strong, based on the frequency of calls. However, some of his links are weaker due to the infrequency of contact. Suppose that Karl, like John, has a small average distance between all of his connections.

Surprisingly, John and Karl may have similar measures of power based on closeness centrality. Their average distance from the other nodes in their networks might be quite similar, leading the network analysis to view them as equally central in this particular social structure. Theoretically, they are. However, their importance, relevance, or power within the social network is clearly different, because John has only a few connections, and Karl has a large social network assigned to him.

Specifically in regard to business applications, this makes a huge difference in terms of marketing and sales campaigns.

In order to differentiate the data in this scenario, a metric called eigenvector is applied. The eigenvector calculation determines the closeness centrality of the nodes in a social structure, based on the smallest average distance from other members, both in terms of local subnetworks and global networks. The computing process for the eigenvector assigns higher value to global networks. In other words, eigenvector computes the closeness centrality measure of power, taking into consideration the average geodesic distances among the nodes depending on the size of the particular subnetwork.

In that case, nodes with similar closeness centrality but with distinct eigenvector measures should be interpreted in different ways. A greater eigenvector might represent more nodes that can be reached with the same amount of effort. In the example of John and Karl, although they may have similar closeness centrality, because Karl has an eigenvector that is greater than John's, he is able to reach more customers than John with the same effort. In a diffusion process, such as a bundled sales campaign, this particular measure can make all difference in terms of span.

MEASURING THE POWER BY BETWEENNESS CENTRALITY

Considering the star network shown in Figure 4.1, node A is between any two pairs of nodes in that particular social structure. For any node within the network to reach any other one, it must pass through node A. Node A works like a bridge or a hub in this social network. If node B needs to contact node C, it must do it through node A. If information needs to flow throughout the network, from node E to node F, it must go through node A. Node A is located at the very center of this social network.

Node A is also able to isolate all other nodes in this social structure. If it is removed from the network, the other nodes will no longer be able to reach any other node. Node A is a broker in a structure such as this. For this reason, its importance to the entire social structure is quite substantial.

The third measure of power described in this chapter shows how a particular node is linked to others within a social structure. If a particular node uses several short paths inside a social network, the information that flows through it should flow faster. If a node does not use short paths among pairs of nodes, the information that passes through the network should flow slower. Based on this concept, node A in the star network is able to spread information throughout the entire network faster than any other node.

Considering the social structure based on the line network, shown in Figure 4.2, nodes A and G are at the very edge of the network. They are the end points of that structure. Nodes A and G are not between a pair of nodes, and for this reason, they are not acting as brokers in that network. They have no betweenness centrality in that particular case. The other nodes, B, C, D, E, and F, are between a pair of nodes, and, thus, they have the same measure of power based on betweenness centrality.

In the social structure based on the circle network, shown in Figure 4.3, all nodes have the same power to act as a broker. All of them are located between two nodes, serving as a bridge for at least one pair of nodes. For this reason, all nodes in the circle network have the same measure of power based on the betweenness centrality. All of them have the same importance or relevance in terms of betweenness, which means that all of them can move information at the same speed through the social network.

Social network analysis takes into consideration several network measures to compute the influence or importance of the nodes within a social structure. The measures of power described in this chapter—degree, closeness, and betweenness—are a few of the network measures used to identify the nodes that are relevant for a particular business application. All of them indicate some specific knowledge about the social structure in study.

SUMMARY

Social network analysis is a relevant tool for exploratory analysis, for investigation, and mostly to create useful knowledge about the behavior assigned to social structures. General knowledge about groups of friends, students, employees, or customers is defined by clustering models, which usually recognize similarities among the members of a particular group by their individual attributes. These clusters are, therefore, created based on individual characteristics. As long as the individuals within a social structure have similar attributes, they are fitted into the same cluster.

Social network analysis allows the establishment of a distinct method of understanding social structures, based on the relationships among their members instead of individual attributes. In this method, how the members of a particular social structure relate to each other is more important than any individual characteristic. These individual characteristics are important in order to assign value to the links among members, but the focus of the analysis, and hence the pattern recognition, is always on relationships. A relationship between two important members may also be quite important. Similarly, a particular relationship between two unimportant members may be unimportant. Regardless of the individual attributes or how important the member, this sort of information is used to assign different levels of power to the links.

This chapter presented some basic concepts about social network metrics, including those related to the measurement of power. Power within a social structure is assigned to the individual nodes, but it is calculated based on their position inside the network. Their position within the network is determined by the relationships among the nodes. Thus, the relationships within the social structure define the measurement of power for the nodes.

Three fundamental measurements of power were discussed in this chapter: the degree of centrality, the closeness of centrality, and the betweenness of centrality. The degree of centrality gauges the power of a particular node according to the number of connections it holds. These connections may or may not be directional. In directed graphs, where the direction of the relationship counts, the measurement of power based on the degree of centrality can be split into two distinct measures, the in-degree, for incoming links, and the out-degree, for outgoing links. The degree of centrality can be measured based on different levels of connections, such as first order, second order, and so on. First-order centrality is the number of direct connections among the nodes. Second-order centrality is the number of direct connections that the nodes connected to the original node have. First-order centrality is commonly referred to by the question "How many friends do I have?" Second-order centrality can be addressed by asking "How many friends do my friends have?"

The second measurement of power is closeness centrality. It is also based on the relationships among the nodes. This measurement gauges how close a particular node is to its related nodes. It can be understood as the average number of steps that a particular node needs in order to reach its correlated nodes. This is known as the average length of path a node needs to diffuse information through its social network. The closeness centrality indicates how far information can spread through the network.

Finally, the third measurement of power is known as betweenness, which is also based on relationships among the nodes. It gauges how central a particular node is within the social structure. A short distance between two nodes is the smallest path connecting them. Considering different levels of connections, node A might reach node B by a distinct path, passing through several different nodes on the way. The smallest distance between those two nodes is the short path between them. If a node partakes of several short paths within the social structure, it is considered to be more central, and its betweenness is high. If not, the node's betweenness level, and thus its position within the network, is lower. The betweenness centrality indicates how fast information can flow throughout the network.

NOTE

1. Robert A. Hanneman and Mark Riddle, *Introduction to Social Network Methods* (Riverside, CA: University of California, Riverside, 2005). Available at http://faculty.ucr.edu/hanneman/nettext/Introduction_to_Social_Network_Methods.pdf (accessed November 3, 2010).

PART

II

Social Network Analysis Case Study

The second part of this book presents a case study based on the concepts presented previously. This case study puts in place most of the concepts described in Part I and is aimed to create a customer influence factor according to particular business events, such as churn and bundle diffusion. Chapter 5 presents the current telecommunications scenarios, and how social network analysis can help companies in their business. Chapter 6 shows how the customer influence factor was modeled by using the telecommunications data, the business issues, and the SAS capabilities. Chapter 7 presents the social network model assessment, by comparing its outcomes in relation to some particular business events such as churn and bundle diffusion. This process is quite related to the model adjustment and fitting due to the event it had been chosen. Chapter 8 describes the social network results in terms of business. How did the customer influence factor perform in comparison to the traditional approaches when applied to retention campaigns and sales activities? Finally, Chapter 9 wraps up Part II, presenting some additional possible applications in terms of product and service choice, and in future works in terms of social network analysis deployment.

CHAPTER 5

Telecommunications Environment

The highly competitive telecommunications market demands that companies establish and maintain a good customer relations process. There are several traditional approaches to address business issues using behavioral segmentation and predictive models. These traditional approaches, such as clustering and predictive models, are well-established unsupervised and supervised learning approaches, respectively. Although these models can be quite effective in terms of predictions or even in terms of customer understanding, they only present an isolated view of customers. They do not consider customers' relationships or the influences among the customers, especially over time. Social network analysis can be used to enhance knowledge about customers' influences in an internal community. New propositions to evaluate customers can clearly distinguish aspects of the virtual communities inside the telecommunications networks, allowing companies to deploy more effective action plans to better spread their products and services. The evolutionary perspective should consider network behavior in distinct time frames, allowing a more complex cross-analysis and also the opportunity to establish a correlation between the strength of the relationship and the influence over time for some particular business events, such as bundle diffusion. Remembering that influence happens first when the relationship is stronger can enable companies to prepare a marketing campaign to optimize the bundle diffusion targeting the right subset of customers.

NEW CHALLENGES IN THE TELECOMMUNICATIONS MARKET

Telecommunications is characterized by an increasingly competitive market. In order to keep the customer base growing, or at least stable, all companies should provide valuable offerings, suitable plans, original and innovative bundles, and, most important, a range of pricing discounts. Very often these actions are based on customer behavior and also their individual values to the corporation. These aggressive offerings can be quite expensive in terms of costs for companies. Due to this fact, an effective customer loyalty program, created within a good-performing customer relationship management system, can make companies more competitive, effective, and, most important in these sort of markets, more sustainable.

In addition, advertising new products and services and diffusing some telecommunications bundles can be very difficult. The process of targeting the best subset of customers to offer some particular bundles can be quite expensive in time and money. Using the concept of social network analysis it is possible to target the best subset of customers, based on not just their likelihood of purchasing but also on diffusion events. This subset of customers targeted through social network measures can perform bundle diffusion among other customers to whom they are related. Using the right measure of influence, they also can induce other customers rather than just contact them.

Effective processes assigned to customer loyalty and bundle diffusion programs should take into account customers' behavior. In this way, a more realistic corporate value of customers can be established. The aforementioned models can address these issues by creating a graph about customers' interactions and connections and identifying a measure of importance or influence about customers, based on how and when they relate to one another.

By using products and services, telecommunications customers leave behind an understandable record of their usages, behaviors, preferences, and needs, thereby showing a company how they interact with it and, possibly, how they would like to. Also, they leave a trail about how they call each other, how they pay their bills, how they acquire and consume new offers, and how often they complain about something. This trail is important to gain an understanding of customer needs and to learn about events, such as churning and bundle acquisition. Monitoring and following all those tracks, learning from them, and applying the knowledge gained from this information is a good way to figure out which subset of customers should be selected to prevent churning, which ones should be selected for acquisition campaigns, and which ones just require some particular relationship contact or message.

Especially in the telecommunications market, customers naturally create a sort of community in terms of when they use telecom products and services, such as short messages, multimedia messages, e-mails, and even in terms of when they make and receive calls. These small—and sometimes big—communities are created by connections among members, whatever the type of connection. These communities can be viewed as social networks, in which each individual has some particular relationship, whether strong or weak, whether frequent or infrequent, with the other members of the community. As in any social community or social network, each individual can exert some influence over other members; some can exert more influence over others, some less. Also, in relation to distinct business events, such as churning or acquisition, these influences can be very specific, which means that some individuals can be influential for one particular business event, such as churning, but not for another, such as bundle diffusion. Similarly, some individuals can be of low influence for some particular business activity, such as service usage, but highly influential for another, such as acquisition. In the end, the influence is assigned to some particular business event. Certainly some individuals can be highly influential for more than one business activity, which just makes those individuals more important to the company.

Ultimately, the social network analysis approach is a straightforward way to learn which customers have more influence than others within a given community.

Influential customers can have an impact on related customers, especially when the business activity occurs in a chain process. Business activities such as churning and purchasing are examples of chain processes.[1] As a chain process, the initial activity can be triggered by a stronger node, that is, in terms of business, by an influential customer.

Companies are usually interested in recognizing the patterns of behavior of their customers, so they establish more focused and direct marketing and sales campaigns. In any highly competitive market, such as telecommunications, it is important to identify who the high-value customers are and who are not the high-value customers. There are several different approaches to define customer value, based on their individual characteristics regarding usage, revenue, profit, demographics and geographic information, credit, risk, and so on. Social network analysis is a suitable approach to establish customers' value based on their relationships, because of their relationships with others inside the telecommunications network. By using social network analysis, it is possible to infer who are the leaders within the social communities and who are the followers. Customer value in this context does not consist only of the attributes described previously; instead, it consists of the importance of the connections—frequency, recency, and strength—and hence the length of the influence. The first attributes are assigned to the links, which compound into the nodes' influence.

The evaluation of customer strengths, in terms of their interactions through the social structure, can reveal the possible influence that some customers can have over the others within their own social networks. Customers identified as central, close, or strong nodes, based on their links inside the social structure, can be selected as targets for special campaigns and special offers, such as loyalty programs and sales promotions. These customers, according to particular business activities, are selected not based on who they are but rather based on what they represent to their own communities and therefore to the companies of which they are customers. The important fact here is to understand how they can influence other customers to follow them in particular business activities and how they interact within their own small communities.[2]

In addition to the degree of influence, it is important to understand how quickly all these influences occur within the social structure. In order to achieve useful outcomes, an overall social network analysis approach should be put in place over time, looking at distinct network metrics for a particular social structure and comparing those metrics over different time periods. It is necessary to consider an influential customer at a particular time and what happens with all customers with whom that influential customer relates over a period of months, weeks, or days. Do other customers perform the same original business activity as this seed customer? If that influential customer decides to purchase a wireless data service, do the related customers decide to acquire the same service afterward? This sort of analysis helps to explain the evolution of social communities within the telecommunications networks and then to prepare marketing and sales campaigns based not on just the behavior of the social networks but also on their possible evolvtion.

The telecommunications market is quite antagonistic. It is highly competitive in some particular services, such as mobile wireless data streaming, and it is very stable in other services, such as landline. Strategies for those different markets should be distinct, and the understanding of overall customer behavior should be unique. In general, the strategy for landline marketing is focused on customer retention. The strategy for mobile marketing is much more complex, and it is focused on cross-selling, up-selling, acquisition, and also retention. Because the process of acquiring new customers is quite expensive, the first action of a mobile marketing strategy should be a loyalty program, establishing a shield to protect current customers. Once those customers are protected, companies are able to search for additional customers and also to increase their relationships with customers with effective cross-selling and up-selling campaigns.

In the highly competitive telecommunications market, an active customer loyalty program can turn into a real competitive advantage, and it might allow companies to retain not just the best customers but also their related consumers. By doing this with the information gained from social network analysis, it is also possible to retain more than the good, or profitable, or even high-usage customers but also their social communities, which probably represent a substantial gain in corporate terms.[3]

By retaining the best and most profitable customers of the telecommunications base, companies are able to improve their sales campaigns, increasing revenue by offering more plans, bundles, promotions, and even new services and products. Clearly, it is easier to sell products and services to good customers than to bad ones. By keeping the good customers loyal, the benefits accrue not just to the existing customer base but also to the sales campaigns aimed at new customers. According to the social network approach, marketing and sales activities can be indirectly applied to the social community of a particular customer. In other words, the social network approach increases significantly the possible earnings from corporate sales and marketing campaigns.

The social network analysis approach can also help the loyalty program. It can support the process of cross-selling and up-selling products and services through a diffusion approach, thereby increasing the performance of these kinds of initiatives.

Likewise, future revenues of telecommunications companies can come from new products and services. Voice and other traditional services are no longer a stable or even an increasable source of revenue. New products and services embedded in distinctive bundles should be launched in order to achieve revenue growth. New technologies are crucial to boost new revenue. New technologies also bring the need for new processes and, therefore, new approaches to manage and handle customers.

The retention and sales campaigns can be substantially augmented by accurately targeting the customer base, which means selecting the right clients or prospects for responses, thereby reducing the costs of operations and increasing profit.

SOCIAL NETWORKS IN THE TELECOMMUNICATIONS ENVIRONMENT

Relationship is the basis of any sort of community. Social networks are created by the relationships among their members. The challenge in regard to social network analysis is to identify properly the roles assigned to actors and edges—in other words, the nodes and the links.

Based on different types of problems to solve and using the same data, distinct nodes and links can be created. In telecommunications, for instance, there are several different types of information that can be turned into links, such as calls, short messages, multimedia messages, access data, e-mails, and so on. Similarly, there are also several different types of information that can be turned into nodes, such as telephone numbers, customers' identification, addresses, companies, and so on. Even very small and highly connected communities could be turned into nodes in order to analyze community relations.

As long as new technologies continue, options for new relationships will continue in the telecommunications market. All those new tablets, smart phones, personal device assistants, and so on create new types of communications among people and, therefore, new types of relationships. Because of these continuing new scenarios, it is possible to create more types of virtual communities, making social network analysis for telecommunications companies more complex. These new virtual networks ultimately imply more opportunities.

Several types of events in communications can be observed as occurring in a chain process, particularly the number of different bundles consisting of distinct products and services. These events can occur over the time, increasing substantially the complexity mentioned earlier. They make the social network more dynamic, and they require studying social interactions in a temporal framework.

By assuming that particular business events, such as churning, acquisition, and others, occur in a chain process, it is possible to assume that those chain events are triggered at some point in the network and also in some period of time. The main goal in this approach is to identity the nodes that are likely to trigger such chain events, when they will trigger them, and, perhaps, why. Network metrics compute and generate data about the network, basically about the nodes, and these data can identify a distinctive approach to answer some of these questions, especially the one related to why. The question about when chain events occur is assigned to predictive models rather than to exploratory or investigative models such as social network analysis.

All those network measures, calculated mostly for nodes, reveal a particular combination of values that explain why a particular node triggers a chain event within a social network. Based on historic (temporal) information, it is possible to observe the correlation between a particular set of network measures and thresholds and the business event being studied.

The relevance of the nodes in terms of strength and the thickness of the links in terms of frequency and importance describe the social network behavior and how the nodes interact with one another by their links. This knowledge can be used to create more effective business actions in relation to events that take place in a chain, such as churning and acquisition. By doing this, companies are able to create a relevant competitive advantage in marketing.

Based on the high association between telephone numbers and customers, particularly in the mobile market, techniques such as social network analysis are suitable to exploit social communities' behaviors. By understanding the nodes' relevance and the links' strength, it is possible to identify which nodes—or customers—are likely to trigger some particular business event inside the network and, additionally, which nodes are likely to follow the same sort of event over time.

In practical terms, by utilizing a social network analysis approach within telecommunications companies, it is possible to improve the retention process by identifying the customers who are likely to churn and then to lead some of their related customers to follow them. Similarly, it is possible to increase substantially overall revenue while decreasing costs of operation by choosing customers who are likely to buy particular products or services and who will lead some of their related consumers to purchase similar products or services after them.

Ultimately, social network analysis helps to target the best customers for particular business events and marketing and sales campaigns.

TRADITIONAL PREDICTIVE MODELS BASED ON ARTIFICIAL NEURAL NETWORKS

Artificial neural networks can be used as supervised models to predict churn or bundle acquisition events that usually happen in telecommunications companies, especially in mobile operations. Data about churning or bundle acquisition can be collected in historical databases and the observation window used to track and validate how the neural network can vary in terms of time. Because of market and behavior dynamics, it is possible to develop predictive models based on artificial neural networks using 12 months, more or less. A shorter period can produce incomplete information or misunderstandings of behavior, and a very long period can mix different behaviors passing through different time frames.

Predictive modeling based on supervised techniques, such as decision trees, artificial neural networks, or linear regression, are suitable to establish the likelihood of occurrence of known business events. Based on these known events, the supervised model is trained to predict the behavior of the target variable, which is the business event being studied. The business event could be directed to churning, acquisition, bad debt, fraud, and so on. Previous occurrences of these business events are important to determine the role the target variable will play. Along with the target variable, a set of additional attributes is included as descriptive variables so that the model can learn about the correlation between the set of descriptive attributes and the target variable. This is the learning process of the supervised model.

Those predictive models are applied to determine the likelihood that each customer will leave a company, that is, will cease consuming some product or service, will not pay bills, will be fraudulent, and so on.

Based on these scores, companies are able to define practical and focused business actions to retain their customers, avoid the cessation of consumption, avoid insolvency, and prevent occurrences of fraud.

A combination of scores is also possible so that companies are able to retain (based on the churning score) their best customers (based on the customers' value) and improve finances and business actions in terms of efficiency. Different offerings could be put in place according to the score for churning and the score for customer value. Good customers with a high propensity to leave could receive aggressive promotions to stay with the company. However, good customers with a low likelihood to leave do not require such aggressive actions.

Aiming to optimize the customer loyalty program, and consequently keep good customers, all sort of companies, especially telecommunications ones, need to know how to evaluate their customers in terms of corporate value. Also, companies need to know how likely a customer is to stop using their products and services. By knowing how important customers are in terms of social interactions and the likelihood of churning, companies are able to define a more focused retention program based on distinct offerings of different values for different subsets of customers. A similar approach can be followed for bundle diffusion, focusing on different subsets of customers with distinct offerings of products and services.

There are several ways to establish this customer value, based on average billing, revenue, usage, or even behavior. This type of customer value can be determined by clustering models or even by simple statistical processes. The combination of the customer value and the score assigned to a particular business event, such as churning or bundle acquisition, allows companies to recognize good customers who are likely to leave or to purchase a bundle and then take action to prevent the churn or to support the sale.

COMBINED MODELING APPROACH

The methodology of social network analysis can be applied to particular business events, such as churning and purchasing, as shown so far. The study of social interactions and their consequences over the community needs to be correlated to some particular event. The main focus in this approach is to recognize the customer behavior and the associations among business events, such as the ones described earlier. When a specific business event is studied, these correlations can reveal how influential particular consumers are.[4]

The combination of traditional models to predict business events like churning or bundle acquisition and the social network analysis to realize the magnitude of impact and influence of particular customers over others can lead companies to establish effective processes for determining customer loyalty and bundle adoption.

It is possible to develop and implement distinct models, such as artificial neural networks, to learn about customer behavior. Other techniques can be put in place to develop predictive models, such as decision trees and regressions. All models can achieve good results, and the choice of which to use is based on the type and format of the data and the data miners' experience. However, a specific model is usually suited to a specific goal, such as predicting churn or bundle acquisition events in the telecommunications scenarios. In order to assess the impact and the correlation among those business events inside the database, it is important to analyze the events in a chain perspective.

The perspective of a chain process should be addressed using social network analysis rather than traditional models. Nevertheless, binding both models—the traditional one based on artificial neural networks to predictive modeling and the social network analysis to learn about the customer's behavior in a chain's process—will achieve a more effective and accurate methodology to prevent churn and to better diffuse a set of particular bundles.

There are several studies about social network analysis aimed at better understanding consumer behavior and the correlation between business events that happen inside a community and their ramifications. As stated previously, the traditional techniques are very useful to predict those events, but they are not quite suitable to estimate the correlation among them. The combination of both techniques can establish the correct knowledge so that companies can understand the impact of events in a chain process.

Social network analysis is a technique that uses the relationship between events to establish and recognize patterns inside large databases. It is used to map and measure the relationships among people, groups, and organizations, among others. Every type of organization of people who may be considered a social network can be the focus of this methodology, which provides a visual and mathematical analysis of human relationships.

Figure 5.1 shows how some particular customers can play an important role in terms of event diffusion, considering business activities, such as churning or bundle acquisition.

The telecommunications market is extremely competitive. Companies in that market offer communications services, including fixed and mobile calls, text, broadband, and others, and they are constantly seeking new ways to attract new customers and keep the current ones with innovative promotions, bundles, and plans.

The most important variables to direct this research are the ones related to the calls. The call-detail records are the main source in the

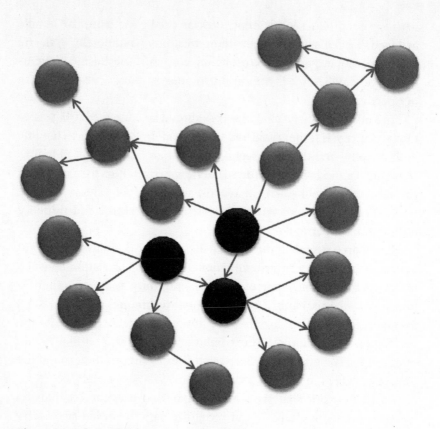

Figure 5.1 Influential Customers in a Social Network

telecommunications database to provide useful information to establish the links and correlations among the network nodes and to recognize customer behavior in terms of usage and event influences. Additionally, demographic and account information should help to define customer behavior and the reasons for the length of influence between the network nodes, that is, the central and powerful customers.

The same attributes, prepared in a different format, can be used to develop the predictive model. The suggested artificial neural network model can use the call-detail records to define a customer's churn behavior as well as demographic information. The difference here is the way the dataset is prepared and the algorithm is applied to discover the specific information. The first model is oriented to recognize the customer's influence, and the second one is oriented to score the likelihood of churn. A similar approach can be used on the bundle- or product-adoption process, where an analytical model assigned to the purchase likelihood can be combined with the customer-influence factor to establish a better target of clients to be contacted.

Data assigned to the churn and sales events can be extracted from distinct information systems, such as customer relationship management, call center, billing and collection, and others. All this information is quite useful to establish the amount of influence that one customer can exert over others. In other words, the churn or the bundle-acquisition record can be used to link the business events inside the telecommunications database, helping to creating an understanding about how some particular business events impact other customers in a chain.

Knowledge of customer influence can be used to define customer value in terms of corporate overview. Understanding corporate value for customers, considering their social interactions, allows companies to establish more focused marketing and loyalty campaigns. This new perspective significantly changes the way companies handle their customers, by evaluating them in terms of social communities rather than as single isolated attributes, such as billing and revenue information. In that way, some customers who spend less than others could be considered as of higher value, not because of the amount of money they directly represent but because of the length of influence they might have. This distinct sort of approach can lead companies to substantial changes in terms of marketing and sales. The total amount of money in relation to the social network or in relation to a social network assigned to a particular influential customer can represent more revenue at the end.

FEASIBLE ACTION PLAN BASED ON THE COMBINED APPROACH

The telecommunications market is becoming continuously more competitive. To keep up their profitability, companies should improve their operational processes, which include, besides quality of service, new packages and bundles and special offerings, to ultimately achieve excellent customer loyalty. As long as the market continues to become more difficult, companies increasingly need to differentiate themselves to raise their competitive advantage. There are several distinct approaches to achieve this goal; the conjunction of some of these approaches could lead to more valuable results.

The traditional predictive modeling approaches—by using artificial neural networks, decision trees, or regression—can uncover knowledge behind the data and establish an accurate likelihood for business events such as churning or bundle adoption that can be attributed to the customer. These customer scores can be used to define and perform different actions in order to retain good customers. This approach can save a huge amount of money in the loyalty process. However, predictive modeling is a method to discover the propensity of each customer to execute some action or event. Nevertheless, these scores are calculated for every customer in the company's database, regardless of their value to the corporation. There should be a way to differentiate, in conjunction with the predictive score, the good customers from the bad ones or, in the corporate sense, the profitable or valuable customers from the unprofitable ones. This differentiation could be determined by clustering models that can establish different groups of customers, according to their characteristics, behaviors, and usage. Also, some simple approaches, such as average billing or type of products and plans, can be used to categorize customers into distinct segments. The prediction score assigned to the client's segment can be a good way to define and perform distinct actions for customer retention, thereby decreasing the costs related to loyalty campaigns.

Although the previous approach is quite mature and widely used in the market, there is a distinct way to categorize customers based on a different value than just revenue or another particular feature. This new type of weight to classify the customer, especially in events like churning and sales, which can be performed in a chain process, represents their possible influence over other customers within a social network.

The customer's loyalty process aims to keep as many customers as possible in the company's base, because acquiring customers is much more expensive than retaining them. Also, billing, revenue, or even some specific feature is an isolated way to evaluate customers. Using a measure that allows companies to visualize just the customer and allows a comparison based on just that kind of measurement allows detached assessments. The customer's influence measure also allows the company to compare a set of customers simultaneously. The customer's influence could raise the value assigned to a specific customer, not because of that customer's amount of billing but because of the sum of values assigned to the satellite customers who spin around the base customer in a social network scenario. The summarized value can be tremendously higher than the isolated one. Some events occur in a chain. In this way, one particular business event—such as churning or purchasing—can trigger several other similar events thereafter. In such cases, it is very important to understand the actors and their relationships over time. By doing this, companies can keep not just the higher-value actors or customers but the whole structure assigned to those actors—the related customers—who are the base customers' social networks.

Additionally, by considering the influencer's measure, companies are able to keep not just more customers in their databases but those customers who have a certain relationships with others, which consequently means more usage of services like call, text, and Internet access. In that way companies will keep the social networks that exist behind the databases and the physical networks. These social networks ultimately mean more people, more revenue, and more extended customer life cycle.

By using this methodology, it is possible to gather outcomes from both analytical models: the likelihood in relation to a particular business event, such as churning or purchasing, and the knowledge about how a business event can possibly spread over the social structure. In terms of individual customers, this combination can predict how likely a particular customer is to leave, for example, and if it is likely, how many people that customer can possibly lead to follow. The score that represents the likelihood of churning/purchasing is drawn by artificial neural networks, and the score that indicates the number of possible consumers affected is drawn by social network analysis.

Therefore, each combination of models makes it possible to establish a different type of business action, as shown in Table 5.1.[5]

This example is about a churn event, but a similar action plan can be established for sales campaigns and cross- and up-selling initiatives.

Table 5.1: Combined Analytical Scores in Order to Establish a More Focused Business Action Plan

Likelihood of Churn	Customer's Influence		
	Level 1	Level 2	Level 3
0–25	Bundle offerings	Product offerings	Service offerings
25–50	Relationship campaign **plus** small discount in bundle offerings	Relationship campaign **plus** small discount in product offerings	Relationship campaign **plus** small discount in service offerings
50–75	Anti-attrition campaign **plus** discount in bundle offerings	Anti-attrition campaign **plus** discount in product/ service offerings	Anti-attrition campaign
75–100	Retention campaign **plus** free bundle offerings	Retention campaign **plus** discount in bundle offerings	Retention campaign

Considering level 1 as the highest influence and level 3 as the lowest influence, and that the likelihood is in percentage of churn probability, the cells in the middle of the table describe the possible actions to be taken by companies. In that way, customers who have more influence over others, level 1, and have the highest likelihood to leave the company, between 70 and 100, will receive the strongest retention promotion to stay longer with the company, which could mean more call time or free texting or more megabytes to download and upload in broadband packages and the like. Similarly, customers who have the lowest influence and have a low probability of leaving the company will be subject to a weak shield campaign to keep them. Additionally, customers who have no propensity to churn don't receive any action.

Using this approach, companies are able to establish different kinds of actions in order to keep the good or influential customers in their databases based on their likelihood to churn. This type of focused business action can represent a substantial gain in terms of cost of operations and a better retention hit rate.

BENEFITS FROM THE COMBINED MODELING APPROACH

There are several business issues that can be addressed by using a combined-model approach. Because of the high predictive capacity of the artificial neural networks, for instance, it is possible to assign distinct likelihoods to each customer in terms of churn prediction or bundle acquisition propensity. Also, due to the strong pattern recognition capability related to social network analysis, it is possible to assign, for each customer, a level of influence and impact that can be exerted inside some particular community. Both business event prediction and customer influence scores can be combined to achieve best results in corporate environments.

This combined-model approach emphasizes the best features of each type of prediction and pattern recognition models. As described in Table 5.2, artificial neural networks are very good models to predict particular events, such as churning or bundle purchase. Also, this approach is adaptable to changes in database or data flows, something very useful in telecommunications. Neural networks also can be replicated to be used in different scenarios, and they can be deployed in a production environment. As a supervised learning model, neural networks can use previous premises to direct the model toward to some particular business need. Specific characteristics of telecommunications can be highlighted in such a process. Finally, neural networks are based on historical data, which can be very effective in events that vary over time, such as churn or product adoption.

Social network analysis, however, is a good technique to recognize patterns of behavior in large amounts of data, typical for the telecommunications industry. As an unsupervised model, it does not require that there be previous premises, which are necessary in order to understand current customer behavior in a virtual network or a small community. It can establish an overall overview about the relationships among customers, which can provide additional knowledge about usage behavior. This type of model defines a comprehensive view about the community's behavior, not just in terms of usage but also in terms of influence. This knowledge allows companies to use that sort of model as a decision-making support for many different business issues. Also, social network analysis is an interpretable model where

Table 5.2: Benefits from the Combined-Model Approach Considering the Predictive Model and the Social Network Analysis

Features	Models	
	Artificial Neural Networks	Social Network Analysis
Suitable to predict target variable based on historic past events	Yes	No
Suitable to recognize patterns and behaviors over the time	Yes	Yes
Suitable to be built over historical data	Yes	It can be
Suitable to be built over snapshot or freeze photos over the time	No	Yes
Suitable for further interpretation	No	Yes
Suitable for further deployment process	Yes	Yes
Suitable for learning adaptive process	Yes	Yes
Supervised learning	Yes	No
Unsupervised learning	No	Yes
Suitable to score databases	Yes	Yes

rules can be described in simple sentences, understandable by business analysts, and deployed in a production environment. This characteristic is important because business analysts can understand the rules behind the knowledge and act on it.

The distinct benefits expected to be achieved through the combination of the predictive and pattern recognition models are listed in Table 5.2.[6]

Different types of approaches can be used to model some scenarios. For example, there are pure mathematical models that are composed of equations and data-mining models that are based on data. For the second type of models, the ones based on data, the data are absolutely relevant. In that case, when data changes, the model needs to be refreshed. As a matter of fact, data models are cyclic processes; once the model is developed and applied in an operational environment it will affect the end the current data. Suppose some particular telecommunications company is faced with a high rate of churn. A predictive model can be developed to understand the churn event and thereby predict churn before it happens again. Once a company is aware that there is a high likelihood that customers will leave, the model triggers a retention process to keep these customers. A special offering is prepared for those customers according to their churn score. After company puts the retention campaign in place, some customers decide to remain, and some decide to leave anyway. Regardless of the effectiveness of the business action, the campaign changes the churn scenario once it modifies the customers' behavior. Once the behavior has changed, the data assigned to this scenario changes as well. Finally, once the data have changed, the model is refreshed in order to reflect the new behavior, which is defined by these new data.

Both models can score the company's database in order to tailor an action plan to the business needs. Using neural networks and social network analysis, companies can establish a different methodology to improve the customer loyalty program and increase product adoption, gaining additional benefits from both effective analytical models.

The combined-modeling approach makes it possible to use the predictive score of churn or bundle acquisition to tailor the retention process or the bundle—adoption campaign for customers who have a high propensity to churn or purchase bundles. Simultaneously, it is possible to use the social network's knowledge to recognize the customer's influence and, therefore, rank business actions for the most important or influential customers, the ones who have more influence over the community. In this way, it is possible to increase substantially the rate of accuracy assigned to the business process, avoid churn, and increase bundle purchase, and also reduce the cost of the operation.

Telecommunications consumers can be ranked based on their score of churn or purchasing. Additionally, these customers can also be ordered according to their corporate value based on the influence factor in terms of the social network analysis. This type of assessment drives companies to focus business actions both to retain profitable customers and also to sell products and services to consumers more likely to purchase them. The influential customers can spread the boundaries of those actions, reaching far beyond the original expectations by a diffusion process among the network of consumers.

The innovation in the case study is the definition of the customer's value by using social network analysis. Also, the network metrics were combined in a distinctive way based on the need to handle churn and bundle diffusion.

SUMMARY

This chapter has presented the overall telecommunications scenario and how a new approach to understanding customers behavior can help companies to personalize their relationship programs. The usual methodology to understand customers behavior is based on customers' own personal attributes, by analyzing their telecommunications service usage, along with some demographic attributes, and some inferred variables.

Social network analysis is a new approach that captures the relationship behavior of customers inside the telecommunications network. The customers' isolated attributes, as described earlier, can also be captured and used in order to understand their behavior. However, the major difference about the social network analysis approach is the recognition of the relationship behavior. How do customers relate to one another, and how can those relationships affect business events inside the telecommunications network? Does the telecommunications network have leaders and followers? What are the relationships between leaders and followers? How do they affect the entire network?

By answering these questions, telecommunications companies are able to personalize their customer relationship programs.

NOTES

1. C. A. R. Pinheiro and M. Helfert, "Artificial Neural Network and Social Network Analysis Combined to Enhance the Customer Loyalty," Second International Workshop on Data Management for Wireless and Pervasive Computing, United Kingdom, 2009.

2. C. A. R. Pinheiro and M. Helfert, "Social Network Analysis Evaluating the Customer's Influence Factor over Business Events," *International Journal of Artificial Intelligence & Applications* 1 (4) (October 2010).

3. C. A. R. Pinheiro and M. Helfert, "Neural Networks and Social Network to Enhance the Customer Loyalty Process," in *Innovations and Advances in Computer Sciences and Engineering*, ed. Tarek Sobh (New York: Springer, 2010).

4. C. A. R. Pinheiro and M. Helfert, "Creating a Customer Influence Factor to Decrease the Impact of Churn and to Enhance the Bundle Diffusion in Telecommunications Based on Social Network Analysis," SAS® Global Forum, 2010.

5. Pinheiro and Helfert, "Neural Networks and Social Network to Enhance the Customer Loyalty Process."

6. Ibid.

CHAPTER **6**

Social Network Modeling*

ocial network analysis can reveal possible correlations between business events, such as churn or purchasing, and other events within the social structure. Much of the following two topics are based on the work of Pinheiro and Helfert, published in the SAS® Global Forum in 2010. This work presented the first advances in the social network analysis method to increase bundle diffusion and decrease churn in the telecommunications industry.[1] This correlation proves that there is a stronger impact when an event is triggered by an influential node in the social structure and a weaker impact when it is triggered by a noninfluential node. Influence is defined as the number of customers who follow an initial business event in a chain process or the percentage of related customers affected by an influential node.

Monitoring and analyzing social structures over time, particularly networks that are interconnected, allows companies to evaluate the impact of business events within the network in terms of revenue. According to the likelihood of churn events and the amount of

---

influence assigned to customers, telecommunications companies can take straightforward actions to decrease churn and increase bundle diffusion in a chain of events.

Social network analysis, when applied to telecommunications, can help companies recognize the behavior of their customers and then predict the strength of links between customers and the possible impact of events among them. In this particular scenario, it is more important to retain an influential customer than an ordinary customer. In fact, it is important to identify the strength of influence, which can indicate the size of the chain reaction that is triggered. In the same way, it is more important to sell a bundle to an influential customer than to an ordinary customer. The difference here is that the influential customer can lead other customers to churn or purchase more than an ordinary customer can.

CUSTOMER-INFLUENCE FACTOR MODELING

In order to assess the correlations between the churn and bundle acquisition events, it is important to analyze the events from a chain's perspective. Are the events related to each other? Is the correlation assigned to the events related to any customer attributes? Do some correlations concern the strength of the links and business events?

These questions can be addressed using social network analysis rather than traditional analytical models.

Due to the huge complexity involved in human relationships, the main challenge of social network analysis is the ability to recognize patterns of behavior among individuals and the impact that each event can hold in terms of an individual's influence.

Information about the extent of customers' influence can be used to define a new corporate value, allowing companies to establish loyalty and sales campaigns. This new perspective can substantially change the way companies manage their customers, evaluating them based on their influence on the correlation between business events instead of their isolated revenue information. Particularly in the telecommunications market, this new approach can be tremendously relevant because of the natural social networks hidden within the data.[2]

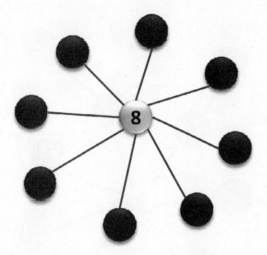

Figure 6.1 First-Order Centrality

In order to highlight the influential customers against the ordinary ones, a social network approach must be applied to the data, basically the call-detail records. Differences among the customers can be defined by this technique, identifying customers' influence and hence the kind of business action that should be performed in terms of customer retention or marketing campaigns. The influence factor can reveal the customers who are able to trigger events in a chain process. This kind of information is more relevant in telecommunications than traditional attributes, and allows companies to execute more effective actions for business processes.

The most traditional measures used to depict a social network are first-order centrality and second-order centrality. First-order centrality describes the number of direct connections from a particular node. Second-order centrality describes the number of connections that the nodes related to the original one have. Figure 6.1 presents the first-order centrality assigned to the white node, in the center of the network.

Once the central node is directly connected with eight customers, the first-order centrality assigned to this node is 8.

Figure 6.2 presents second-order centrality in relation to the white node, in the middle of the network. The eight nodes directly

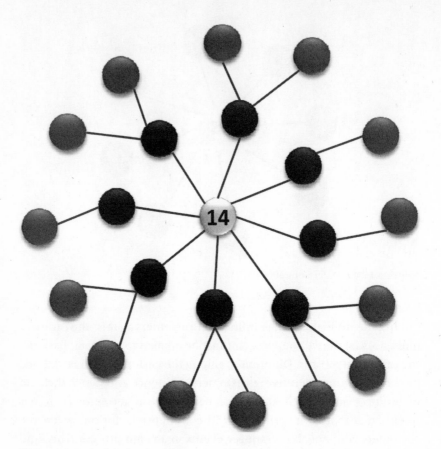

Figure 6.2 Second-Order Centrality

connected to it hold an additional 14 connections. Therefore, the second-order centrality assigned to the central node is 14.

All black nodes directly connected to the white node in the center represent first-order centrality, and the gray nodes directly connected to the black ones or indirectly connected to the white node represent second-order centrality.

These two measures of network topology are used to compose the customer-influence factor because they represent how many connections a particular customer can reach directly and how many customers can be reached indirectly.

Because first-order centrality represents the number of nodes directly connected to a particular node, this measure is quite relevant for events in which a direct influence is involved. It is well known how many friends a particular customer has and can directly influence. Churn can be considered as this type of event. Second-order centrality shows the number of nodes indirectly connected to the customer, which is applicable to events for which direct influence is not required. Events that require spread diffusion, such as bundle acquisition or product adoption, can be thought of as these types of events. This measurement is identified by how many connections the friends of a particular customer have. Both types of events will be the focus of later examples.

Even though these two measures of social network analysis are used most commonly, the majority of applications using social network analysis do not consider two directions of relationship. When social network analysis is applied to coauthorship or friendship networks, the edges between nodes do not require a bidirectional vector. If node A is friends with node B, node B is also a friend of node A. The link between them doesn't need a direction in order to establish who is friend with whom. They are simply friends. The same thing happens with coauthorship. In spite of the order of appearance, authors publish together; in that way, the direction of the edge is not required. They simply publish in conjunction.

However, in the telecommunications industry, it is important to consider the direction of the relationship. Node A, or customer A, is not connected only to customer B. In telecommunications, customer A is connected to customer B and customer B holds another connection with customer A. The bidirectional vector should be taken into consideration. In this case, customer A can make 10 times more calls to customer B than customer B does to customer A. This differentiation in the edge shows that customer A is more active in terms of making calls than customer B. Customer B in this case receives more calls than customer A. In terms of network activity, and also in terms of revenue generation, customer A can be considered more important than customer B.

Additionally, the two different directions in relation to the connections have distinct values in the telecommunications scenario. Incoming calls are valued differently than outgoing calls. Because a particular customer can make and receive calls inside the network,

How the customers place originating calls

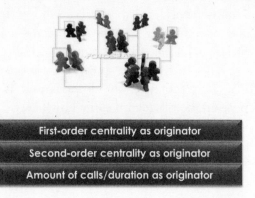

Figure 6.3 Customer-Influence Factor Attributes for Originating Calls

both incoming and outgoing calls are taken into consideration, but have distinct values in the final influence factor calculation.

Therefore, the formula used to calculate customer-influence factor must consider first- and second-order centrality data of the incoming and outgoing calls separately. The number and duration of calls between customers is considered as well, as a method to establish the strength of the relationship between customers. An equation dividing call duration by the total number of calls between a pair of customers can be used to establish the strength of the relationship between them.

Therefore, in this way, the customer-influence factor takes into consideration the way in which customers are originating their calls, providing a good sense of how they function inside the social network. Figure 6.3 illustrates this concept.

Three distinct attributes are being considered to calculate the customer-influence factor: first-order centrality, second-order centrality, and an equation of call duration divided by the amount of calls. All these attributes are related to originating calls only, depicting how customers make calls inside the social network.

The same attributes are taken into consideration when customers receive calls, depicting the role they play as a call receiver. Figure 6.4 illustrates this concept.

First-order centrality, second-order centrality, and duration factor are included in the customer-influence factor formula in order to

How the customers place receiving calls

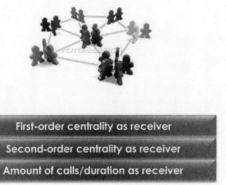

Figure 6.4 Customer-Influence Factor Attributes for Receiving Calls

represent customer behavior when receiving calls within the social network.

However, outgoing calls hold a different value than incoming calls when some corporate dimensions are considered. In terms of revenue, outgoing calls are of higher value to companies than incoming calls. In this way, first-order centrality, second-order centrality, and duration factor are being considered with different weights, based on their value to the company. Figure 6.5 displays different values in relation to calls.

Because the important thing here is to establish a differentiation between incoming and outgoing calls, it is possible to use values, such as the retail price of calls, cost, profit, and so on. Due to the complexity involved in establishing measures like call cost or, even worse, profit, it is easier to simply use the cost of the calls to define the relationships between these two types.

It can also be interesting to consider the number of calls in relation to incoming and outgoing calls. The relationship between values of the calls must take into consideration the value and the number of calls for each of the two types.

It is important to notice that the values of calls vary according to the time of day and whether they take place on a weekday or weekend.

In this case, considering all these distinctions, the connection between incoming and outgoing calls is 12.215. This means that

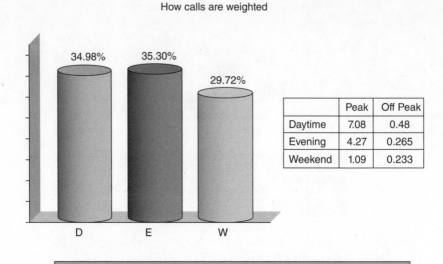

How calls are weighted

	Peak	Off Peak
Daytime	7.08	0.48
Evening	4.27	0.265
Weekend	1.09	0.233

Revenue relation between incoming and outgoing calls = 12.215

Figure 6.5 Attributes Weighting for Outgoing and Incoming Calls

all components in relation to the incoming calls, such as first-order centrality, second-order centrality, and the relation between the number of calls and the total duration, must be divided by 12.215 to differentiate the two types of calls in terms of corporate value.

Finally, one additional factor is included in the customer-influence formula. The values of the attributes can vary widely, due to large distinctions in customer behavior. It is quite common to find a very large difference between the values of two particular customers in terms of the number of outgoing calls, incoming calls, or total call duration. In order to normalize the calculations, the coefficient of variation for some specific factors inside the formula is used. Figure 6.6 displays how the coefficient of variation works to decrease the variable dispersion.

Therefore, the coefficient of variation is applied to the first-order centrality, second-order centrality, and the relation between the number of calls and total duration in order to normalize the magnitude of the measures. This process allows distinct measures, such as first- and second-order centrality and the relation between the number

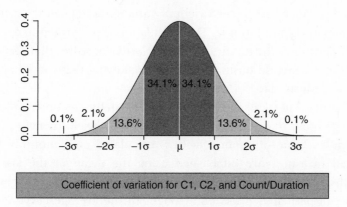

Figure 6.6 Decreasing the Dispersion of the Attributes in Relation to the Customer-Influence Factor

of calls and the total duration, to be compared and used in a single formula.

The social network related to telecommunications companies holds internal and external connections. For instance, considering just the residential customers from a particular telecom operator, customers can communicate with other residential customers using telephones from other operators as well. Although residential customers can exert influence over other residential customers, all networks should be considered in order to estimate the extent of customer influence. In that way, the relations between residential customers have some type of value, and other connections between residential and nonresidential customers, including those from outside the network, have another value in the influence-factor formula.

To summarize the calculation process, first- and second-order centralities are taken into account as well as the sum of calls and total duration. These measures are calculated for both internal residential networks and the entire network. In addition, these measures are calculated separately to consider incoming and outgoing calls. A multiplying factor is applied to all measures assigned to the incoming network in order to differentiate the value of incoming and outgoing calls.

Finally, in order to normalize the magnitude of the measures so it is possible to use them in a massive process, which considers the entire customer base, a coefficient of variation is applied to particular components in the formula. This calculation is performed to decrease the dispersion of the metrics in order to arrive at scores that are applicable for real-world business problems, allowing them to be applied to a single formula.

Figure 6.7 presents the components used in the customer-influence factor in order to calculate the extent of customer influence.

The customer-influence factor is calculated on a monthly basis, and all measures are established using the mean of the last four months. This is done to discard outlier numbers and to lessen the impact of particular peaks and troughs in the average curve of customer behavior.

The customer-influence factor is used by corporations to improve customer loyalty and the bundle diffusion initiative. Considering a time period of six months prior to events of churn and bundle purchasing, a set of correlation measures has been established to prove the relationship between the customer-influence factor and some business events.

DATA EXTRACTION PROCESS FOR SOCIAL NETWORK ANALYSIS MODELING

The whole process of social network analysis was developed from the SAS® platform. Following SEMMA methodology—Sample, Explore, Modify, Model, and Assess—the first step in the development of the model was to extract the data required to create social network analysis. The most important piece of information in respect to social network analysis is the data that establish the edges of the nodes. In telecommunications, this consists of customer call records, which represent the way customers relate to each other. These records are called CDR, Call Detail Record. These data are stored in a corporate data warehouse, which makes the extraction process much easier.

Therefore, the first step toward making the data available for social network analysis is to extract the call-detail records from the corporate data warehouse, as shown in the next code.

residential network	outgoing calls	first-order centrality
		second-order centrality
		amount of calls
		total duration
	incoming calls	first-order centrality
		second-order centrality
		amount of calls
		total duration
entire network	outgoing calls	first-order centrality
		second-order centrality
		amount of calls
		total duration
	incoming calls	first-order centrality
		second-order centrality
		amount of calls
		total duration

Figure 6.7 Components Used to Calculate the Customer-Influence Factor

```
proc sql;
  create table dcu_cdrs as
    select b.*
      from cdw_prod_teraminer.dcu_customers a,
          cdw_prod_bv.rated_call_history_v by
```

```
      where  (trim(a.std) = trim(b.std)
        and trim(a.telno) = trim(b.telno)) or
            (trim(a.std) = trim(b.area_code) and
              trim(a.telno) = trim(b.called_no))
        and (b.call_date between date '2009-01-01'
and '2009-01-31');
quit;
```

Due to the huge amount of data contained in the call-detail records, it is necessary to extract the data on a monthly basis. Furthermore, because the social network analysis must be deployed in a production environment, periodically refreshing the data is required. In order to establish a good sense of customer behavior, the process will be performed every month, extracting data and calculating the average factor considering the last four months of information, as mentioned.

The most relevant information to build a social network analysis model is the call-detail records. However, in order to establish correlations with business events as well as an analysis that is understandable from a corporate perspective, some additional data must be extracted from the corporate data warehouse.

Information about customer attributes, such as where they live, how long they have been customers, which products they have purchased and when, and so on, is always important in order to build an overview of customer behavior and to recognize particular patterns in the customers' base.

Structured Query Language (SQL) presents the code required to extract information about customers. The structure of telecommunications data is usually established through different layers of information, in which one customer can have more than one line, product, or service. It is necessary to combine different tables in order to collect the right information about customers and their current services.

```
proc sql;
  create table dcu_customers as
    select a.std, a.telno, a.acc_no, a.acc_dist,
a.soc_cat, a.prov_date,
```

```
b.acc_stat_date, b.cust_cr_rating, b.addr_rmndr,
b.bal_os, c.segment
      from cdw_prod_bv.line_info_v a, cdw_prod_
bv.acc_info_v b,cdw_prod_bv.common_tis_account_v c
         where a.acc_no = b.acc_no
           and b.acc_no = c.acc_no
           and a.cust_line_stat = 'A'
           and b.acc_stat = 'A'
           and b.cust_typ = 'R'
           and c.segment in (41,42,43,44,45,46);
quit;
```

Social network analysis is a concept that is closely related to customer influence; thus, the analytic data model was developed according to residential customers only. These customers have the ability to exert influence over others.

Historical billing information or payment behavior is necessary in order to establish important correlations with particular business events, such as churn and bundle acquisition, and the impact that actions can have inside the corporate structure.

The next code presents the SQL used to extract billing information from the data warehouse.

```
proc sql;
  create table dcu_billing as
    select b.*
      from cdw_prod_teraminer.dcu_dublin_customers a,
          cdw_prod_bv.acct_bill_mth_tot_new_v b
        where a.acc_no = b.acc_no
          and b.cdw_year = '2009'
          and b.cust_typ = 'R';
quit;
```

It is important to notice that the corporate data warehouse in this particular example is based on Teradata. SAS is well integrated with this technology, which allows the direct extraction from the database in the SAS environment. In addition, SAS and Teradata are strengthening their partnership, which produces benefits for companies and users alike.

DATA PREPARATION PROCESS FOR SOCIAL NETWORK ANALYSIS MODELING

Following the use of SEMMA methodology, a data preparation process is required in order to prepare all data extracted from the corporate data warehouse, to ensure that it is used properly in the social network analysis.

The data preparation process consists of gathering all information collected from the data warehouse and observing them from a unique perspective. At this point, information about customers, accounts, fixed lines, call-detail records, products, and billing history is collected from the data warehouse. However, all of this information is completely dispersed. It is necessary to organize the data in a single document.

Social network analysis is based on relationships, which are based on communication among customers. Calls represent the connections among customers—in other words, the relationship among the customers' telephone numbers. In this way, the centric view should be the telephone number and all related information should be aggregated around it.

In order to perform the data integration process, SAS® Enterprise Guide® was used. This tool provides a huge set of capabilities in terms of collecting, gathering, transforming, and analyzing the available data. It is very user friendly, allowing users to execute a vast range of functions, including data manipulation, statistical tests, and quality analysis. These procedures are significant in creating a better understanding of the data and allowing important business insights.

Figure 6.8 presents the SAS Enterprise Guide workspace.

The Enterprise Guide is used to prepare the data and gather different types of information and sources in a single customer view. In this particular case, the centric view is based on telephone numbers rather than the customer account.

Therefore, using the data manipulation capabilities provided by the Enterprise Guide, a data sample process was performed, creating a random statistical sample for the development of the model. A random statistical sample is required in order to test and validate

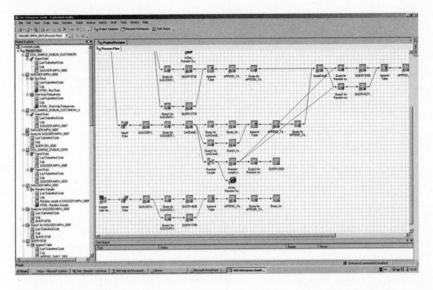

Figure 6.8 SAS Enterprise Guide to Analyze and Prepare the Data for the Model

combinations of attributes and values in the customer influence formula. It is not necessary in this sort of modeling to use three different samples in the supervised learning model, one for development, one for the test, and one for validation. The social network analysis model does not require such an approach because it can be considered an unsupervised model, with no previous premise involved. Nevertheless, the data sample is quite useful in order to create the model development approach and to test set combinations of attributes and values to be used in the formula.

The data sample is defined based on telephone numbers. Therefore, it is necessary to extract the related information from the call-detail records, the products and services attached to the numbers, and the billing history. These data are combined using the Enterprise Guide functionalities in an easy and direct way. Very often the model development process requires a single table, so that all information extracted and gathered according to the data sample is stored in a single dataset.

Finally, the data preparation process includes some additional steps in respect to the related content. Each attribute is analyzed in terms of distribution, and the outliers are removed from the sample in order to guarantee a more normalized sample. Missing values are discarded or replaced based on their particular cases and importance to the model.

Once the dataset for the model development process is created, it is possible to start the modelling activity.

However, it is vital to recognize the importance of the data preparation stage. All procedures related to data cleansing, data enrichment, and data profiling should be performed in this phase, preparing the data for analytical modeling and further analysis, most of which depends on evaluation of the results.

COMPUTING THE BASIC SOCIAL NETWORK MEASURES

Based on the telephone number information gathered from the previous steps, it is now possible to start the modeling the data.

Social network analysis modeling is generally based on relationships, which in this case are the call-detail records. The information required to start the model is quite simple, and is summarized here in order to make the process easier.

The very first step of the modeling process is to establish frequency among the numbers. Because social network analysis takes customers' relationships into consideration—or, more specifically, the relationships among customers' telephone numbers—the frequency among the connections is extremely relevant.

Treating the customer-influence factor as an ongoing process, the whole set of measures is calculated on a monthly basis. In this way, the first step is to declare which month of processing and variables should be used to calculate the formula.

```
%global cdrdate filesource customerdataset;
%let cdrdate=0409;
%let customerdataset=sasuser.customers_residential;
```

The general measures in respect to social network analysis, such as first- and second-order centrality, are calculated using the link analysis capability provided by SAS. There are a set of procedures that can be used in this way, calculating the basic social network dimensions in distinctive ways.

The links-analysis procedures require a set of initial steps. First, you must compute the frequency of outgoing numbers, incoming numbers, and the sum of both.

```
data calls (index=(anumber bnumber));
set sasuser.cdrs&cdrdate;
keep anumber bnumber;
run;
```

When the call-detail records consist of distinct information about the calls, the relevant information about the relationships is selected. The calling number and the receiving number are kept in the frequency statement, as shown in the preceding code.

Based on the data selected in the previous step, the frequency of the numbers can be calculated.

```
proc sort data=calls out=callsab;
by anumber bnumber;
run;

proc freq data=callsab noprint;
by anumber bnumber;
table anumber*bnumber / out=abn;
run;

proc sort data=calls out=callsa;
by anumber;
run;

proc freq data=callsa noprint;
by anumber;
table anumber / out=an;
run;

proc sort data=calls out=callsb;
by bnumber;
run;

proc freq data=callsb noprint;
by bnumber;
table bnumber / out=bn;
run;
```

In order to reduce the number of missing values and improve the speed of calculation, the dataset for the frequency process is sorted by numbers, as follows: the combination of the calling and the receiving numbers, only the calling numbers, and then only the receiving numbers.

Once the data required for the link-analysis procedures have been created, it is possible to proceed with the computation of the basic social network measures.

```
filename code catalog 'sashelp.dmlink.macros.source' ;
%include code ;
%_rawnodes(append=0,outds=nodesab,inds=an,var=anumbe
r,role=id,format=$11.) ;
%_rawnodes(append=1,outds=nodesab,inds=bn,var=bnumbe
r,role=target,format=$16.) ;
%_rawlinks(append=0,outds=linksab,inds=abn,var1=anum
ber,format1=$11.,var2=bnumber,format2=$16.) ;
%_rawmerge(nodes=nodesab,links=linksab,missing=0) ;
%_rawstats(train=sasuser.cdrs&cdrdate,freqvar=,node
s=nodesab,links=linksab) ;
%_centrality(nodes=nodesab,links=linksab,weigh
ted=1) ;
%_centrality(nodes=nodesab,links=linksab,weigh
ted=0) ;
%_prefix(inds=nodesab,var=VALUE,prevar=PREFIX,pnum=0,
pchar='/') ;
%_final(nodes=nodesab,links=linksab,outnodes=nodesme
asures&cdrdate,outlinks=linksmeasures&cdrdate,
maxobs=100000000,desc=1) ;
```

The first two lines are necessary to externally label the Enterprise Miner, which contains the macros related to the link analysis. The macro *%_rawnodes* establishes the nodes according to the frequency previously defined in the *proc freq*. This macro defines the output dataset, creates an index of unique nodes, and establishes the role that the node plays in the relationship and the format of the content. Because the relationships among customers in the telecommunications networks have two distinct directions, outgoing and incoming, the role in that macro holds an extremely important position, indicating whether the nodes make or receive the call.

Because of the distinctive directions of the calls among the customers, the macro **%_rawnodes** is executed twice, once for the originating nodes and again for the receiving nodes. In this way, it is possible to create two distinct datasets of nodes and hence two distinct datasets of social network measures. This is the preferred method of extracting data about customers' calling habits, giving a different value to incoming and outgoing calls.

The macro **%_rawlinks** performs a similar function to that of macro **%_rawnodes**. It defines the output dataset, creates an index of unique links, establishes the origin node and its role, establishes the destination node and its role, and determines the formats assigned to the contents. Basically, this macro creates the edges between the customers, identifying the caller and the receiver in the relationship.

The macro **%_rawmerge** combines the information about the nodes and the links in terms of customer relationships. It prepares the next step regarding the basic statistics that must be performed in order to calculate the main social network measures.

At this point, all raw information about the social network is ready to be used. The macro **%_rawstats** establishes the fundamental analysis that computes the social network measures. All frequency measurements in respect to the originating nodes, the destination nodes, and the links are performed in this stage. It is important to note that a training dataset is assigned to the original call-detail records database. This is done in order to define how many calls each customer makes and receives, to whom, from whom, and how often. These sorts of measures are required in order to compute the social network measures.

Finally the main social network measures can be computed using the macro **%_centrality**. This macro calculates, based on the datasets of nodes and links created previously, first- and second-order centrality for each node, or customer. In addition, first- and second-order centrality can be calculated using different values.

Centrality can be computed with a parameter that uses the value variable in the links dataset. This value may represent a geographic distance, a logical distance, or even a relative value such as time, revenue, number of calls, or call duration of the link. This value is a simple multiplier in the formula.

The %_prefix macro is used to extract a common prefix string from the nodes. This happens frequently with Web server data, where all text strings have a common prefix, such as "http://myserver.mydomain.com/". This step can simplify the data analysis of the nodes and their content. In the case of telecommunications, and in relation to call-detail records, this does not happen often.

Finally, the %_final macro establishes the final output dataset regarding social network measures. The maxobs parameter controls how many links you may keep in the final output dataset, and the desc parameter controls the direction of the relationships of those links. For instance, it is possible to have as many as 10,000 nodes that generate 100 million links. However, it should be possible to keep just the top 10,000 links, based on descending sort order of the count column.

COMPUTING THE CUSTOMER-INFLUENCE FACTOR

The customer-influence factor is a measure of customer behavior, hence it should present average consumer habit, payment history, telecommunications services in terms of outgoing and incoming calls, and so on. Because average behavior can change over months as customers move to different locations, take vacations, go away for holidays, and so on, a mean of usage behavior is calculated. This is a good way to decrease the variations of usage over time. Therefore, customer-influence factor is calculated by considering the last four months of usage, computing the mean of customer behavior.

```
proc sql;
  create table nodesmeasuresid&cdrdate as
    select a.* from nodesmeasures&cdrdate a
      inner join &customerdataset b
        on a.value = b.anumber
          where a.role = "id";
quit;
```

```
proc sql;
  create table nodesmeasurestarget&cdrdate as
    select a.* from nodesmeasures&cdrdate a
      inner join &customerdataset b
        on a.value = b.anumber
          where a.role = "target";
quit;

proc sql;
  create table nodesmeasuresidtarget&cdrdate as
    select a.value as valuei, coalesce(a.c1,0) as
c1i, coalesce(a.c2,0) as
          c2i, coalesce(a.count,0) as counti,
b.value as valuet,
          coalesce(b.c1,0) as
          c1t, coalesce(b.c2,0) as c2t, coalesce(b.
count,0) as countt
      from nodesmeasuresid&cdrdate a
        full join nodesmeasurestarget&cdrdate b
          on a.value = b.value;
quit;
```

The first SQL selects the company's customers from the dataset of nodes that act as call makers. In the nodes dataset, they are indicated with an *id* value. This dataset considers the entire network, in other words, the customers who have been making calls inside and outside of the network as well as customers who have been receiving calls from inside and outside the network. Because of that, the nodes included in the dataset do not have to be customers of the telecommunications company. The customer-influence factor should be calculated just for the telecommunication company customers once they are able to exert some sort of influence over the network.

The second SQL performs a similar function, separating the telecommunications company's customers, but in this case those who receive calls. In the nodes dataset, the customers who act as call receivers are indicated with a *target* value.

Finally, the third SQL merges the social network measures assigned to both relationship directions, that is, call makers as well as call receivers. This is intended to compile both roles that customers can play in the telecommunications networks.

The *proc means*, displayed below, calculates several distinct measures for a particular dataset. In this case, it is used to compute the coefficient of variation for the variables assigned to first-order centrality, to second-order centrality, and to the relationship between the number of calls and the total call duration. The coefficient of variation is calculated from these measures regardless of whether a customer is a call maker or receiver. In the nodes dataset, those customers are indicated as *id* or as *target* in the role attribute.

```
proc means data=nodesmeasuresidtarget&cdrdate
noprint;
  var c1i c2i counti c1t c2t countt;
  output out=nodesmeasurescv&cdrdate cv=cvc1i cvc2i
cvcounti cvc1t cvc2t
                                    cvcountt;
run;
```

The following code presents a way to keep in memory the coefficients of variation for the first- and second-order centralities as well as the relation between the number of calls and the call duration in regard to incoming and outgoing calls so they can be used in the formula for each node's measures.

```
data _null_;
  set nodesmeasurescv&cdrdate;
  call symput ('mcvc1i',put(cvc1i,10.4));
  call symput ('mcvc2i',put(cvc2i,10.4));
  call symput ('mcvcounti',put(cvcounti,10.4));
  call symput ('mcvc1t',put(cvc1t,10.4));
  call symput ('mcvc2t',put(cvc2t,10.4));
  call symput ('mcvcountt',put(cvcountt,10.4));
run;
```

Finally, the formula is applied to the available row data. First-order centrality is considered the most relevant measure in this formula. For this reason, it is calculated in a straightforward manner, merely being divided by its coefficient of variation. Second-order centrality is less relevant, but it is still included in the formula for the customer-influence factor, with its square root taken into consideration. In the same manner as first-order centrality, the measure is divided by its coefficient of variation, meaning that the square root is computed according to the relationship between its second-order centrality and coefficient of variation. The third component in the formula is the relation between the number of calls and total duration. This attribute is applied to the formula in the same way: as the square root of the relation between the row measures, the number of calls over the total duration, divided by its coefficient of variation.

The fourth, fifth, and sixth components in the formula are similar to the first three, but take into account first-order centrality, second-order centrality, and the relation between the number of calls and the total duration assigned to the incoming calls. In other words, those last three components are assigned to customers' behavior when they play the role of call receivers.

Due to incoming calls being calculated with a value 12 times less than outgoing calls, the attributes assigned to the call receivers are divided by 12.215.

Therefore, the sum of first-order centrality divided by its coefficient of variation, the square root of second-order centrality divided by its coefficient of variation, and the square root of the relation between the number of calls and the total duration divided by its coefficient of variation are divided at the end by 12.215.

```
data nodesmeasuresuniquetmp&cdrdate;
  set nodesmeasuresidtarget&cdrdate;
  if valuet=. then value=valuei;
  else value=valuet;
  gc=round(((c1i/&mcvc1i)+sqrt(c2i/&mcvc2i)+sqrt(coun
ti/&mcvcounti)+
    (((c1t/&mcvc1t)+sqrt(c2t/&mcvc2t)+
    sqrt(countt/&mcvcountt))/12.215),0.1)*10;
run;
```

The very last step in this code is the selection of the measures for all customers of the telecommunications company. The dataset containing the customer-influence factor measure is merged with the customers database in order to select just the telecommunications company's customers, especially the ones who are able to exert influence over the social network.

```
proc sql;
  create table nodesmeasuresunique&cdrdate as
    select a.* from nodesmeasuresuniquetmp&cdrdate a
      inner join &customerdataset b
        on a.value = b.anumber;
quit;
```

As noted previously, in order to discard any type of variation in the customers' behavior over time, the customer-influence factor is calculated using the mean of the last four months of usage.

In this way, a simple code was written to calculate the mean of the last four customer-influence factor measures. The isolated customer-influence factor is calculated on a monthly basis, and a regular mean is used in order to decrease the variation of customer behavior.

```
%global cdrdate1 cdrdate2 cdrdate3 cdrdate4;
%let cdrdate1=0109;
%let cdrdate2=0209;
%let cdrdate3=0309;
%let cdrdate4=0409;
proc sql;
  create table nodesmeasuresuniquetmp as
    select * from nodesmeasuresunique&cdrdate1
      outer union corr
    select * from nodesmeasuresunique&cdrdate2
      outer union corr
    select * from nodesmeasuresunique&cdrdate3
      outer union corr
    select * from nodesmeasuresunique&cdrdate4;
quit;
proc sql;
  create table nodesmeasuresunique as
    select distinct value,
```

$$
\text{General Centrality} = \frac{\dfrac{C1_{org}}{C_V(C1_{org})} + \sqrt{\dfrac{C2_{org}}{C_V(C2_{org})}} + \sqrt{\dfrac{CouDur_{org}}{C_V(CouDur_{org})}} + \dfrac{C1_{rec}}{C_V(C1_{rec})} + \sqrt{\dfrac{C2_{rec}}{C_V(C2_{rec})}} + \sqrt{\dfrac{CouDur_{rec}}{C_V(CouDur_{rec})}}}{12.215}
$$

Figure 6.9 Customer Influence Factor Formula

```
    (round((avg(gc)),1)) as gc,
    (round((avg(c1i)),1)) as c1i,
    (round((avg(c2i)),1)) as c2i,
    (round((avg(counti)),1)) as counti,
    (round((avg(c1t)),1)) as c1t,
    (round((avg(c2t)),1)) as c2t,
    (round((avg(countt)),1)) as countt
from nodesmeasuresuniquetmp
  group by value;
quit;
```

This code establishes the four months to be calculated. The four datasets containing the measures of the customer-influence factor are appended, and a mean procedure is computed considering the appended dataset.

This simple approach discards strong variations in customer behavior and considers their average usage as well as their importance inside the social network.

The final formula assigned to the customer-influence factor can be summarized as shown in Figure 6.9, which considers the components in relation to first-order centrality, second-order centrality, and relation between the number of calls and total duration. All three measures are computed for incoming and outgoing calls.

The further steps assigned to the calculation of customer-influence factor have less to do with the computation itself and more to do with the usability of the formula. It is important to establish a customer-influence factor that holds a significant correlation to particular business events. This makes the customer-influence factor useful to the company and applicable in terms of business actions.

ADJUSTING THE INFLUENCE FACTOR ACCORDING TO PAST EVENTS

Analytical models based on social network analysis can easily recognize some relevant aspects of groups or communities and gather information in terms of human behavior. What matters is how people relate to each other.

In this way, social network analysis can be considered an unsupervised model, in which there is no expected outcome. Patterns recognized from the social network analysis model can gather information, even if it proves useless.

This sort of unsupervised model is quite good for understanding the patterns assigned to a particular scenario. In this case, the scenario is the telecommunications industry and the way individuals connect to others. The kind of relationship, the frequency, the recency, the average duration, and the types of people connected are very important in order to establish a good understanding about the communities that form inside the networks.

However, as an unsupervised model, social network analysis is not particularly useful in making predictions or even correlating social and individual behavior with a particular event, be it marketing, operations, finance, or even fraud.

In order to assign the information gathered from the communities and their behavior, especially if it is in relation to a particular business event, a distinct method of analytical modeling should be used. Social network analysis recognizes information about general community behavior in terms of all different types of business events which are happening inside the network. There is no correlation between network behavior and a particular business event, such as fraud, churn, insolvency, or purchasing.

Nevertheless, predicting models are characterized by a target class, which defines earlier information about a particular subject of interest. As a supervised approach, predicting models are developed, trained, and tested according to a known target class. This target class represents earlier information about a business event such as fraud, payment, bad, or purchases. Due to previous occurrences of business events, it is possible to develop, train, and test an analytical model to capture this information and apply it to future events.

A sort of predictive modeling can be used to direct the information gathered by social network analysis to a subject of interest, such as marketing, finance, or revenue assurance.

In this type of approach, regular social network analysis is used, gathering general information about the internal communities and the relationships among the individuals within the network. This information is compared to a particular business event and information about its previous occurrences. For instance, imagine a purchasing process for a specific product or service. It is possible to track past events in order to gather information about the purchasing process, who bought this product, when, under what circumstances, and, most important, the neighbors who bought the same product later on. In this method, social network analysis is directed toward one particular business event, not all of them, due to earlier information about the specific subject of interest.

This social network analysis technique is used to analyze the links among nodes in terms of statistical measures, such as frequency, distance, and importance. This establishes a set of metrics about the network. Also, considering individual measures assigned to nodes, such as distance and importance, it is possible to define distinct groups of nodes. These groups can be understood as clusters, established according to a measure of distance between the nodes. Each cluster can hold the same set of metrics as the entire network. In this way, it is possible to obtain general metrics for the entire network as well as each subgraph identified as an individual cluster. The whole network or its subgraphs can be analyzed in terms of statistical measures gathered by the same technique.

By using the predictive modeling approach to direct social network analysis toward a particular business event, it is possible to create distinct measures of importance or influence according to the business event being studied. For instance, when social network analysis is used to create general measures about a community, metrics such as closeness, betweenness, and centrality are assigned to the entire network. However, if the social network analysis is used to study a particular business event, such as churn, the set of statistical metrics created is assigned and weighted according to the social network's behavior in terms of churn.

Social network analysis can answer some questions, such as who is the most central node? Who is the broker? It is possible to translate those metrics to business, such as defining the most influential customer or the most valuable client. However, in real life, importance or influence can be relevant to a particular type of event or, from a corporative perspective, to a specific business occurrence.

The previous questions or answers are modified based on who is the most central node when a churn event is taking place or who is the broker during the purchasing process. Based on this information, it is possible to say there are some nodes, or individuals, who are influential during churn events but not for purchasing. This means that this central or influential customer is able to diffuse his influence when he decides to create churn. In other words, he can exert influence on related customers when he leaves the company, causing other customers to follow him. Perhaps he does not have the same influence when he purchases a particular product. A different customer can be central or influential when he decides to buy something. He can be influential by merely purchasing a product, causing related customers to buy it or a similar product. However, if he leaves the company, he is not able to influence other customers to follow him.

It can be quite relevant that the customers in this study can be influential in some events but not others. According to this premise, it is sufficient to apply the social network analysis measures to specific business events, such as churn or purchase. The influence in this case is assigned to a business event rather than to a particular person.

Several distinct methodologies can be put in place to adjust the social network measures of business events. It is possible to use a set of statistical approaches to fit the values into the formula for influence factor in order to extract the best results from it or, in other words, to determine the highest correlation between the formula and the business event. Optimization models, even though they are based on operational research, can be deployed in order to find the best values in the formula to define the correlation between the influence factor and the business event being analyzed. Distinct sets of values can be tested in order to find the best components of the formula to determine the correlation between the influence factor and the particular business event.

What really matters here is the correlation between some measures of the network—influence factor, for example—and the business event in question, such as churn or purchase. This correlation should reveal how influential the customer can be in relation to the business event being analyzed. For instance, looking at past purchasing events, it is possible to create a general formula assigned to the customers' influence and progressively adjust the values in that formula to find the highest correlation between the purchasing event and the diffusion process, once the initial event is triggered. In other words, one particular customer can be defined as the most influential when social network analysis is applied. However, this particular customer may hold less power of diffusion in a chain process such as purchasing. Another customer may have more power of diffusion when he purchases a product. The general social network measure—centrality, for instance—for the first customer could be greater than that for the second customer, but diffusion power could be higher for the second customer than for the first. This means that the overall influence factor is higher for the first customer but the influence factor for purchasing is higher for the second customer. In this way, influence or importance in the social network is always assigned to a particular event, always considering past events.

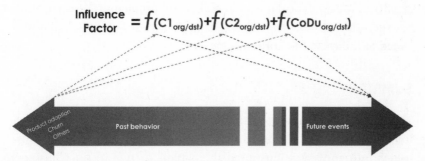

$$\text{Influence Factor} = f(C1_{org/dst}) + f(C2_{org/dst}) + f(CoDu_{org/dst})$$

Figure 6.10 Tuning the Customer-Influence Factor Formula According to Past Business Events

Figure 6.10 presents an overview of this approach, in which the values of each component in the influence factor's formula are based on past events. This recalls the approach used to develop predictive models. The known events contribute to the creation of specific information about past occurrences and make it possible to teach and train the analytical model in a supervised approach.

The learning process in a supervised model is always based on past events, in which a target variable is assigned to a distinct class, such as fraud. According to past events of fraud, this class, zero for fraud and one for nonfraud, can be used to train the model to predict future occurrences. Similarly, looking at past events of a particular business occurrence like churn or purchasing makes it possible to gather information based on the previous observations and, therefore, fit and adjust the model to a particular business event.

Like any type of analytical model, whether supervised or unsupervised, occurrences over time change the overall behavior of the social network as well. This sort of analytical model should be revisited and adjusted periodically, enabling the model to represent the reality behind the data. If the data change, then the pattern also changes. In this way social network analysis, especially when considering adjustments and values based on past events, must take into consideration the time frame assigned to all business events in question. This composite approach to the deployment of a social network model is due to its unsupervised methodology. A fine-tuning of the weights due to the supervised methodology is an effective way to increase the applicability of the analytical model to real-world problems. The correlation between the influence of customers and business events is well established and directed to corporate needs.

SUMMARY

This chapter has presented the methodology used to calculate customer influence in relation to a telecommunications network. Customer influence was illustrated in relation to two distinct business events, which acted as target variables, directing the development of the model to their own particularities.

The events of churn, in which customers leave the company, and bundle diffusion, in which customers purchase a bundle or packet of products and services, were used to illustrate the customer-influence factor.

The development of the model has taken into consideration the main characteristics of each of these two business events and also their consequences over time. What happened when an influential customer leaves the company? What happened when influential customers bought a particular bundle? Did related customers leave the company or buy a similar bundle afterward?

The events following the starting point of analysis are crucial to understanding how influential customers are when considering the business events defined, and hence how the influence factor will be defined.

NOTES

1. C. A. R. Pinheiro and M. Helfert, "Creating a Customer Influence Factor to Decrease the Impact of Churn and to Enhance the Bundle Diffusion in Telecommunications Based on Social Network Analysis" SAS Global Forum, 2010.

2. Ibid.

CHAPTER 7

Assessing the Social Network Model

The most important stage of social network analysis in terms of business is to evaluate the network analysis's possibilities for corporate applications. How can the network analysis be applied to improve the business process? How can the network measures be deployed in order to avoid churn and to improve bundle diffusion?

The network measures are assigned to the nodes and hence to the customers. Ranking the customers by their network measures, such as degree, closeness, betweenness, and influence, it is possible to highlight the influential customers in terms of relationships inside the telecommunications network. However, the influence is most often related to some particular business event. For instance, there are some influential customers who can lead others in churning. Although these customers can be recognized as leaders in terms of churning, they may not be leaders in terms of another business event, such as purchasing.

Because of this, for each business event analyzed in this particular case study, an evaluation process was performed on the network measures. Therefore, two distinct assessments for the network measure were performed separately, one for churning and another one for bundle diffusion.

Further topics will present an explanation about the codes developed to evaluate the outcomes of the network analysis according to the business events established earlier. All codes assigned to the case study are also assigned to the algorithms presented in the previous chapter. Although the codes presented are specific to the case study, they can direct readers toward methods of analyzing network measures.

ASSESSING THE CUSTOMER-INFLUENCE FACTOR DUE TO BUSINESS EVENTS

In this case study, the customer-influence factor is aimed at establishing strong correlations to particular business events, such as churning and bundle acquisition. In this way, it established some procedures to evaluate the strength of those correlations, relating the customer-influence factor to past events of churning and bundle diffusion.

As in the previous steps, the first action is to establish the months of processing with respect to the correlation assessment proposed. Additionally, some particular correlation analyses need to be linked with the customer base and the call-detail records.

```
%global cdrdate1 cdrdate2 cdrdate3 cdrdate4
dbcalls dbcustomers;
%let cdrdate1=0109;
%let cdrdate2=0209;
%let cdrdate3=0309;
%let cdrdate4=0409;
%let dbcalls=sasuser.cdrs0109;
%let dbcustomers=sasuser.customers_residential;
```

In relation to past events, it is important to define the concept of churning. Churn, particularly in telecommunications, takes place when a customer requests a disconnection of his line, when a customer interrupts his usage of traffic—calls or data—or when he leaves the company completely. In the case studied here, churn is considered an interruption of usage.

Therefore, the code that follows presents a set of procedures for establishing the dataset of customers who left the company in a particular month. All future analysis of correlations will be performed based on this dataset of customers and will consider subsequent months.

```
proc sql;
  create table nodesmerged as
    select nm1.valuei as valuei1,
           nm1.c1i as c1i1,
           nm1.c2i as c2i1,
           nm1.counti as counti1,
           nm1.valuet as valuet1,
           nm1.c1t as c1t1,
           nm1.c2t as c2t1,
           nm1.countt as countt1,
           nm1.value as value1,
           nm1.gc as gc1,
           nm2.valuei as valuei2,
           nm2.c1i as c1i2,
           nm2.c2i as c2i2,
           nm2.counti as counti2,
           nm2.valuet as valuet2,
           nm2.c1t as c1t2,
           nm2.c2t as c2t2,
           nm2.countt as countt2,
           nm2.value as value2,
           nm2.gc as gc2,
           nm4.valuei as valuei4,
           nm4.c1i as c1i4,
           nm4.c2i as c2i4,
           nm4.counti as counti4,
           nm4.valuet as valuet4,
           nm4.c1t as c1t4,
           nm4.c2t as c2t4,
           nm4.countt as countt4,
           nm4.value as value4,
```

```
              nm4.gc as gc4,
              nm4.valuei as valuei4,
              nm4.c1i as c1i4,
              nm4.c2i as c2i4,
              nm4.counti as counti4,
              nm4.valuet as valuet4,
              nm4.c1t as c1t4,
              nm4.c2t as c2t4,
              nm4.countt as countt4,
              nm4.value as value4,
              nm4.gc as gci4
        from nodesmeasuresunique&cdrdate1 as nm1
          full join nodesmeasuresunique&cdrdate2 as nm2
            on nm1.value = nm2.value
              full join nodesmeasuresunique&cdrdate3 as
nm3
                  on nm2.value = nm3.value
                    full join nodesmeasuresunique&cdrdate4
as nm4
                  on nm3.value = nm4.value;
quit;
```

The preceding code merges all information about the customers over the time considered for the correlation analysis.

All customers who have some usage in a particular month and do not show usage in subsequent months will be considered customers who left the company. Once again, those customers who did not leave the company but interrupted their use of service—calls or data—will no longer be considered customers.

```
proc sql;
  create table nodeschurn as
    select * from nodesmerged
      where value1 not is missing and value2 is
missing and
          value3 is missing and value4 is missing;
quit;
```

All correlation analysis was performed considering the top influential customers against random ones and, in some cases, the top revenue customers.

Basically, the analysis is performed on a particular business event that happened in the past and subsequent events in a specific time frame. For instance, in relation to churning, a particular month is considered, and then all customers who left the company in that month are included in the dataset of starters or trigger customers. Subsequent events are analyzed considering the related customers, which means the customers who have some relationship with the starters or the triggers. The correlation analysis is basically the evaluation of how many customers, from the related ones, have followed the starters or the triggers in the same event. More specifically, if customer A left the company in month 1 and, in that month, he was related with ten more customers, the correlation assessment is the evaluation of how many customers from those ten left the company in the subsequent months.

The code that follows establishes the number of customers who will be considered in the analysis as top customers.

```
%global topbottom;
%let topbottom=1000;
```

The next code defines the top influential customers who left the company in a particular month. The top influential customers are extracted from the entire number of customers who left the company in that month.

```
proc sql outobs=&topbottom;
  create table nodeschurntop as
    select value1 as value from nodeschurn
      order by gc1 descending;
quit;
```

Therefore, all customers who have had relationships with the initial top influential customers who left the company are included in a specific dataset. They are the related customers.

```
proc sql;
  create table nodeschurntoprel as
```

```
    select distinct cdr.bnumber as number from
nodeschurntop as nct
      inner join &dbcalls as cdr
        on nct.value=cdr.anumber
    union
    select distinct cdr.anumber as number from
nodeschurntop as nct
      inner join &dbcalls as cdr
        on nct.value=cdr.bnumber;
quit;
```

The preceding code establishes the size of the entire social network of the first top influential customers who left the company. However, some of these relationships could not belong to the telecommunications company. In other words, from this entire social network, there is a subset of customers and another subset of noncustomers.

In this way, another dataset containing only the related customers is created. This dataset consists of the related customers who can be affected or influenced by the initial top influential customers, the ones who left the company in that particular month.

```
proc sql;
  create table nodeschurntoprelcust as
    select distinct nctr.number from
nodeschurntoprel as nctr
      inner join &dbcustomers as cl
        on nctr.number=cl.anumber;
quit;
```

Finally, from the related customers, all customers who left the company in subsequent months is determined. In terms of influence, this analysis checks the number of customers who followed the initial top influential customers from the triggered churn.

The code presents the Standard Query Language (SQL) that extracts the related customers who left the company in subsequent months.

```
proc sql;
  create table nodeschurntoprelchurned as
```

```
    select distinct nctr.number from
nodeschurntoprel as nctr
      inner join nodesmerged as nm
        on nctr.number=nm.value1
          where nm.value2 is missing or nm.value3 is
missing;
quit;
```

In order to compare the performances of the customer-influence factor and the traditional measures of social network theory, the same analysis is performed for the top influential customers but ranked by first-order centrality. Similarly, the correlation assessment is performed evaluating how many related customers have followed the influential ones in the same event in subsequent months.

```
proc sql outobs=&topbottom;
  create table nodeschurnfoc as
    select value1 as value from nodeschurn
      order by cli1 descending;
quit;

proc sql;
  create table nodeschurnfocrel as
    select distinct cdr.bnumber as number from
nodeschurnfoc as ncf
      inner join &dbcalls as cdr
        on ncf.value=cdr.anumber
    union
    select distinct cdr.anumber as number from
nodeschurnfoc as ncf
      inner join &dbcalls as cdr
        on ncf.value=cdr.bnumber;
quit;

proc sql;
  create table nodeschurnfocrelcust as
    select distinct ncfr.number from
nodeschurnfocrel as ncfr
      inner join &dbcustomers as cl
```

```
      on ncfr.number=cl.anumber;
quit;

proc sql;
  create table nodeschurnfocrelchurned as
    select distinct ncfr.number from
nodeschurnfocrel as ncfr
      inner join nodesmerged as nm
        on ncfr.number=nm.value1
          where nm.value2 is missing or nm.value3 is
missing;
quit;
```

The same analysis is performed for the random subset of customers, evaluating how many related customers have followed them in the same event in subsequent months.

```
proc surveyselect data=nodeschurn out=nodeschurnran
  method=srs
  n=&topbottom
  noprint;
  id value1;
run;

proc sql;
  create table nodeschurnranrel as
    select distinct cdr.bnumber as number from
nodeschurnran as ncr
      inner join &dbcalls as cdr
        on ncr.value1=cdr.anumber
    union
    select distinct cdr.anumber as number from
nodeschurnran as ncr
      inner join &dbcalls as cdr
        on ncr.value1=cdr.bnumber;
quit;

proc sql;
  create table nodeschurnranrelcust as
    select distinct ncrr.number from
nodeschurnranrel as ncrr
```

```
      inner join &dbcustomers as cl
        on ncrr.number=cl.anumber;
quit;

proc sql;
  create table nodeschurnranrelchurned as
    select distinct ncrr.number from
nodeschurnranrel as ncrr
      inner join nodesmerged as nm
        on ncrr.number=nm.value1
          where nm.value2 is missing or nm.value3 is
missing;
quit;
```

Also, the same analysis is performed for the top revenue customers, ranked by average billing for the last four months of activity, evaluating how many related customers have followed them in the same event in subsequent months.

```
proc sql outobs=&topbottom;
  create table nodeschurnrev as
    select value1 as value from nodeschurn as nc
      inner join &dbcustomers as clr
        on nc.value1=clr.anumber
      order by revenue descending;
quit;

proc sql;
  create table nodeschurnrevrel as
    select distinct cdr.bnumber as number from
nodeschurnrev as ncr
      inner join &dbcalls as cdr
        on ncr.value=cdr.anumber
    union
    select distinct cdr.anumber as number from
nodeschurnrev as ncr
      inner join &dbcalls as cdr
        on ncr.value=cdr.bnumber;
quit;

proc sql;
  create table nodeschurnrevrelcust as
```

```
    select distinct ncrr.number from
nodeschurnrevrel as ncrr
        inner join &dbcustomers as cl
          on ncrr.number=cl.anumber;
quit;

proc sql;
  create table nodeschurnrevrelchurned as
    select distinct ncrr.number from
nodeschurnrevrel as ncrr
        inner join nodesmerged as nm
          on ncrr.number=nm.value1
            where nm.value2 is missing or nm.value3 is
missing;
quit;
```

One important analysis of relevance is the average revenue involved in subsequent events of churning, considering the random customers, the top revenue customers, and the most influential customers, based on both social network measures, the traditional first-order centrality, and the proposed customer influence factor, a general centrality.

The following code presents a way to establish the average revenue with respect to those perspectives previously mentioned. The comparison of these amounts of revenue reveals the financial impact of subsequent events of churning. Hence it allows companies to create a more directed business plan to retain good or influential customers.

```
proc sql print;
  select sum(clr.revenue) from
nodeschurntoprelchurned as nctrc
        inner join &dbcustomers as clr
          on nctrc.number=clr.anumber;
quit;

proc sql print;
  select sum(clr.revenue) from
nodeschurnfocrelchurned as ncfrc
```

```
    inner join &dbcustomers as clr
      on ncfrc.number=clr.anumber;
quit;

proc sql print;
  select sum(clr.revenue) from
nodeschurnranrelchurned as ncrrc
      inner join &dbcustomers as clr
        on ncrrc.number=clr.anumber;
quit;

proc sql print;
  select sum(clr.revenue) from
nodeschurnrevrelchurned as ncrrc
      inner join &dbcustomers as clr
        on ncrrc.number=clr.anumber;
quit;
```

An approach similar to analyzing the impact of churning events in a chain process, especially about events triggered by the influential customers, can be performed to analyze the impact of bundle acquisition.

When the event is related to consuming, the spread of the product or service usage can be considered as a diffusion process. In that way, the impact of subsequent events, in a chain process as well, triggered by influential customers can disclose important information to improve the diffusion process and hence increase the effectiveness of some business actions.

The code that follows presents a set of procedures similar to those shown earlier to analyze the impact of churning in a chain process. This code establishes the months of processing and the bundle events related to a particular month—the event that triggered the chain process—and also defines the number of customers to be compared in the cross-analysis of relevance and correlation in term of events and influence.

```
%global bundles01 bundles1234;
%let bundles01=sasuser.bundles_jan;
%let bundles1234=sasuser.bundles_janfebmarapr;
```

Similarly, a dataset containing the customers who acquired some bundle in a particular month is created. This dataset is the initial process in a chain perspective.

From those customers who bought some bundle in a particular month, a subset of influential customers—ranked by the customer-influence factor—was extracted. This subset of customers contained the top influential customers who bought some bundle in the month of analysis.

```
proc sql outobs=&topbottom;
  create table nodesbun as
    select n.value from nodesmeasuresunique as n
      inner join &bundles01 as b
        on n.value=b.anumber
    order by n.gc descending;
quit;
```

An additional dataset was created, containing customers related to those who had bought some bundle in the initial month. The top influential customers who acquired some bundle in the initial month of analysis relate, on average, to a particular number of distinct customers. This last dataset consists of all customers who were related with the top influential customers.

```
proc sql;
  create table nodesbunrel as
    select distinct cdr.bnumber as number from
nodesbun as nb
      inner join &dbcalls as cdr
        on nb.value=cdr.anumber
    union
    select distinct cdr.anumber as number from
nodesbun as nb
      inner join &dbcalls as cdr
        on nb.value=cdr.bnumber;
quit;
```

The social network of the influential customers who bought some bundle in the initial month consists of several distinct contacts; some of them are customers, and some of them are noncustomers. The nodes—or contacts—who can be influenced by the influential nodes are the ones who are customers as well.

Hence, a subset of the related contacts is filtered to contain just customers from this particular telecommunications company.

```
proc sql;
  create table nodesbunrelcust as
    select distinct nbr.number from nodesbunrel as nbr
      inner join &dbcustomers as c
        on nbr.number=c.anumber;
quit;
```

Now, from all those related contacts that are customers and have some relationship with the initial influential customers who bought a particular bundle, a subset of the influenced customers is extracted. This subset consists of the related customers who bought some bundle in subsequent months, after the process was triggered by the initial influential customers.

```
proc sql;
  create table nodesbunrelcustbun as
    select distinct nbrc.number from
nodesbunrelcust as nbrc
      inner join &bundles1234 as b
        on nbrc.number=b.anumber;
quit;
```

The same analysis is executed for the influential customers, according to their customer-influence factor, but it is ranked by the traditional first-order centrality. Again, this procedure is important in evaluating the relevance of the new measure, the general centrality, or the customer-influence factor against the traditional attribute of the social network analysis concept.

```
proc sql outobs=&topbottom;
  create table nodesbun as
    select n.value from nodesmeasuresunique as n
      inner join &bundles01 as b
        on n.value=b.anumber
```

```
      order by n.c1i1 descending;
quit;
proc sql;
  create table nodesbunrel as
    select distinct cdr.bnumber as number from
nodesbun as nb
      inner join &dbcalls as cdr
        on nb.value=cdr.anumber
    union
    select distinct cdr.anumber as number from
nodesbun as nb
      inner join &dbcalls as cdr
        on nb.value=cdr.bnumber;
quit;
proc sql;
  create table nodesbunrelcust as
    select distinct nbr.number from nodesbunrel as
nbr
      inner join &dbcustomers as c
        on nbr.number=c.anumber;
quit;
proc sql;
  create table nodesbunrelcustbun as
    select distinct nbrc.number from
nodesbunrelcust as nbrc
      inner join &bundles1234 as b
        on nbrc.number=b.anumber;
quit;
```

Once more, the same analysis is performed on random customers, or on the average behavior in the customer base. This represents, from the customers who had bought some bundle in the initial month, how a subset of random customers affect or influence their related contacts or customers to follow them in a particular business event in a chain process. In other words, it shows us how many customers related to the random ones have bought some bundle in the months subsequent to the initial event.

```
proc surveyselect data=&bundles01 out=nodesbun
  method=srs
  n=&topbottom
  noprint;
  id anumber;
run;

proc sql;
  create table nodesbunrel as
    select distinct cdr.bnumber as number from
nodesbun as nb
      inner join &dbcalls as cdr
        on nb.anumber=cdr.anumber
    union
    select distinct cdr.anumber as number from
nodesbun as nb
      inner join &dbcalls as cdr
        on nb.anumber=cdr.bnumber;
quit;

proc sql;
  create table nodesbunrelcust as
    select distinct nbr.number from nodesbunrel as nbr
      inner join &dbcustomers as c
        on nbr.number=c.anumber;
quit;

proc sql;
  create table nodesbunrelcustbun as
    select distinct nbrc.number from
nodesbunrelcust as nbrc
      inner join &bundles1234 as b
        on nbrc.number=b.anumber;
quit;
```

The code that follows is the same as the previous analysis but considers the top revenue customers.

```
proc sql outobs=&topbottom;
  create table nodesbun as
```

```
   select n.value from nodesmeasuresunique as n
     inner join &bundles01 as b
       on n.value=b.anumber
   order by revenue descending;
quit;
proc sql;
  create table nodesbunrel as
    select distinct cdr.bnumber as number from
nodesbun as nb
       inner join &dbcalls as cdr
         on nb.value=cdr.anumber
     union
    select distinct cdr.anumber as number from
nodesbun as nb
       inner join &dbcalls as cdr
         on nb.value=cdr.bnumber;
quit;
proc sql;
  create table nodesbunrelcust as
    select distinct nbr.number from nodesbunrel as
nbr
       inner join &dbcustomers as c
         on nbr.number=c.anumber;
quit;
proc sql;
   create table nodesbunrelcustbun as
    select distinct nbrc.number from
nodesbunrelcust as nbrc
       inner join &bundles1234 as b
         on nbrc.number=b.anumber;
quit;
```

The preceding set of codes establishes the correlation between the customer-influence factor and the subsequent events considering the same business action, that is, the bundle acquisition.

The figures with respect to the customer-influence factor and the churn and bundle acquisition events in a chain process are presented next. It is possible to observe that the influential customers exert some influence over those whom they relate to, not just in terms of absolute numbers but also in terms of hit rate.

PLOTTING THE SOCIAL NETWORK

All correlation analysis performed in the previous steps is quite important and supports the relevance of the customer-influence factor, especially when some business events can be considered as a chain process, such as churn and bundle acquisition.

However, a very good analytic approach is always visualization. In order to understand the overall social-network behavior and also recognize the network structure, it helps to see what the social network looks like.

SAS provides a set of visualization tools to perform this sort of analysis. A particular tool— a macro—is quite useful to understand the social network structure and then analyze some particular aspect of its overall behavior.

The macro *%ds2const* aims to draw the network structure. It also provides a small set of functionalities for graph visualization and data manipulation.

```
goptions reset=all;
ods listing;
%ds2const(ldata=nodesbunrelbun6,
          ndata=nodesbundle6,
          datatype=assoc,
          labels=y,
          layout=auto,
          colormap=y,
          nodeshap=circle,
          linktype=arrow,
          fntname=arial,
          fntsize=8,
          fntstyl=plain,
          nodebdr=none,
          width=1680,
```

```
        height=1050,
        codebase=C:\Program Files\SAS\Shared Files\
applets\9.1,
        htmlfile=C:\MyDocuments\DCU\PostDoc\
top100bun6.htm,
        archive=%str(sas.graph.constapp.jar, sas.
graph.nld.jar,
                    sas.graph.j2d.jar ),
        lfrom=anumber,
        lto=bnumber,
        nid=number,
        nlabel=number,
        nvalue=gc,
        ncolor=nc);
```

The parameters *ldata* and *ndata* indicate the datasets assigned to the links and to the nodes, respectively. The parameter *datatype* establishes the type of the graph that will be drawn. This macro is able to build the network structure in some distinct shapes, such as arcs, or from an association or hierarchical perspective. The parameter *nodeshap* specifies the shape of the node in the network drawing, as a circle, diamond, square, or triangle. In the same way, the parameter *linktype* specifies the type of the links or edges, whether as a simple line or as a narrow band. It is also possible choose the style and size of the font used in the labels and the width and the height of the graph, using the parameters *fntname*, *fntsize*, *width*, and *height*, respectively.

The parameter *htmlfile* defines the file that contains the HTML code for the network drawing.

The parameters *lfrom*, *lto*, and *nid* are important to establish the origination and the destination of the links and the nodes themselves, respectively. *Nlabel*, *nvalue*, and *ncolor* establish the labels in the drawing, the size of the nodes, and their color.

Figure 7.1 shows a social network structure plotted by using the macro **%ds2const**, including the nodes and their related links.

Any type of visualization analysis is important to enhance understanding of a business issue. For example, if those network drawings are put together in distinct snapshots over the time, it is possible to

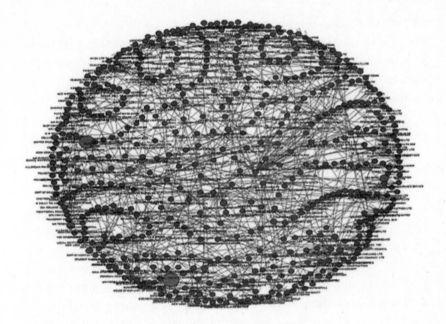

Figure 7.1 Social Network Structure

see what is happening in the network, the direction in which it is moving, and its strengths, and thereby to predict or foresee the next events inside the social network behavior.

ESTABLISHING THE DISTANCE FOR CUSTOMERS BASED ON SIMILARITY

From the understanding of the social network structure, and based on the way the nodes establish and maintain their relationships, it is possible to gain some relevant business knowledge.

In this particular case, the network structure reveals how the customers call each other and in what frequency. Then the network depicts the strength of the relationships inside the social network. These strengths can indicate how solid the social network is and can provide some important business information that can be used to understand customer behavior and predict further events.

However, an additional visual analysis can be performed using the similarities among customers. The graph assigned to the structure of the network can reveal how the social network behaves but not how the customers behave in pairs. Similarities among the customers can be used to describe their relationships in terms of strength and frequency, and also in relation to their proximities. In other words, it enables us to perceive how close or how far one customer is from another. According to their proximity, or distance, how strong or weak is their relationship? Finally, based on the strength of their relationship, how does their relationship correlate with some business events?

In order to answer those questions and create additional information about the social network and customers' relationships, it is possible to plot the network structure based on customer similarities.

The first step is to create customer similarities based on distinct pairs of customers. This means that for each pair of two customers, a distance according to their similarity is computed. Certainly the bigger the customer base, the greater the size of the matrix required to calculate distances. As a matter of fact, this sort of calculation has a practical limitation for real business problems. When that matrix contains all the pairs of customers, a medium-size customer base with 1 million customers could produce a distance matrix with 1 trillion cells, or, in other words, 1 trillion combinations of similarities. This is definitely a real limitation for practical business applications. However, it is possible to apply this approach for a small subset of customers, allowing a better understanding of a particular social network.

For instance, in order to describe the use of this approach, a small subset of customers can be plotted according to their similarities. This small set of customers was chosen based on customer-influence factor ranking.

The code that follows selects the top 1,000 highly influential customers according to the customer-influence factor, or their general centrality.

```
proc sql outobs=1000;
  create table topcustomers as
    select value from sasuser.nodesmeasuresunique;
quit;
```

Based on the subset of top influential customers, it is possible to select all calls assigned to their pairs. In this way, the relationships of the top influential customers are extracted from the call-detail records database, and the customer similarities, by pairs of customers, can be calculated. The customer similarities will indicate the distance between the customers and hence the strength of their relationship.

The next two blocks of SQL codes extract the related calls among the top influential customers and their pairs and also establish the attribute that represents their similarity. The similarity can be calculated based on any attribute, such as, in this particular telecommunications scenario, the number of calls, the length of the calls, the relation between the number of calls and the length of the calls, or any other possible variable that has some business relevance.

```
proc sql;
  create table calltmp as
    select cdr.anumber, cdr.bnumber from
topcustomers as tc
      inner join sasuser.cdrs0109 as cdr
        on tc.value=cdr.anumber
    union
    select cdr.anumber, cdr.bnumber from
topcustomers as tc
      inner join sasuser.cdrs0109 as cdr
        on tc.value=cdr.bnumber;
quit;
proc sql;
  create table call as
    select anumber, bnumber, count(*) as value from
calltmp
    group by anumber, bnumber;
run;
```

The calls among the top influential customers and their related pairs are the single piece of information required to perform the similarity calculation. Based on these similarities, by each pair of two customers, a set of virtual coordinates will be computed, describing the possible distances among the customers in the social network perspective.

The following code creates the similarity matrix from the call details related to the top influential customers.

```
proc sql;
  create table callab as
    select distinct anumber as anumber from call
    union corr
    select distinct bnumber as anumber from call
    order by anumber;
quit;

proc sql;
  create table callba as
    select anumber as bnumber from callab;
quit;

proc sql;
  create table matrixab as
    select anumber, bnumber from callab, callba;
quit;

proc sql;
  create table matrix as
    select m.anumber, m.bnumber, coalesce(c.
value,0) as value
      from matrixab m
        left join call c on
          (m.anumber=c.anumber and m.bnumber=c.
bnumber) or
          (m.anumber=c.bnumber and m.bnumber=c.
anumber)
      order by m.anumber, m.bnumber;
quit;
```

The procedure *transpose* creates the final matrix containing all combinations of pairs of customers. The coordinates will be computed accordingly, considering all those pairs.

```
proc transpose data=matrix out=matrixmds;
  by anumber;
  id bnumber;
run;
```

Finally, the procedure *mds* creates the coordinates in relation to all those pairs of customers included in the final matrix. The procedure *mds* uses the multidimensional scaling approach in order to calculate the customers' coordinates. This method estimates coordinates for a set of objects in a space of specified dimensions.

```
proc mds data=matrixmds
  condition=matrix
  level=absolute
  coef=diagonal
  dimension=2
  fit=distance
  alternate=matrix
  fit=distance
  shape=square
  similar
  pconfig
  pcoef
  pfinal
  pdata
  out=posmds outres=posmdsres;
  id anumber;
run;
```

The procedure *mds* in this case was used to create the coordinates of each object in a Euclidian space with two dimensions. The Euclidian distances are weighted according to the dimension coefficients. The dimension coefficient used here is diagonal. In that way the weights are the squares of the dimension coefficients.

Once all coordinates in relation to the top influential customers' relationships are computed, it is possible to plot all those customers according to the proximities—similarities distances—in a two-dimensional space. This approach can disclose some specific information about customer behavior as well as about customer relationships.

The code that follows draws the social network in terms of similarity coordinates. As mentioned earlier, the visualization analysis in terms of customer proximities can disclose the strength of the customer relationships and thereby create a new method for customer-relationship management.

The SAS® procedure used to plot the customers in this particular code is the macro **%plotit**.

```
title1 'Customers' landlines positions';
%plotit(data=posmds(where=(_type_='CONFIG')),
datatype=mds, plotvars=dim1
      dim2);
run;
```

Another way to plot the customers in a two-dimensional space is by using the procedure **gplot** as shown next.

```
title1 "Customers" landlines positions';
axis1 label=(angle=90 rotate=0) minor=none
/*order=(0 to 5 by 1)*/;
axis2 minor=none /*order=(0 to 5 by 1)*/;
proc gplot data=posmds;
  plot dim1*dim2/vaxis=axis1 haxis=axis2 frame
cframe=ligr;
run;
```

In addition, customers' coordinates can be used to cluster customers into distinct groups with similar relationship strengths. Because the distance among the customers can be considered to indicate the strength of the relationship, these coordinates can plot customers' positions not only in terms of proximity but also by clustering them into groups of similar characteristics. The most valuable characteristic for this approach is undoubtedly the proximity of customers.

The **modeclus** procedure clusters observations based on a dataset by using an algorithm of nonparametric density estimates. The data used in the **modeclus** procedure can be coordinates or distances. The customer coordinates computed previously can, therefore, be used in that clustering process.

This clustering is an additional way to visualize customer behavior and gain an understanding of the customer in terms of business events and practical actions. By grouping customers according to the strength of their relationships and their closeness in the social network, particular features of the network are revealed, allowing future optimization processes. If it is clear that several influential customers talk to each other and then spread their conversation with other customers in the social network, it might be interesting to contact some of those influential customers instead of all of them, thereby optimizing the process of contacting customers and reducing the cost of the whole operation.

SUMMARY

This chapter described in detail the process of social network analysis. The network outcomes, particularly the network measures, were computed and evaluated in terms of the business events of churning and bundle diffusion. The customer-influence factor was built based on the network measures, weighted by their call value, and normalized by the coefficient of variation. The customer influence factor was computed for each node inside the network, considering its average behavior over the last four months.

The evaluation process of network outcomes took into consideration the following six months of similar business events of churning and bundle diffusion. Basically, the assessment was based on the comparison of the most influential customers, based on their influence factor, with a random subset of customers, like a control group.

For each influential customer who left the company, an evaluation of the following six months was performed, identifying the number of correlated customers who left the company as well. A similar process was performed for the event of bundle diffusion. At the same time, for each random customer who left the company, an evaluation of the following six months was performed, identifying the number of correlated customers who also left the company. This comparison was performed in absolute terms, considering the number of correlated customers who left the company in the following months, but also on a relative basis, considering the percentage of customers who left the company in the following months.

The exact figures in relation to this particular comparison will be presented in the next chapter, describing the business results achieved by the social network analysis model.

8

Evaluating the
Business Results

C hapter 5 described the telecommunications environment, presenting the business issues that most telecommunications
companies are facing. A distinguishing factor of a good
customer-relationship program is the way a company understands its
customers, not just in their demographic attributes or in usage, but
also in terms of their relationships with one another. The way the
customers relate to one another can reveal quite relevant information
about them.

Chapter 6 presented the methodology to calculate the customer-
influence factor according to a particular business event, specifically
with regard to churn and bundle diffusion. That chapter dealt with
how to create an influence factor, taking into consideration the customer relationships within the network.

Chapter 7 presented the code to analyze the network outcomes,
showing how to calculate the influence factor based on behavior
over four months and the cascade events based on the next six
months.

In contrast to Chapters 6 and 7, which dealt with technical
approaches, Chapter 8 returns to the business approach, presenting
the business results in terms of the social network analysis model.

This chapter explores how this model effectively improves business processes in terms of bundle diffusion and decreases the impact of churn over time.

CORRELATION BETWEEN CUSTOMER INFLUENCE AND PAST EVENTS OF CHURN

The most important information gained from analytical models is its relevance to business goals. The customer-influence factor is a distinctive approach to understand customer behavior. By using the social network analysis methodology, it is possible to understand more than just customer behavior but how customer relationships happen and how important those relationships are to the company.

In spite of the relevance of the customer-influence factor by itself, in terms of business perspective, it is important to create practical actions from the analytical models and hence applicable information in terms of business goals.

The customer-influence factor is a measure that indicates how important the customer is in a social network structure, but is it correlated with additional objectives or even with business needs? In order to answer this question, a set of cross-analyses between the customer-influence factor and some business events, such as churn and bundle acquisition, were performed. According to these analyses, it is possible to prove that even more important than the measure of customer influence is the correlation that measure holds with some particular business events, such as churn and product adoption. All those correlations, which will be described later, allow companies to establish an effective action plan in terms of business processes, using the customer-influence factor in a realistic way to change the corporate environment and the business scenarios.

Correlation between the customer-influence factor and business events will be further described for churn as well as for the bundle acquisition. Both events can be understood as happening in a sequence of events, or within a time frame that is, as a chain process. This last characteristic reinforces the importance of influential customers within a social network, and the knowledge of the central nodes can be used to improve business actions in a corporate scenario.

Using the customer-influence factor measure based on the last four months of network data and considering the next six months to establish the correlations, the next figures are about customer influence in terms of churn events.

The average customer-influence factor was calculated using 769,104 residential customers. In a specific month, 10,624 left the company.

Taking 1,000 residential customers randomly, they relate with another 5,076 distinct phones in the entire network; of that number, 1,262 are residential customers of the telecommunications company. Considering the subsequent three months, 18 residential customers from those 1,262 left the company as well. In other words, those 1,000 random residential customers usually relate with another 1,262 residential customers, all of whom can exert some sort of influence. From these relationships, just 18 residential customers have followed them in the same event, the churn, in subsequent months. This study considers that those 18 residential customers who churned have been led by those random 1,000 original residential customers in the chain process in some specific way.

Taking the same 1,000 residential customers but ranking them now by the average revenue in the company, they relate with another 6,955 distinct phones; of that number, 1,156 are residential customers of the same telecom operator. From these relationships, 19 residential customers left the company in the subsequent three months.

Now, considering the same 1,000 residential customers but ranking them by the influence factor, they relate with another 16,991 distinct phones; of that number, 5,018 are residential customers who belong to the same telecom company. From that amount, 130 residential customers have churned in the subsequent three months.

Figure 8.1 presents the numbers with respect to the relationships and the subsequent churn events.

Considering the almost 11,000 residential customers who left the company in a specific month, a random 1,000 residential customers from that number have led additional 18 residential customers to churn. The top 1,000 residential customers have led an additional 19 residential customers to churn. Finally, the top 1,000 influential residential customers from the same 11,000 residential customers who

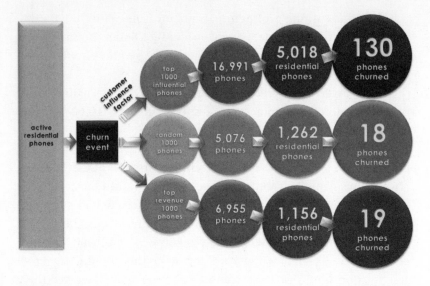

Figure 8.1 Numbers of Customers in Subsequent Churn Considering the Events in a Chain Process

left the company have led an additional 130 residential customers to churn.

In terms of capacity to span their actions, considering the subset of 1,000 residential customers who have left the company in a particular month, from the random process, every 56 residential customers who left the company have led another 1 to follow them in the churn event. From revenue ranking, every 53 residential customers who left the company have led another 1 residential customer to follow in the churn event. Finally, from the influence-factor ranking, every 8 residential customers who left the company have led another 1 to follow in the churn event.

Figure 8.2 presents the relationship between the number of customers required to affect or influence an additional one, using randomly targeted customers, the revenue-ranking selection, and finally the customer-influence factor selection.

In terms of business actions, if the company intends to deploy a retention process, it should be aware that every 56 residential customers, on average, will affect or lead another one residential customer

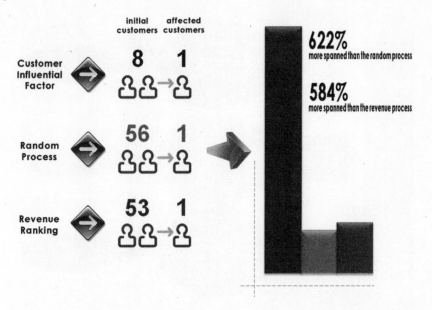

Figure 8.2 Relation between the Number of Customers Who Initially Perform the Event and the Number of Related Customers Who Follow Them in the Same Event

to churn. Every eight influential residential customers will affect or lead another residential customer to churn. That is undoubtedly a big difference in terms of span when a company is concerned with retaining customers or increasing their loyalty.

Although the performance in terms of span is greater when influential residential customers are considered—622 percent higher than the random process—the hit rate of the influence factor is also more effective.

Certainly, as the influential customers have relationships with a higher number of other customers, it should be expected that they influence more individuals in absolute terms. In another perspective, it is expected that a higher number of related customers churn when they are related to the influential customers than if they are related to randomly chosen or average customers. Comparing both subsets of customers, there are more than 5,000 customers related to the influential ones and just a little bit more than 1,000 customers related to the randomly chosen or average ones. It should be expected that, from those 5,000 related customers, a higher number of individuals churn in comparison with the 1,000 subset.

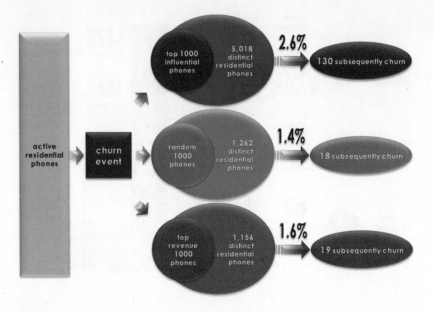

Figure 8.3 Numbers of Related Customers Influenced by the Initial Subset of Customers Using the Churn Events in a Chain Process

In spite of the higher absolute number of subsequent events associated with the influential customers, they also have a better performance in a relative analysis. Even taking into consideration those 5,000 related customers, 130 churned in the subsequent months, which represents 2.6 percent of the possible customers affected. Considering the random subset of customers, from the 1,000 related customers, just 18 customers churned in the subsequent months, representing just 1.3 percent of the possible affected customers.

Figure 8.3 shows the relationship between the number of customers affected, or influenced, and the possible customers who can be influenced, which means the customers who were related to the initial target of customers, considering the random ranking, the revenue ranking, and finally the customer-influence factor ranking.

Like the figures presented in relation to the number of customers required to influence an additional one considering churning, Figure 8.4 presents the relative numbers with respect

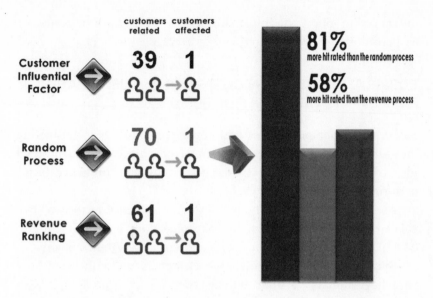

Figure 8.4 Percentages of Related Customers Affected in Subsequent Churns Using the Events in a Chain Process

to their relationships and subsequent churns, but from a hit rate perspective.

This graph shows that for each 39 related customers who have a relationship with the initial target, or the initial customers who left the company in a specific month, 1 customer is influenced in subsequent months. This relation is with respect to the initial target ranked by the customer-influence factor. Using the random-ranking process to target the subset of initial customers, this means that, for every 70 related customers—the ones who have a relationship with the initial customers who left the company—1 customer is influenced. Finally, considering the initial target ranked by the revenue rule, for every 61 related customers, 1 customer is influenced to follow the same event (i.e., churn).

Using the relative performance, for every 70 related customers assigned to the random subset, just 1 is affected by the initial event of churn. However, using the related customers assigned to the influential ones, for every 39 possible customers affected, 1 is influenced to follow the initial churn. This represents a performance 81 percent better than the random or average customers.

CORRELATION BETWEEN CUSTOMER INFLUENCE AND PAST EVENTS OF BUNDLE DIFFUSION

Based on similar procedures performed previously, but considering the bundle-purchasing event instead of churning, we can proceed to a correlation analysis with respect to customer-influence factor performance.

As mentioned previously, the customer-influence factor was calculated from 769,104 residential customers. In a specific month, 20,480 purchased a bundle of particular services of the company.

Similarly, taking 1,000 residential customers randomly from those who have purchased some bundle, they relate to another 29,216 distinct phones considering the entire network; of those, 6,847 are residential customers of the telecommunications company in that particular study. Considering the subsequent three months, another 885 residential customers with a relationship to those 6,847 residential customers have purchased some bundle as well. In other words, those 1,000 random residential customers usually have relationships with another 29,216 residential customers, all the customers who can exert some sort of influence, and from those relationships, another 885 residential customers have followed them in the same event—the bundle purchasing—in subsequent months. Similarly, in this study we are considering that those 885 residential customers who have purchased some bundle were led in some way by the original 1,000 randomly chosen residential customers in this chain process.

Taking the same 1,000 residential customers, now ranked by average revenue, they have relationships with another 47,041 distinct phones in the entire network; of those, 9,235 are residential customers with the same telecom company. From these relationships, 1,165 residential customers have purchased some bundle in the subsequent three months.

Now, considering again the same 1,000 residential customers, but ranked by the influence factor, they have relationships with another 64,366 distinct phones in the entire network; of these, 21,558 are

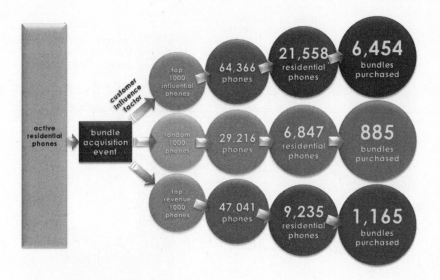

Figure 8.5 Numbers of Customers Influenced in a Subsequent Bundle-Purchasing Event Using the Events in a Chain Process

residential customers who are with the same company. Of that number, 6,454 residential customers have purchased some bundle in the subsequent three months.

Figure 8.5 presents the numbers with respect to the relationships and the subsequent bundle-purchasing events.

Considering the almost 27,000 residential customers who have purchased some bundle in a specific month, a random 1,000 residential customers from that number have led an additional 885 residential customers to purchase some bundle. The top 1,000 residential customers according to the average revenue from that same number have led an additional 1,165 residential customers to purchase some bundle. Finally, the top 1,000 influential residential customers from the same 27,000 residential customers who purchased some bundle have led an additional 6,454 residential customers to purchase some bundle.

Similar to the churn-event process, the bundle-purchasing event has good performance in terms of capacity to span, considering the same subset of 1,000 residential customers who have

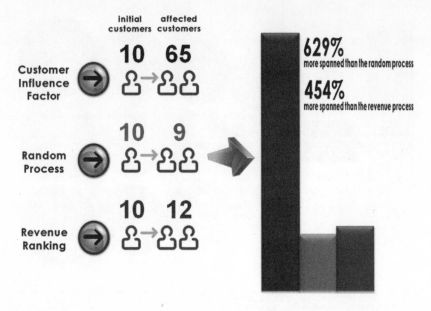

Figure 8.6 Percentages of Affected Customers in a Process of Subsequent Bundle Purchasing Using the Events in a Chain Process

purchased some bundle in a specific month. From the random process, each 10 residential customers who purchased some bundle have led another 9 residential customers to follow them in the bundle acquisition. From the revenue ranking, each 10 residential customers who purchased some bundle have led another 12 residential customers to follow them in the bundle-purchasing event. Finally, from the influence-factor ranking, each 10 residential customers who purchased some bundle have led another 65 residential customers to follow them in the same event of acquisition.

Figure 8.6 presents the relationship between the numbers of customers required to influence additional customers to follow them in the same business event.

Again, in terms of business actions, if the company intends to launch a bundle diffusion campaign, it should be aware that every 10 residential customers on average will affect or lead another 9 residential customers to acquire some bundle. However, every 10 influential residential customers will affect or lead 65 additional residential customers to acquire some bundle in future months. That is undoubt-edly a huge difference in terms of span.

Although the performance in terms of span is significantly greater when influential residential customers are considered—629 percent higher than the random process—the hit rate of the customer-influence factor is also more effective when the event is analyzed from the per-spective of a chain process.

Using the same line of reasoning as the churn event, as the influ-ential customers relate to a higher number of other customers, it should be expected that they influence more individuals in absolute terms. In other words, it is expected that a higher number of related customers will purchase a bundle when they are related to the influential customers who also bought a type of bundle than they would with randomly chosen or average customers. Comparing both subsets of customers, more than 21,000 customers related to the influential ones and almost 7,000 customers related to the randomly chosen or average initial customers bought a bundle in the initial event in a chain process. It should be expected that, from those almost 22,000 related customers, a greater number of individuals acquire a type of bundle than compared to the almost 7,000 initial customers.

In spite of the higher absolute number of subsequent events asso-ciated with the influential customers, they also have a better perfor-mance in a relative analysis, taking into consideration the hit rate of influenced customers they relate to. Even considering those almost 22,000 related customers, more than 6,400 customers have purchased some bundle in subsequent months, which represents 30 percent of the possible related customers who might be influenced. Using the random subset of initial customers, from the almost 7,000 related customers, fewer than 900 related customers have purchased some bundle in subsequent months, representing 13 percent of the possible related customers who might be influenced.

Figure 8.7 shows the relationship between the number of custom-ers affected, or influenced, to the possible customers who can be influenced, which means the customers who hold a sort of relation-ship with the initial target customers, using random ranking, revenue ranking, and finally the customer-influence factor ranking.

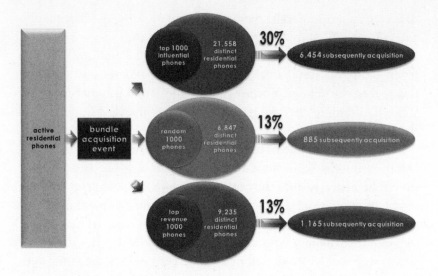

Figure 8.7 Relationship between the Number of Customers Who Initially Perform the Event and the Number of Related Customers Who Follow Them in the Same Event

Using the 885 residential customers from the 6,847 related customers who have followed the original 1,000 random-purchaser customers—the 1,165 residential customers from the 9,235 related customers who have followed the original top 1,000 purchaser customers in terms of revenue—and the 6,454 residential customers from the 21,558 related customers who have followed the original 1,000 influential purchaser customers, the relationship between the number of customers required to influence other customers is presented as follows.

Like the figures presented previously in relation to the number of customers required to influence an additional 1 customer in the bundle acquisition event, Figure 8.8 presents the relative numbers in respect to the relationships and the subsequent bundle purchases, but from a hit rate perspective.

The figure shows that from each 3 related customers who hold a relationship with the initial target, or the initial customers who had purchased some particular bundle, 1 distinct customer is

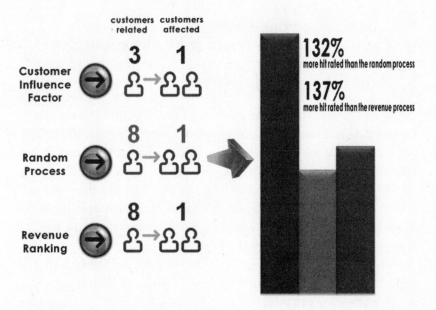

Figure 8.8 Percentages of Customers inside a Process of Subsequent Bundle Purchasing Using the Events in a Chain Process

influenced in the subsequent months to acquire some bundle as well. This relationship is about the initial target ranked by the customer-influence factor. Using the random-ranking process to target the subset of initial customers, for every 8 related customers—the ones who are related to the initial customers who bought some bundle in a particular month—1 customer is influenced in the subsequent months. Finally, considering the initial target ranked by the revenue criteria, for each 8 related customers who bought some bundle in the initial event, 1 customer is influenced to follow them in the same event of purchase.

Taking into consideration the relative performance, for every 8 related customers assigned to the random subset, just 1 is affected by the initial event of bundle acquisition. However, considering the related customers assigned to the influential ones, for every 3 possible customers to be affected, 1 is influenced to follow the initial event of bundle acquisition. This represents a performance 132 percent better than the random or average customers.

THE SOCIAL NETWORK'S EVOLUTION IN A CHAIN PROCESS PERSPECTIVE USING BUSINESS EVENTS

In order to compare the effectiveness of the social network analysis model, a comparison was established to analyze the performance of events in a chain process. The business event is the bundle acquisition. Considering the same example presented earlier, where 20,480 customers acquired some bundle in a particular month, a subset of just 100 customers was created randomly. In addition, from the same 20,480 customers who bought a bundle, the top 100 influential customers were included in another subset. The customer-influence factor was used to rank those 20,000 customers and select the top 100 more influential ones due to their influence factor.

As noted earlier, the procedures to plot the customers and their links with other customers have a physical limitation. Using the procedure *mds* to calculate coordinates based on their similarities has a practical limitation in terms of the number of customers who can possibly be plotted. The square matrix to compute the similarities among all those pairs of customers has a computational memory limitation, not allowing that a large number of customers have been the calculated coordinates. Even the direct way to plot the customers and their connections with the other customers by using the macro *%ds2const* is limited in computational terms. It is not possible to plot a large number of customers using that macro because the Java script and the amount of memory required could be very high.

Regardless of those limitations, a visual analysis based on directed graphs is always more intuitive than any spreadsheet. It is possible to execute some social network calculations and a network structure drawing considering the nodes and their links, or, in other words, the customers and their connections with related customers. Taking into consideration a small subset of customers—the top 100 more influential ones, for instance—this sort of visual analysis can be more effective for some particular business needs than traditional cross-analysis.

Therefore, even with just a small subset of customers to analyze, the network structure visualization can be quite relevant. For instance,

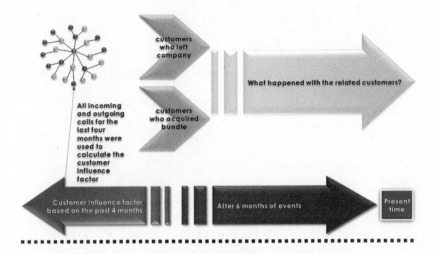

Figure 8.9 Timeline, Using Past Events to Calculate Customer-Influence Factor and Subsequent Events to Analyze the Correlation between the Influence Factor and Subsequent Events

analysis over time—showing how the social network behaves, how it grows, changes, and evolves over time—is possible by using this kind of directed graph analysis.

The main idea in this analysis over time is to compare the performance of those two groups of customers, the top 100 influential ones and also the random set of another 100 customers. The analysis about future events was performed using the subsequent six months.

Figure 8.9 presents the process of customer-influence factor calculation, by using past events, and future analysis, using subsequent events in subsequent months.

Figures 8.10 and 8.11 present the performance assigned to the influential customers compared to the random ones. The analyses were viewed from a cumulative perspective, summarizing customers who purchased some bundle over the preceding months, and also from the perspective of an individual month, using just the number of customers who bought some bundle in a specific month.

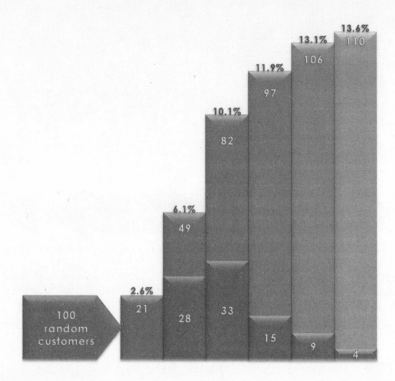

Figure 8.10 Hit Rate and Span of Random Customers in Terms of Bundle Diffusion

Therefore, using the period six months after the initial event of bundle purchasing, the subset of random customers who were influenced in the following six months was 21, 28, 33, 15, 9, and 4. From a cumulative perspective, the subset of random customers who were influenced was 21, 49, 82, 97, 106, and 110 in the subsequent six months.

The cumulative perspective gives an overview about the span of influence using the random customers in the subsequent six months.

Figure 8.10 shows the related customers influenced by the initial random 100 customers in the bundle purchase events.

Similarly, using the subset of the top 100 influential customers, they have influenced the following related customers in the subsequent six months: 396, 600, 542, 370, 265, and 222. Proceeding with the same cumulative analysis, the subset of the top 100 influential

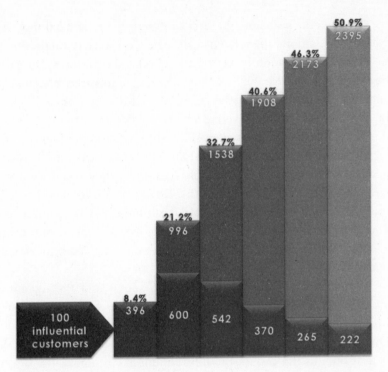

Figure 8.11 Hit Rate and Span of Influential Customers in Terms of Bundle Diffusion

customers who influenced related customers in the following six months was 396, 996, 1,538, 1,908, 2,173, and 2,395. This is the length of the span related to the top influential customers over time. As they are only the top 100 influential customers and hold a huge number of connections with related customers among them, it is predictable that they would influence a larger number of related customers in the bundle acquisition process, diffusing the product through their own social networks. They talk more to more people, so it is expected that they can probably influence more related customers as well.

Again, the cumulative perspective gives an overview about the span of influence using the top 100 influential customers in the subsequent six months.

Figure 8.11 shows the related customers influenced by the initial top 100 influential customers in the bundle purchase events.

The percentages below the bars represent the individual monthly relationships among the related customers who were influenced over the subsequent six months versus all the related customers. Similarly, the percentages above the bars represent the cumulative relationships among the numbers of related customers who were influenced over the following six months versus all the related customers. After six months of bundle purchase events, the subset of 100 random customers have influenced a few more than 100 related customers, which means 13.6 percent of the possible customers they could influence (i.e., the customers they relate with). However, considering the same time frame for the top 100 influential customers, they have influenced more than 2,000 related customers, which means 50.9 percent of the customers they could possibly influence (i.e., the customers with whom they hold some kind of relationship).

In both cases, based on the random subset and the top influential customers, the impact of the influence is higher in the first three months than in the last three months, even though, in relation to the random subset of customers, the third month is the highest one. In the case of the top influential customers, the second month is the highest. However, in both cases, there is a trend indicating that the influence tends to be stronger after the initial event and to decrease over time.

Figure 8.12 shows the trends graphically. In both cases, the monthly number of customers influenced has decreased over the time.

Certainly the top influential customers usually relate to a greater number of distinct customers, and, thus, they are more likely to influence a greater number of other customers. Even if we consider those events as a coincidence, there will still be more customers acquiring bundles who are related to the top influential customers than to the random ones. This fact could just be associated to the high number of relationships of the influential customers in comparison to the random customers. On average, each 1 of the 100 influential customers relates to another 46 distinct customers. The average number for random customers is to relate to just 8 other customers. Therefore, it is possible to correlate the higher number of customers purchasing bundles at the end of the process just because there are a higher number of customer relationships at the beginning.

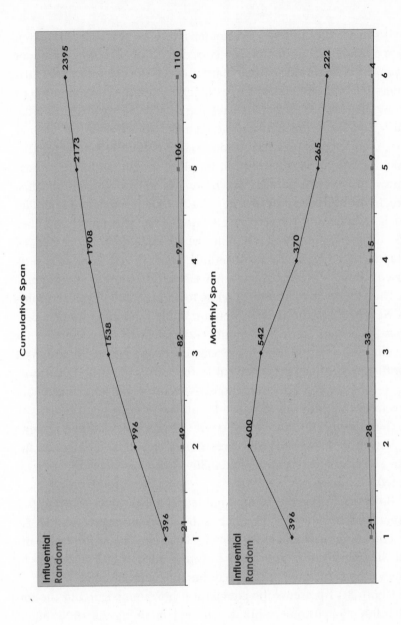

Figure 8.12 Span of Influential Customers and Random Customers in Terms of Bundle Diffusion

However, the hit rate of customer influence is also higher when the top influential customers are considered rather than the random ones. At the beginning of the chain process, the top influential customers relate to 4,697 distinct customers. In the next month, 396 of those initial related customers have acquired some particular bundle, which equates to an 8.4 percent hit rate. Similarly, in the second month, another 600 related customers have purchased some bundle, which equates to 12.8 percent. In the third month, another 542 customers purchased a bundle, which equates to 11.5 percent of influence. In the fourth month, another 370 customers purchased a bundle, which equates to a 7.9 percent hit rate. In the fifth month, another 265 customers purchased a bundle, which equates to 5.6 percent of influence. Finally, in the sixth month, another 222 customers purchased a bundle, which equates to a 4.7 percent hit rate of influence.

The 100 random customers relate to another 809 distinct customers. Nevertheless, the same process using the random customers performs 2.6 percent in the first month—21 customers from the 809; 3.5 percent in the second month—28 customers; 4.1 percent in the third month—33 customers; 1.9 percent in the fourth month—15 customers; 1.1 percent in the fifth month—9 customers; and finally 0.5 percent in the sixth month—just 4 customers.

Considering a cumulative overview, the random customers achieve 14 percent of the initial related customers, which means they influence 110 customers from the initial 809 customers to whom they are related.

However, using the same cumulative perspective, the top 100 influential customers achieved a substantial number—around 51 percent—of influence over the initial related customers, which means that they have influenced 2,395 from the initial 4,697 customers to whom they are related at the beginning of chain process.

Figure 8.13 presents the comparison hit rate assigned to the top 100 influential customers and the subset containing the 100 random customers. The comparison is shown in the cumulative and monthly perspectives.

According to those graphs, it is possible to observe that the performance of the influential customers is higher in terms of absolute numbers than the average or random customers, when the bundle

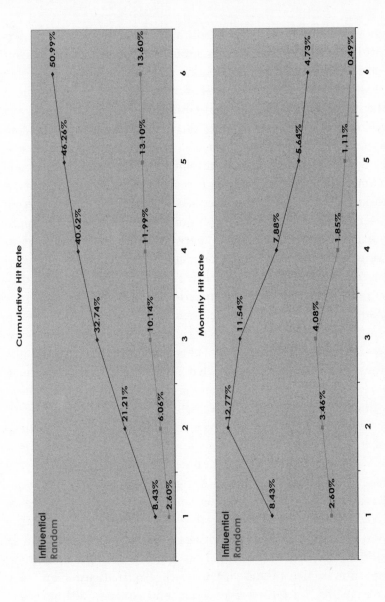

Figure 8.13 Hit Rate of Influential Customers and Random Customers in Terms of Bundle Diffusion

185

acquisition event is considered, but, also, the influential customers have a better hit rate, which represents their relative influence over the possible related customers they can affect.

It is important to note that the number of customers influenced by the initial subset of influential customers, when considering the bundle acquisition event, is larger than the initial subset of random customers. The percentage of possible related customers affected is also larger when the influential customers and the random customers are compared. However, both figures are quite relevant in terms of business actions. The absolute numbers of related customers affected represents the possible number of customers who might be influenced by the influential customers in an event of bundle diffusion. Regardless of whether they have a higher influence factor when compared to the random or average customers, at the end of the process, they affect more customers than anyone else.

Assuming that there is no influence in respect to that, which means that the percentage of affected customers over the related customers is the same for the influential and the average customers, the final number of customers contacted and hence influenced is much larger for the influential customers than for the average customers. This single fact may support a decision to first target the influential customers for a bundle diffusion campaign. However, the percentage of related customers affected over the entire amount of related customers is even greater for the influential customers than for the average or random ones. This percentage of influence may be considered as an influence factor and proves that there really is an influence movement inside a particular social network. Considering again the previous example, after six months from the initial event of bundle acquisition, the top 100 influential customers have affected half their relationships, which means that, for each 2 related customers, they affect 1 whereas for the average or random customer, this rate is just about 13 percent, which means, considering the same time frame of six months, for each 10 related customers, slightly more than 1 is affected.

In summary, the influence factor indicates customers who might contact more distinct customers in a diffusion campaign, like product adoption, but also customers who probably might affect more related customers to move toward them in the same event or to follow them in the same business action, such as bundle acquisition.

THE BUNDLE DIFFUSION PROCESS ANALYZED OVER TIME

With respect to the customer-influence factor, the top 100 influential customers have exerted a higher influence over their relationships, more than the group of random customers. The hit rate is undoubtedly quite relevant, and it shows a real correlation between the influential customers and some particular business events, such as product and service acquisition. However, in terms of marketing, and also in relation to the operational performance, a span perspective can show how the actions associated with the influential customers should be spread in contrast to those of ordinary customers.

One important type of observation is of the customers' behaviors over time. How do they relate to one another when the influence occurs? How long does it take to influence other customers after the initial event in a chain process? All those questions can be answered by a visual analysis using the social network's behavior over time.

Using the same number of 100 customers, this case study has shown that the subset of random customers has contacted on average 809 other customers, influencing just 110 of them. The same number of 100 customers, ranked by the influence factor, contacted on average 4,697 other customers, influencing the huge number of 2,395 of them. At the end of the process, the important figure is that, from one group of 100 regular, or random, customers, it was possible to diffuse the bundle to another 110 different customers. Using the same number of 100 initial customers who bought some bundle in a particular month, but who were ranked by the influence factor, they were able to diffuse the bundle to an additional 2,395 distinct customers. This is a huge improvement of performance in terms of product adoption or bundle diffusion.

Figure 8.14 presents the evolution of the social network in terms of relationships (i.e., how the initial subset of random customers influenced their relations in the same business event over the time). The images of the social networks show the behavior starting from the initial event of bundle acquisition from the first month through

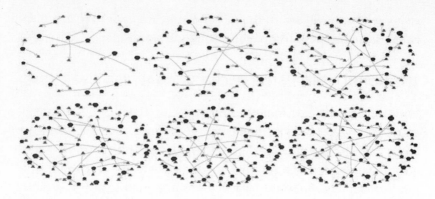

Figure 8.14 Bundle Diffusion Process Viewed from a Network Evolution Perspective for Random Customers

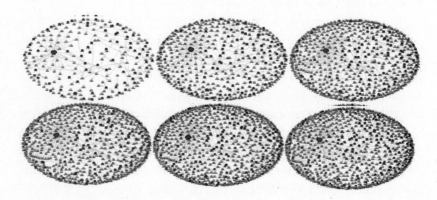

Figure 8.15 Bundle Diffusion Process Viewed from a Network Evolution Perspective for the Top 100 Influential Customers

the sixth month, considering the event of bundle acquisition triggered by the initial subset of random customers.

Those images show how the social network spreads out over time and how the initial subset of random customers has influenced their relations in terms of the same business event (i.e., the bundle acquisition).

Similarly, Figure 8.15 presents the evolution of the network's behavior in terms of relationships and how the initial subset of influential customers has affected their relationships over time. The images show how the related customers have followed the initial top influential customers after the bundle acquisition event has been triggered. The network evolution is related to the first month after the original bundle event and goes through the sixth month.

It is important to compare these two distinct images, the first one of the subset of random customers and the second one, below it, of the subset of influential customers. It is easy to note how the influential customers have spread out their relationships and also have influenced the people connected to them to follow the same business event. At the end of the business process, those images show how the bundle diffusion has performed starting from the random customers and from the influential ones.

It is easy to see how dense the influential customers' network is in comparison to the random customers' network. The dark shaded nodes are the original customers who had acquired some particular bundle in a specific month. The very darkest color in the image represents the nodes assigned to the initial 100 random customers in the first network and the top 100 influential customers in the second network. The other nodes, with different shades, are the ones assigned to the customers who have acquired some bundle in the subsequent six months after the initial event of purchase. Each shade in both network images represents one particular month, from light to dark shades. The lightest shade is the first month and the darkest shade is the last month of analysis. The different shades describe visually the evolution of the social relations among the customers over time, showing that the peak of influence for the random customers is the third month and the peak of influence for the top influential customers is the second month.

Figure 8.16 shows the difference between the two bundle diffusion approaches, using the initial subset of random customers and the initial subset of influential customers. The social network image at the left represents the final network reached by the random customers in terms of influence. The social network image at the right shows the final network reached after six months from the initial event of bundle acquisition triggered by the influential customers.

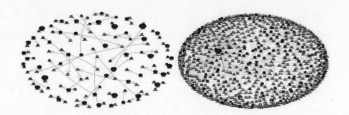

Figure 8.16 Comparison between the Bundle Diffusion Process from a Network Evolution Perspective for a Random 100 Customers (left) and the Top 100 Influential Customers (right)

Noticing the different shades assigned to the nodes around the initial subset that have triggered the business event, we can see that the closest customers are influenced first in the timeline. The sequence of network images shows the light nodes as the customers who acquired the bundle in the subsequent first month, and all of them are very close to the initial subset of influential customers who had triggered the business event. The darker nodes are the customers who were influenced in the second month after the initial event; they are still close to the initial subset. Sequentially, the other shades, from light to dark, show that the closer the customers, the higher the speed of influence among them.

Using the calls as the connections among the customers and the total duration of those calls as the closeness measure, it is possible to verify that the customers who relate more with the initial subset of influential customers were influenced first. The length of the customers' relationships decreases over time, but even so, the average number of minutes between the initial subset of influential customers and the customers they have influenced is greater than the entire average using their social networks.

For instance, the mean of the total duration assigned to the call between a pair of customers, considering the entire residential network, is just about 6.5 minutes monthly. Taking just the top 100 influential customers, the mean of the total duration assigned to the calls among them and their relationships is about 24.6 minutes monthly. Once more, if the length of the customers' relationships can be considered

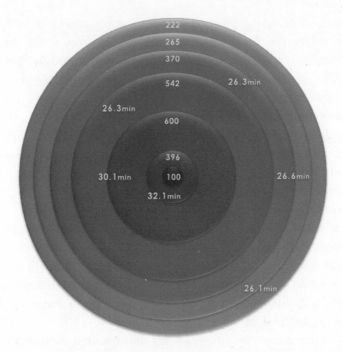

Figure 8.17 Closeness Comparison in Relation to the Bundle Diffusion Considering the Strength of the Customers' Relationships

based on the total duration assigned to their calls, the top 100 influential customers hold relationships almost four times greater or stronger than the random customers.

The number of related customers influenced by the top 100 influential customers, over time, is 396 in the first, 600 in the second, 542 in the third, 370 in the fourth, 265 in the fifth, and, finally, 222 in the sixth month. In addition to the correlation between the influential customers and the following events of bundle acquisition, it was observed that the influence factor also holds a correlation between the subsequent events and the strength of the relationship. The relationship in this particular telecommunications case study can be measured by the frequency and the duration of the calls among the customers.

Figure 8.17 shows the mean total duration between the initial subset of the top 100 influential customers and all other related customers they have influenced. For example, the 396 customers influenced in the first month by the original top 100 influential customers have a mean total duration of about 32.1 minutes monthly. The 600 customers influenced in the second month after the initial event have a mean total duration of about 30.1 minutes monthly. In other words, the first 396 customers influenced have more contact, or relationship, from a quantitative perspective, than the 600 customers influenced in the second month. Therefore, it is possible to assume that those 396 customers were influenced first because of their stronger relationship with the initial top influential nodes. Subsequently, the 542 customers influenced in the third month have a mean total duration of about 26.3 minutes. For the 370 customers influenced in the fourth month, the mean is the same, about 26.3 minutes. The 265 customers influenced in the fifth month have a mean a bit higher, about 26.6 minutes, and the last 222 customers, influenced in the sixth month, have a mean of about 26.1 minutes total duration.

The comparison over time shows that the first customers influenced by the original top influential nodes have the higher mean of total duration associated with their calls. We can see that gradually, as duration of calls increased among the customers, the higher and faster is the influence of the bundle acquisition events over time.

Taking into consideration the average duration of the calls between the top 100 influential customers and the customers related to them, regardless of whether they have influenced the related nodes in the bundle acquisition event, the duration is about 24.6 minutes monthly. Again, the analysis of these figures reveals that the related customers affected by the influential customers hold a higher number of minutes in terms of relationships than the customers who were not influenced. The average duration between the influential customers and the influenced ones is from 26.1 to 32.1 minutes monthly, increasing as long as the influence event happens first.

Figure 8.18 presents the number of minutes of relationship among the customers over time, considering when they were influenced, the overall mean of the influential calls, and, also, comparing those numbers with the average duration in relation to the entire residential network.

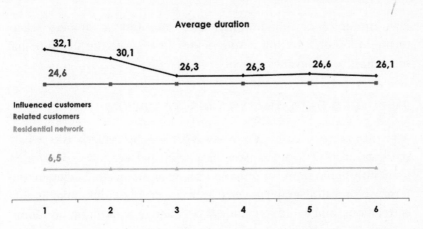

Figure 8.18 Closeness Comparison in Relation to the Bundle Diffusion Considering the Customers' Relationships

The average duration between the residential customers is just 6.5 minutes monthly. However, using the top 100 influential customers, the average duration of their calls is 24.6 minutes monthly. This means that the average duration among the top 100 influential customers and those 4,697 related customers is about 24.6 minutes monthly. Nevertheless, the average duration of calls for those 2,395 related customers who were influenced in the bundle acquisition event in the subsequent six months is about 32.1 minutes for the first month, decreasing gradually to 26.1 minutes for the last (sixth) month.

The total duration assigned to the calls among the customers can be considered here as a measure of closeness. This measure is calculated according to the customers' dissimilarities (i.e., the greater the duration, the smaller the distance). Therefore, as the distance shortens, the closeness increases. In that way, the closer the customers are, the greater the likelihood of influence in terms of this particular business event, the bundle acquisition.

The previous figures presented a high correlation between the customer-influence factor and the events that happen in a chain process, such as churn and bundle acquisition. This fact is important to understand how the social network behaves in the telecommunications environment and also how customers relate to one another, exerting a sort of influence over the network for some particular business events.

ENHANCED DATA ANALYSIS VISUALIZATION

A picture is worth a thousand words. This is particularly true when statistical analysis is taking place. In spite of all data analysis performed previously, presenting information about customer behavior in the form of statistical graphs—such as bars, pies, scatters, and lines—correlations, and evolution analysis over the time, nothing says more than an image embedding a particular data analysis.

Several data analyses take into consideration geographic information, such as address, counties, cities, and even countries. Analyzing the distribution of some particular business event or population can help our understanding of how the set of observations is behaving for a specific scenario.

Tracking the movements of a set or subset of a particular population can reveal the pattern assigned to some business event and helps predict the next steps.

It is very common to analyze important business events using graphs. Information about how some particular product has been purchased throughout the country is regularly assessed by graphs using bars or pies. However, evaluating the data in relation to this selling process plotted over a country's map can be more intuitive and more easily understood.

Considering the case study depicted in this book, using country and county maps can significantly assist the understanding of how customers are behaving from a geographic perspective. Social network analysis exploits the relationships among the customers and attempts to bring some understanding about how they can impact or exert influence over others. From the links among the customers, it is possible to see how close they are and how strong the relationships are. It is also possible to plot the social network structure based on the strength of the customers' relations and then recognize the virtual distance among the nodes. However, the simple but quite important information about where they are, geographically speaking, which counties have more influential customers, which neighborhoods have more sequences of events of churn, which particular areas have more frequent occurrences of purchasing, and so on, can disclose significant information about the customers' behavior and, therefore, their possible future movements.

In this case study, information about the influential customers—where they are, what are the densities of influence, the rate of selling and churn for each geographic area—all of this information help companies to better establish and position their marketing campaigns, logistics, and also supply chains. What kind of advertising should a company perform in some particular neighborhood? Perhaps in a neighborhood with a low density of influential customers, just an outdoor marketing campaign is enough to achieve retention. Perhaps in a neighborhood with a high density of influential customers, a more one-on-one marketing campaign would be necessary. Whatever the sort of strategy in relation to the marketing campaign, geographic information about current customers linked to statistical metrics about their value can assist companies in deploying more effective operational processes.

Plotting data over maps is quite simple and straightforward by using the SAS® capabilities. Basically, some setting should be defined, such as colors, title, border, font type and size, legends, and so on. The **proc gmap** should be used to plot the data about some particular subject of interest over a specific map. There are usually two datasets to use in the map plotting. The first one is the coordinates of the counties for a particular country. It is necessary to link the information about the data about some particular subject—for example, the business or corporate data—and the coordinates about the counties' boundaries. Usually, based on some particular fields from the address, it is possible to merge and join the coordinates in order to plot the business data onto the maps. It is important to have some of this information, such as street name, neighborhood, city, county, or even geographic coordinates. Based on detailed information like coordinates or street name plus some additional fields, it is possible to extract the county. Sometimes it is possible to extract the county from the neighborhood, and certainly from the city. Once the county is assigned to the business information, joining the coordinates of the map, it is possible to draw a map and then plot any business information on it.

The following code shows how simple it is to establish the coordinates from the country map's information and then to plot the corporate information.

```
goptions reset=all;

goptions reset=global gunit=pct noborder cback=white
         colors=(blue green lime pink cyan red)

colors=(Blue,BlueViolet,BurlyWood,CadetBlue,Chocola
te,CornflowerBlue,Crimson,DarkBlue,DarkCyan,DarkGold
enRod,DarkOliveGreen,DarkRed,DarkSalmon,DarkSeaGree
n,DarkSlateBlue,DarkSlateGray,DimGray,DodgerBlue,Fo
restGreen,Gold,GoldenRod,GreenYellow,Indigo,Orange,
RoyalBlue,SteelBlue)

ctext=black ftext=swiss htitle=2 htext=2;

title1 'Top 1000 influential customers';

 percentannomac;

percentmaplabel(maps.ireland,maps.ireland2,labctnam
e,idname,id,font=swiss,color=black,size=1,hsys=3);

legend1 label=('Number of Customers');
legend2 label=('Total Influence Factor');
legend3 label=('Average Influence Factor');
proc gmap data=sasuser.top1000irlagg
  map=maps.ireland all;
  id id;
  prism count / levels=all coutline=lightgrey
annotate=labctname
  description='Customers Distribution'
legend=legend1;
run;
quit;
```

The first procedure *goptions* defines some basic settings, such as colors, borders, and background. It is possible to set up a significant range of attributes in relation to the maps. Also, the palette of colors can be defined in order to plot the corporate data through the procedure *colors*.

The macro *%maclabel* defines the country's map, the reference table with the country coordinates' map, the name of the attribute to be plotted, its identification, and visual components like color, font, background, size, and scale.

The command *legend* defines the different legends to be used in the map as long as the corporate information is plotted.

Finally, the procedure *gmap* defines the dataset that contains the corporate information: which country's map should be used, the unique identification of the business data, the type of map visualization, how many levels of data are taken into consideration, the type of the line, any referenced annotated dataset, the title, and the legend of the map. Naturally there are additional settings that can be configured in order to create the most personalized map possible. Once again, the most important step here is the linking of the corporate information and the coordinates of the map.

Figure 8.19 presents a visualization data analysis based on the map. In this example, the most influential customers were plotted through the map in order to get an overview about the geographic distribution of customers.

In the figure, it is easy to see the most important counties in terms of absolute numbers of influential customers.

Being aware of the number of influential customers in each county is quite relevant, as is the total customer-influence factor, which represents indirectly how important the county is.

Figure 8.20 presents the total amount of customer-influence factor for each county, and gives a clear view about the value and importance of the counties.

Absolute numbers sometimes can drive attention in the wrong direction. In order to avoid misunderstanding the corporate data, it is important to analyze the same set of information from different points of view.

One type of data analysis evaluates the same set of information according to its density. Figure 8.21 shows the counties and the density of influential customers for each county.

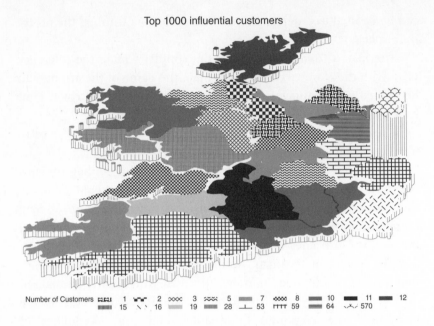

Figure 8.19 Visualization Analysis about the Customers' Distribution

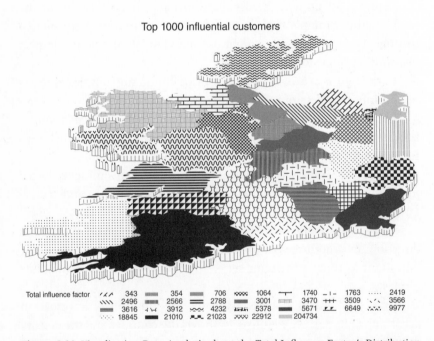

Figure 8.20 Visualization Data Analysis about the Total Influence Factor's Distribution

Top 1000 influential customers

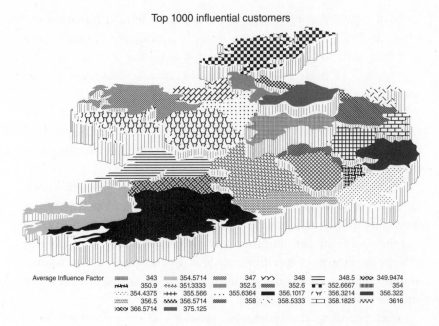

Average Influence Factor		343		354.5714		347		348		348.5		349.9474
		350.9		351.3333		352.5		352.6		352.6667		354
		354.4375		355.566		355.6364		356.1017		356.3214		356.322
		356.5		356.5714		358		358.5333		358.1825		3616
		366.5714		375.125								

Figure 8.21 Visualization Analysis about the Average Influence Factor's Distribution

In this way it is possible to recognize some particular counties or neighborhoods that hold a good number of influential customers, even though they do not have large populations. The average influence factor is high when compared to other counties or neighborhoods. This information can change the marketing strategy by directing some particular campaigns to this small but highly valued set of customers.

GEOGRAPHIC VISUALIZATION ANALYSIS

There is a set of SAS features available to plot business and corporate data over maps, using different levels of granularity, such as country, county, and neighborhood. It is a useful and good approach to improve the quality of the data analysis. It helps to better understand some particular distributions and to realize how customers are behaving and—most important—where they are.

Besides the possibility of plotting corporate and business data on the maps using SAS capabilities, there is another option to plot those kinds of data. By using open maps and public domain functions and procedures to plot data on these maps, it is possible to analyze business data based on georeferential maps like Google Maps.

Figure 8.22 presents an example of corporate data plotted in an open map in order to analyze the customers' distribution.

This type of analysis can be very useful to understand the real customer distributions in a very high degree of detail. By using address reminders, it is possible to analyze particular distributions based on streets and small geographic areas.

The close-up map shown in Figure 8.23 presents high-level detail information of customer distribution. It is possible to visualize where the highly influential customers are concentrated. This sort of analysis is quite useful for defining the marketing strategy and the sequence of steps to perform in specific campaigns. Being aware of the locations of influential customers can enable companies to establish more direct and effective marketing actions.

Understanding the geographic positions of the customers, especially the influential ones, makes it possible to correlate distinct actions because of the influence factor for each customer and the relationships among customers. For instance, two highly influential customers who relate to each other and live in the same neighbourhood or small area can receive different campaigns so they can swap the marketing information between them. If the company knows they are highly influential customers, and they live close each other and also have a strong relationship with each other, it is probable these customers will discuss the marketing campaign. The company can use this knowledge to contact just one or to contact both with distinct campaigns. This can increase the effectiveness of the marketing actions and, at the same time, decrease the cost of operations.

The use of georeferential localization has been increasing and becoming more common. New procedures and functions about geographic data analysis are coming soon and will be used in most companies, especially the ones that are in competitive markets.

Combining data mining and geographic data analysis is a good approach to increase functionalities about performance management and to make marketing campaigns more effective. The

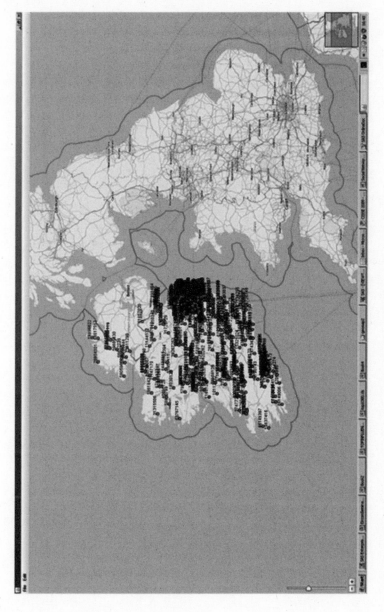

Figure 8.22 Geographic Data Analysis Based on the Address Reminder Data

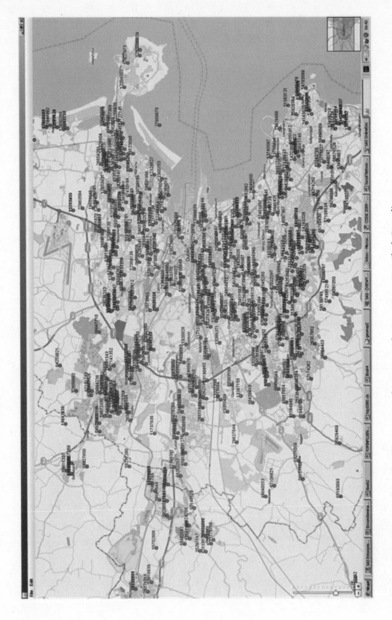

Figure 8.23 Geographic Visualization Analysis Considering More Detailed Coordinates

combination increases information about customers and correlates that information to real and relevant attributes about the customers.

SUMMARY

This chapter presented the process of evaluating the social network analysis outcomes in terms of business applications. The figures in relation to the network measures and the business results were depicted in detail. The chapter described the gain in the number of customers retained in the company using a churn event as well as the gain numbers of customers who were likely to purchase a bundle of products and services. These gains compared random or regular customers with influential customers. By contacting the influential customers, either about churn or bundle diffusion, telecommunications companies are able to improve the effectiveness rate for the customer retention and bundle diffusion processes.

In addition, further visualization approaches were covered in order to present the benefits from this sort of analysis. A network visualization method, using nodes and links, shows the relationships among the customers, highlighting the leaders and the followers for particular business events, such as churn and bundle diffusion, as presented in the case study. Geographic visualization plots the customers and their relationships on geographic positions, allowing companies to compare the relationship similarities against the georeferencing locations. Do customers living in the same area have some strong relationships? Are there some particular locations where the distances and the relationships have some correlation?

The visualization methods, either network relationship or geographic mapping, create a brand-new perspective of customer assessment, allowing recognition of which customers are relevant inside the network in terms of the strength of their relationships and their geographic positions inside the network.

CHAPTER **9**

Final Remarks for the Case Study

This chapter presents the final conclusions of the case study analyzing the telecommunications industry. Although there are several distinct statistical and mathematical methods used to analyze data and, therefore, increase knowledge of customer behavior, most if not all of these methods miss relevant information about the relationships that make up the network.

The regular data analysis method isolates customers' attributes, such as usage and demographic information. Neither of these describes how customers relate to each other or, most important, how relevant these relationships are to some business events.

The case study described in Part II was developed based on telecommunications data concerning two particular business events, churn and bundle diffusion.

The premise for the case study was that both events are impacted in a cascade time scale occurrence. Based on this hypothesis, a framework of analysis was built using several months of data in order to determine average customer behavior and analyze later events caused by the cascade concept.

If a particular customer decides to leave the company, the impact depends on his level of influence. If he is a highly influential customer, the likelihood that he will lead other customers to leave the company is very high. However, if he is not influential, he will probably not lead many customers to follow him. Bundle diffusion is quite similar to churn; influential customers are more likely to affect other customers in their decision to purchase a bundle than regular or non-influential customers.

The information gathered through social network analysis can change the way companies handle customer relationship programs, improving effectiveness and at the same time reducing operational costs. Among several business applications, social network analysis can assist in defining the target subset of customers for particular campaigns and refine the task of establishing distinct approaches to marketing, sales, relationship, retention, and other business activities.

PRODUCTS AND SERVICE CHOICE

Social network analysis can be deployed as an agent-based modeling approach, particularly when it is applied in order to detect customers' behavior in terms of relationships. This topic is based on the work of Baxter, Collings, and Adjali, and briefly describes the agent-based modeling method and its application in terms of business events. Their study can be applied to business operations such as customer relationship management. In this way, social network analysis is viewed as an agent-based modeling approach.

In addition to data mining procedures specific to the social network analysis methodology presented in this book, it is possible to create an entire environment where simulation procedures can take place. By understanding customer behavior according to past events, products, and services, and, most important in this particular case, relationships over time, it is possible to create a more complex scenario of decision making, incorporating features of simulations. This what-if approach allows companies to analyze different targets, waves, paths, and scripts in terms of campaigns, and also different sets of products and services offered.

Simulations of product and service choices can be performed using a theory known as agent-based modeling. Agent-based modeling is not within the scope of this book, but it is a wise way to apply social network analysis outcomes within a corporate environment.

Agent-based models are simulations based on local interactions between members of a population and between members and the environment in which they are contained. This definition can be applied to social network analysis, in which case it is the study of the relationship of members (agents) within a population (environment). When using the information system approach, individuals are usually treated as objects and are limited by a set of parameters and behavioral rules. This set of rules considers any sort of modification that can occur within the environment and use it to establish interactions with other agents in the system. This approach is quite similar to the way social networks are built. Interactions among agents, like nodes in social networks, are crucial to recognizing individual behavior within networks or communities.

When analyzing huge populations and, therefore, a massive number of interactions, pattern recognition in terms of behavior is often quite difficult to define using agent-based modeling. It can be difficult to establish behavior for the entire population, but a concept of microscopic behavior can be defined for small communities inside the network. As in social network analysis, the evaluation of the network over time can point to some interesting trends, not just in terms of the overall market but also about the individuals who make up communities. The agent-based technique is distinct from other modeling approaches in which characteristics are often aggregated and manipulated based on high-level information.

Baxter, Collings, and Adjali state that agent-based models provide a natural framework for capturing spatial and network effects in systems:

> Individuals can be associated with a geometric location and permitted to move around their environment where appropriate. The individuals can be located in a continuous space or restricted to a discrete grid-based geography. Comparisons between the distances among the customers in terms of relationship strength and the geographic locations can reveal for the companies new paths to communicate with the customers. In the fields of social science and computational economics, agent-based modeling has provided an opportunity to move beyond the concept of a rational agent. The reasoning of

individuals can be progressively defined, accounting for their limited knowledge and abilities. An agent-based simulation can also capture the flow of information between agents in a system, a critical factor in the construction of a social simulation. There have been many studies to investigate the links that associate one person with another within a population.[1]

Studies of the general behavior of people who are linked to each other are often related to social network analysis. This sort of study is usually related to the links rather than the nodes. Relationships are the main focus of the analyses. Relationships describe the network structure but also the pattern of behavior assigned to the nodes, or actors, or customers in the case study presented earlier.

Social network analysis based on the agent-based modeling method can be applied to solve several business problems or improve operational processes. The outcome of this methodology can help decision makers anticipate particular market scenarios, especially those characterized by dynamism. In competitive markets such as telecommunications, the ability to anticipate scenarios, predict the best and shortest paths, and identify opportunities and threats can be quite advantageous. Another relevant feature in these markets is simulation. The ability to simulate business scenarios and analyze different perspectives, paths, and parameters helps identify the causes and consequences associated with different levels of decision making. Simulation in social network analysis is a method of analyzing the evolution of behavior among members of communities and populations, which allows trends to be studied. Once again, agent-based analysis based on interactions over time can indicate the direction of the market and allow substantial explanation of these paths.

There are numerous theories in social science, social network analysis, and marketing studies which are focused on product adoption, especially the diffusion of new innovations over time. Most of the diffusion models take a comprehensive approach, and generally establish three possible premises:

1. There are two distinct states of service and product adoption: customers have acquired products and services or they have not.

2. The number of prospects for adoption is basically fixed.

3. In most cases, there are no repeat purchases or multiple adoptions. This assumption is usually defined to make the modeling process simpler.

The adoption of multiple products and services can be described by social network analysis when it is applied to data over time. The method used to understand the behavior of adoption over time is to analyze the network structure as a sequence of snapshots and then compare them in terms of evolution. How do relationships among the members of a particular community affect adoption? Is there any correlation between the network metrics for nodes, links, and adoption? How do these network metrics change over time? What happens when an important node inside the network adopts a particular product or service? Do related nodes adopt similar products or services afterward? Is this node really influential? How does the influence factor correlate to the network metrics, considering both nodes and links? All these questions can be addressed by applying social network analysis and studying the sequence of network snapshots over time.

When business information is gathered by applying social network analysis to historic data, it is possible to understand customer behavior in terms of product and service adoption based on customer relationships. A properly focused marketing campaign can be established by using this sort of information. Well-targeted campaigns can drive performance and high conversion rates. In conjunction with predictive scores for product and service purchase, which indicate the likelihood of customers acquiring a particular product or service, it is possible to define an environment for marketing and sales.

By choosing highly influential customers who are likely to influence others, with a high propensity for purchasing a particular product or service, an entire diffusion process can be initiated throughout the network. Most important this process can be triggered by customers. Information about a particular product or service can flow rapidly through the network via the links among customers. The information about the product or service, or about the campaign itself, is seeded in a particularly influential customer and disseminated through his contacts. This is certainly the best diffusion process in terms of marketing and sales. This is how viral marketing works for businesses.

An agent-based model should represent a particular population of customers. In this case, each node within the population should have a correlated process driving its likelihood of adopting a product or service according to a particular offering. The individuals are influenced by environmental factors, such as market and competition. Those who purchase the product will be exposed to a range of different interactions with the company and also with the other related customers. Agents, or nodes, inside the telecommunications network can share their perceptions about a product or service through their social structure, influencing the decisions of others within the network. This simulation approach controls the key drivers of customer behavior, allowing detailed exploration of system dynamics.

Consumers usually flow within stable phases in terms of a company's lifetime. A full cycle of relationship stages is shown in Figure 9.1. Baxter, Collings, and Adjali described this cycle as follows:

> The first step is the acquisition. During the first stage of the decision process an individual receives information that alters their perception of the product or service on offer. This change of perception is due to a combination of inter-agent communication and external factors such as marketing and competition.
>
> The second step is the decision. The individual now makes the choice of adopting or staying with the product if their perception is sufficiently high.
>
> The third step is the implementation. This step represents the explicit act of adoption or rejection, making the process particularly suitable for repeat purchase models.
>
> The fourth and last step is the confirmation. In this step the agents' parameters are adjusted based on experience of using the product or service.[2]

The process of agent-based modeling is quite similar to predictive modeling in the sense of gathering information from the past and using the analytical model to learn from this information. Sequence analyses of social interactions over time are also similar to the

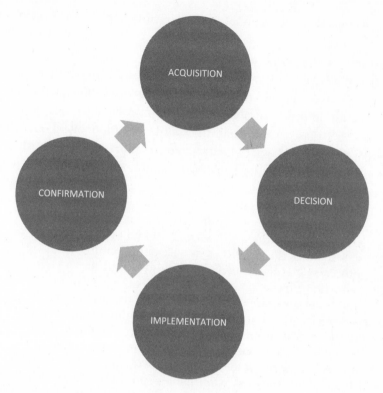

Figure 9.1 Cycle of Stages for Agents

predictive approach, fetching knowledge from the past and using it to teach the next models or to lead further analyses.

Although the results gathered through social network analysis can be used directly for marketing and sales purposes, additional factors should be taken into consideration for corporate applications. In spite of the possibility of finding influential customers within a community, external facts should also be taken into account, such as the quality of the product or service, its price, customer service in relation to sales, and several other market scenarios. A company can find influential customers to be targeted by a campaign, but perhaps the product or service involved in the sale process is not very good, not very attractive, or not very cheap. There are no influential customers who can make this diffusion process work. As a matter of fact, there are no influential customers to acquire this product or service at all.

The outcomes from analytical models including statistical, probability, predictive, and exploratory, such as social network analysis, produce knowledge, not intelligence. Intelligence is the application of information in order to solve some specific problem.

In other words, other than the social network analysis oucomes, there is a long list of external characteristics that can impact business.

Baxter, Collings, and Adjali described those external characteristics in the following way:

> In addition to the procedure described it is important to consider the influence of social fads and other network externalities on product or service adoption. In these processes it is the knowledge of who within the population has adopted that generates the pressure to adopt, rather than the functionality of the product or service itself. The term network externality describes the circumstance where a product's benefit changes as the number of agents consuming it changes. Baxter, Collings and Adjali have presented a classic example of a product that exhibits network externalities such as the fax machine. As more people purchase fax machines, users can communicate with a greater number of people, and the utility of the device increases. This fact also happens nowadays very strongly with social network websites such as Bebo, Facebook, LinkedIn, MySpace, Ning, Flickr, Plaxo, among others. As much users get in, there is more opportunities for interactions among them. Companies are currently trying to capture these social media interactions in order to understand the customers' needs, behaviors and tendencies. By capturing the customers' interactions from social network websites, companies expect to capture as consequence the customers' experience in relation to a particular product or service, or to the company itself.
>
> However, this is unlikely to be realistic for the most products and services available. The concept can alternatively be implemented as an addition to the acquisition stage of the adoption process. At every time step in the simulation, individuals examine their social

network and assess the proportion of their acquaintances that have adopted. For a pure fad the agent will adopt the product as soon as this proportion reaches their individual threshold value. However, in the combined process, changes in the proportion of adopters will simply be an extra influence on the perception of the product.[3]

It is difficult to correlate acquisition with its respective cause. Customers may acquire a product because of a massive advertising campaign, telemarketing, research, or network influence. In the end, it is always hard to measure the reason for acquisitions and assign them to business events. However, it is possible to correlate purchasing with customers over time, recognizing the customers who have more connections buying similar products or services. The reason for purchasing is still unknown, but the correlation between the event and the customers can point to influence.

All these features of service simulation and product choice can be used in a high-level program regarding customer relationship management (CRM). Understanding the interactions among customers makes it possible to create new marketing and sales campaigns, more in tune with customers' needs and behaviors, particularly regarding their relationships within social networks.

According to Baxter, Collings, and Adjali, analysts predict that companies will spend billions of dollars in the next few years on software and services to help manage their customer interactions more effectively. Unfortunately, most organizations do not fully understand how these investments will affect their customer base. Currently only 21 percent of CRM projects meet all expectations, according to a survey conducted by Hewson Consultancy Group in January 2000.

Word of mouth can be a powerful way for businesses to recruit new customers. This premise makes social network analysis even more important, especially in terms of the centrality and strength of nodes and links. People are often suspicious of advertisements and seek opinions from trusted friends and acquaintances before purchasing a product or service. In this way, customer influence is quite important in defining and selecting targets for campaigns. Referrals are effective, as they usually come from someone who is familiar with the product or service but has no financial motive for making the recommendation. Companies generally find that referred customers require less sales time to build trust and credibility and tend to be more loyal than those whose purchases are driven by advertisements, according to a study published by Griffin in 1995. The customers who lead this word-of-mouth process are influencers inside social networks, making social network analysis crucial for diffusion campaigns.

Intelligent CRM tools embed an agent-based customer model using the cognitive process discussed previously. It is a decision support tool that enables organizations to visualize the impact of their CRM strategies and explore the effects of word of mouth on customer recruitment and retention. Social network analysis must be involved in order to effectively implement this sort of approach.

CRM tools should contain a generic model that captures the key drivers of customer behavior and choice and can be used in a consultancy environment to facilitate dialogue. Baxter, Collings, and Adjali claim that it is designed for use with a range of clients and is not specific to any company or sector. Trials show that using such a tool can stimulate discussion and improve understanding of CRM issues. However, a model assigned to CRM is not a precise forecasting tool. The agent-based approach offers a more realistic representation of a customer population, but it is still based on numerous assumptions and simplifications. In reality, many of the parameters required to define a theoretical model are difficult to measure, and specific external events can cause unexpected behavior. Results should be treated as illustrative but can still be used to compare the impact of different CRM strategies, in terms of both market share and financial performance.

FURTHER INFERENCES AND FUTURE WORKS

Telecommunications is a very dynamic industry in which situations can change very quickly. When changes happen in the market, the data tend to change as a consequence. Social network analysis can be used to monitor and assess a company's action plan and apply it to new business realities, which are represented by a new type of data content.[4]

Social network analysis also can adapt in order to consider changes that occur in the industry's data, following customer behavior in terms of events, consumption, and relationships. Adaptability is fundamental in a market characterized by high competition, such as telecommunications. In this market, the conditions of customer behavior can change very rapidly and should be tracked in order to respond to new business needs.

The dynamic characteristics of the industry, especially the retail, telecommunications, and financial markets, can change and impact the customers' environment and should be reflected in corporate data. In this way, any analytical model based on data can recognize change when it studies a period of time.

Ranking consumers according to their influence factors rather than a set of isolated attributes makes it possible to establish and perform business operations in a straightforward way, allowing companies to retain more customers with less effort and diffuse products and services more effectively.

A valuable benefit of using social network analysis is the opportunity to assign a value to customers that considers their influence scores based on their relations with others rather than their isolated characteristics in terms of the market or within the corporation. Considering events that occur in a chain process, such as churn and diffusion, this approach can represent a completely unique way to accomplish important business goals.

The most traditional methods of evaluating customers are often based on demographic information, such as billing, revenue, and usage data. However, because the telecommunications network usually creates natural social structures, they can be quite effective in establishing a distinct method of customer evaluation, considering their influence in those communities. The way customers relate with their connections counts more than their own characteristics in the social network perspective. Somehow, how they act is more relevant than who they are. By using this approach, companies will be able to retain more than just highly valuable customers; they will retain all relations assigned to them, which means more products and services can be sold.

Suppose a customer generates revenue of about $100 but has few connections. Imagine three recurrent pairs of contact. These additional three customers generate an average of $50 in revenue. It is possible to assume roughly $250 in monthly revenue for the original customer. Suppose another customer generates revenue of about $50. However, this particular customer has an extensive social network with 10 connections. Suppose these 10 customers each generate the same $50 of revenue. By this reckoning, you can attribute $550 in monthly revenue to this well-connected customer. A simple analysis of individual characteristics would determine that the first customer is more important or valuable than the second ($100 versus $50). However, because of their social networks, the second customer is certainly more valuable than the first in terms of total revenue generated ($550 versus $250).

Similarly, targeting customers for a marketing campaign to diffuse a new bundle based on the customer influence factor can allow companies to expand their products and services in the best way, through the relationships of their customers rather than sales procedures. These campaigns are able to reach more customers in terms of absolute figures, and influential customers can convert or influence more customers.

The case study illustrated that additional gains in effectiveness and operational performance were achieved due to the customer influence factor. The process of selecting the best customers in order to augment a particular campaign was 81 percent more effective in terms of hit rate when using the influence factor than a random process. When the target was based on the influence factor, the absolute rate was 132 percent better than a random process. The first figure demonstrates effectiveness, and the second shows the practical result.

Nevertheless, gains in terms of effectiveness are quite relevant. Performance in terms of absolute numbers, or the capacity to expand a particular business process, is even better. The use of the influence factor to execute a retention process is 622 percent more effective than a random approach, which means that it is possible to reach seven times more customers in a retention process than through a random approach. Similarly, performance of the influence factor in a bundle diffusion process is 629 percent better than a random approach. Starting with the same number of customers, once again it is possible to reach seven times more customers in order to diffuse some particular bundle when using the customer influence factor instead of a random process.

Assuming that some business events, such as churn and bundle diffusion, occur in a chain process, and considering the importance of relationships in the telecommunications network, social network analysis can play a large role in shaping business strategies, especially when considering the effectiveness and cost of marketing, sales, and retention campaigns.

Social network analysis is very good at establishing new ways to evaluate customers. This approach considers influence among related customers rather than their isolated attributes within the company. Considering the existing social structures inside the telecommunications network, this methodology might succeed more than traditional approaches, which consider only personal information to evaluate customers.

However, features and capabilities assigned to simulation are required to evaluate the best options in terms of actions and campaigns to be triggered, and they will be the focus of research in the future. In order to create a suitable environment to support business decisions, other than the knowledge created from these models, a simulation process is required to improve the evaluation of customers, impacts of churn and diffusion, performance of the process from a chain perspective, retention of central customers, and sell some particular bundle for them.

The simulation should address business questions based on assessments of network chain events, evaluating different impacts according to events such as churn and bundle acquisition. Due to specific events of churn or bundle acquisition, how will social networks behave afterward? How will the simulation of events affect the value of customers and update their importance according to ongoing situations? This kind of simulation process can greatly improve the accuracy of analytical decision support processes. Corporate decisions should be defined by simulation assessments rather than by historical numbers and simple statistical analysis alone.

SUMMARY

Part II presented a case study that was developed and deployed by a telecommunications company, proving the value of the concept in relation to social network analysis. Chapter 5 presented the telecommunications industry, describing the strong correlation between telecommunications and social networks. By viewing telecommunications networks as social networks, it is possible to recognize the interactions among customers and hence highlight the leaders and followers within communities. Leaders and followers can be handled by distinct approaches of relationship management, providing distinct offerings and campaigns according to the type and strength of the customers.

Chapter 6 described the modeling process for social network analysis. How to consider the proper attributes and calculate the influence factor, methods for composing a timeline, and, finally, how to correlate customer influence factor to business events were topics covered in this chapter.

Chapter 7 covered the methodology of assessing the social network analysis model in terms of effectiveness, correlating the customer influence factor to events such as churn or bundle diffusion.

Finally, Chapter 8 presented the outcomes of social network analysis in terms of business yields. The outcomes are in relation to the case study, depicting the benefits of deploying an analytical model such as social network analysis in telecommunications. The results achieved by the modeling process were effective in terms of both absolute and percentage gains.

NOTES

1. N. Baxter, D. Collings, and I. Adjali, "Agent-Based Modeling—Intelligent Customer Relationship Management," *BT Technology Journal* 21(2) (2003): 126–132.

2. Ibid.

3. Ibid.

4. C. A. R. Pinheiro and M. Helfert, "Creating a Customer Influence Factor to Decrease the Impact of Churn and to Enhance the Bundle Diffusion in Telecommunications Based on Social Network Analysis," SAS® Global Forum, 2010.

PART III

SAS Capabilities for Social Network Analysis

The third part of this book presents the most relevant SAS capabilities in order to develop and deploy a social network analysis model in a real problem. Some of these SAS features should be used before the social network analysis modeling, while some of them should be put into place after the model development, basically to analyze the outcomes. Chapter 10 describes the common statistics procures provided by SAS in order to previously understand the data available. Descriptive analysis; including frequencies and distributions; unique and multivariate analyses, and clustering methods are included in this chapter as a way to prepare the analysts to further tasks in addition to the social network analysis.

Chapter 11 shows the Link Analysis Node comprised in the SAS Enterprise Miner, which was used to develop the case study of this book. It presents how to define nodes and links, how to use the macros (this is particularly important to the case study), which measures are available, and how to analyze the networks. Chapter 12 lists some relevant tools to visualize social networks, such as the macro %DSTOCONST and the software Network Visualization Workshop. Finally, chapter 13 describes briefly a brand new procedure provided by SAS to work with graphs and networks. Procedure OPTGRAPH computes a wide range of network measures, as well as performs some relevant group analysis including communities, connected components and biconnected components.

CHAPTER **10**

Basic Statistics

The description of the basics statistics in this chapter is based on SAS® documentation.[1] A very small subset of the statistical procedures available in SAS was used in the development process in relation to the case study presented in this book. For this reason, these statistical procedures are going to be briefly described in this chapter.

The social network analysis approach used in the case study is an exploratory and investigative analysis to understand a social structure's behavior. This approach aims to create a commonsense understanding about the social network structure and, therefore, about node behavior and the relationships within the social structure. The outcome from the social network approach is a set of network measures that describe the importance of the nodes and links within the social structure.

The statistical procedures presented in this chapter usually take place before and after the social network analysis method. Before the network measures computing, it is always necessary to prepare the data, analyze it, modify it, sometimes insert missing information into the input dataset, and, mostly, transform the traditional data into network data for the social network analysis computing process. The statistical procedures are used in order to analyze the network-measure outcome, identifying the most important nodes, the most relevant links, the network distribution, the outliers, the social structure, the communities, and connected groups within the network, among others. According to the business problems to be solved, some subset of network measures are more relevant than others. The outcome analysis is targeted, therefore, because of business purposes, to highlight the relevant measures about nodes and links within the social structure. For instance, for fraud or risk objectives, outliers' nodes, links, and communities are quite relevant. Thus, multiple variable analysis, principal component analysis, and distribution analysis are recommended. For diffusion process, such as products and services sales campaigns, single-variable analysis, and ranking analysis are better directed to identify the most important nodes to trigger the events in a chain process. For churn, single-variable, and ranking analyses, other network metrics are recommended.

Also, in terms of visualization analysis, some particular approaches can lead to understanding the social structure in terms of positioning similarities. As with the clustering process, by analyzing the node and link positions, it is possible to improve the selection of the target nodes for particular campaigns. For example, in sales campaigns, it might be possible to discard very closely positioned influential nodes, if just one of them might trigger a diffusion process. For churn campaigns, influential nodes that are closely positioned might be selected together to reinforce the retention's actions.

Multidimensional scaling is one of the possible algorithms to establish the map of nodes positioned by the strength of their relationships. The similarity variable to create the coordinates for the nodes might be the strength of the links among them.

As described earlier, the traditional data and network data are different. The first step in the social network analysis approach is, as in any analytical process, to prepare the data properly for the modeling process.

As a matter of fact, the very first step in the social network analysis approach is to understand the data available and the business problem to be solved, and, therefore, to identify which information will serve to create the nodes and which will serve to create the links.

By defining which information will comprise nodes and links, a social network that can be analyzed is created.

To carry out the case study presented in this book, a small set of statistical procedures were performed to understand the data in relation to the business issue to be addressed. These statistical procedures are related to sort, frequency, unique variable analysis, multidimensional scaling, and clustering.

DESCRIPTIVE ANALYSIS

Two distinct approaches for statistical analysis are covered in this chapter. The first one is in relation to descriptive analysis, presenting the processes assigned to sort some particular dataset, to create frequencies in data, and to analyze variables in a unique way. The second approach is about more complex processes, such as clustering, recognizing and identifying groups of observations based on similar behavior, and creating virtual coordinates for nodes based on the strength of their relationships. This last model is called multidimensional scaling, and it creates coordinates based on similarities of some particular attribute or set of variables.

Sorting

Several tasks in SAS require a sorted dataset to be used. A sorted dataset improves the performance of some jobs, especially in statistical analysis when comparisons and combinations are required. Tasks such as preliminary data preparation require some sort process to be done in order to use the link analysis macros presented in Part II of this book.

The SORT procedure in SAS orders some specific dataset of observations by a list of values, which can be one or more variables. The SORT procedure can replace the original dataset used as input, or it can create a new dataset with content of the original input dataset ordered.

The next example presents an input dataset with call-detail records, containing just the calling number and the called number in this case, for the sake of simplicity. The SORT procedure replaces, in this

Table 10.1: Calls among Phone Numbers

anumber	bnumber	frequency	duration
84011853	84251406	12	166
84223809	75053478	3	34
23893455	23346789	5	57
87659384	45678769	6	52
34768900	34452311	3	23
98675723	45867399	4	43
34897599	37563544	2	9
23548766	45738239	1	34
88970403	87605767	5	59
45647867	99877659	7	26
26216897	26223099	8	64

example, the original dataset **calls**, just by ordering its content by the variables **anumber** (calling number) and **bnumber** (called number), **frequency** (the number of calls between a pair of numbers), and **duration** (the number of total minutes in calls for a pair of numbers).

```
proc sort data=calls;
  by anumber bnumber frequency duration;
run;
```

Suppose there are 11 observations in the original dataset **calls**, with four variables, the calling number (**anumber**), the called number (**bnumber**), the number of calls between these numbers (**frequency**), and the total duration in minutes (**duration**) among them.

Table 10.1 presents the calls among phone numbers.

The output shown in Table 10.2 presents the results of the SORT procedure using the dataset of preplaced **calls** of the same content

Table 10.2: Calls among Phone Numbers Sorted by Phone Numbers

anumber	bnumber	frequency	duration
23548766	45738239	1	34
23893455	23346789	5	57
26216897	26223099	8	64
34768900	34452311	3	23
34897599	37563544	2	9
45647867	99877659	7	26
84011853	84251406	12	166
84223809	75053478	3	34
87659384	45678769	6	52
88970403	87605767	5	59
98675723	45867399	4	43

ordered by all variables, **anumber**, **bnumber**, **frequency,** and **duration**, in this order.

It is possible to sort the dataset by some numeric variable, from the highest value to the lowest value.

```
proc sort data=calls;
  by descending duration;
run;
```

By doing this, the list of 11 pairs of numbers is ordered by the number of minutes connected between them, as shown in Table 10.3, which presents the calls among phone numbers sorted by frequency.

The SORT procedure comprises an extensive list of options, allowing the creation of new columns, dropping others, defining the

Table 10.3: Calls among Phone Numbers Sorted by Frequency

anumber	bnumber	frequency	duration
84011853	84251406	12	166
26216897	26223099	8	64
45647867	99877659	7	26
87659384	45678769	6	52
23893455	23346789	5	57
88970403	87605767	5	59
98675723	45867399	4	43
34768900	34452311	3	23
84223809	75053478	3	34
34897599	37563544	2	9
23548766	45738239	1	34

memory to be used in the process, establishing the type of algorithm to use in the sort process, and defining the size of the observations, among others. In spite of its simplicity, the SORT procedure is a highly powerful tool to prepare the input data for some particular analytical procedures in SAS.

Frequency

Some particular statistical tasks in SAS might require some data format that the FREQ procedure would accomplish. The FREQ procedure can also transform the original data layout into a new one, more assigned to the statistical requirements for some particular analytical process, making the analysis initiative easier overall. Tasks such as the preliminary data preparation in order to use the link analysis macros presented in the case study covered in this book might require computing some sort of frequencies.

The FREQ procedure produces one-way to n-way frequencies and cross-tabulation tables. In two-way tables, the FREQ procedure can also produce tests and measures of association among the variables available in the input dataset. It might be interesting to calculate the strength of the correlation between particular pairs of variables within an input dataset. There are different measures to test the association in relation to a pair of variables, such as chi-square, binomial proportions, odds ratios, and others. If any of these measures is close to zero, there is no association between the variables. Otherwise, if the measure of association is close to 1, there is a high association between the particular pair of variables.

The following piece of code creates the dataset containing the information used in the previous example.

```
data calls;
  input anumber bnumber frequency duration;
datalines;
84011853 84251406 12 166
84223809 75053478 3 34
23893455 23346789 5 57
87659384 45678769 6 52
34768900 34452311 3 23
98675723 45867399 4 43
34897599 37563544 2 9
23548766 45738239 1 34
88970403 87605767 5 59
45647867 99877659 7 26
26216897 26223099 8 64
;
```

By running a FREQ procedure over the input dataset **calls**, the outcome should be like this:

```
proc freq data=calls;
  tables anumber;
run;
```

The SAS System   16:27 Wednesday,
November 10, 2010 10
The FREQ Procedure

anumber	Frequency	Percent	Cumulative Frequency	Cumulative Percent
23548766	1	9.09	1	9.09
23893455	1	9.09	2	18.18
26216897	1	9.09	3	27.27
34768900	1	9.09	4	36.36
34897599	1	9.09	5	45.45
45647867	1	9.09	6	54.55
84011853	1	9.09	7	63.64
84223809	1	9.09	8	72.73
87659384	1	9.09	9	81.82
88970403	1	9.09	10	90.91
98675723	1	9.09	11	100.00

As all numbers in that dataset occur just once, the frequency and the percentage are the same for all of them.

By running a measure of association based on chi-square for variables **frequency** and **duration**, it is possible to identify if there is any correlation between this pair of variables. The code to perform this task is:

```
proc freq data=calls;
  tables frequency*duration / chisq;
run;
```

Statistics for Table of frequency by duration

Statistic	DF	Value	Prob
Chi-Square	72	79.7500	0.2485
Likelihood Ratio Chi-Square	72	44.4359	0.9956
Mantel-Haenszel Chi-Square	1	7.0379	0.0080
Phi Coefficient		2.6926	
Contingency Coefficient		0.9374	
Cramer's V		0.9520	

As you can see in the results, the value of the measure chi-square is 79.75, which is close to 1, indicating that there is a correlation between the number of calls and the total duration between a pair of nodes. However, this particular dataset is very small. The chi-square may not be a valid test in this particular situation. In reality, people can call each other a few times with long calls, several times with short calls, a few times with short calls, and several times with long calls. A correlation between these two variables relies on plans and promotions for each telecom operator, leading customers to make more calls of short duration or fewer calls of long duration.

The FREQ procedure was used in the case study in order to produce the matrix of links, joining the originating and destination nodes upon the connections inside the telecommunications network. In order to compute the centrality measures, both nodes and links datasets should be created as matrices. To perform this task, the FREQ procedure was put in place. All macros comprised in the link analysis node, such as %_rawnodes, %_rawlinks, %_rawmerge, %_rawstats, %_centrality, %_prefix, and %_final, require the source datasets in a matrix format.

```
proc freq data=callsab noprint;
  by anumber bnumber;
  table anumber*bnumber / out=abn;
run;
proc freq data=callsa noprint;
  by anumber;
  table anumber / out=an;
run;
proc freq data=callsb noprint;
  by bnumber;
  table bnumber / out=bn;
run;
```

The piece of code presented earlier also makes part of the case study covered in the earlier chapters. It aims to prepare the source datasets for the link analysis macros, creating the matrices data in relation to the original links, the originating phone numbers and the destination phone numbers.

Univariate Analysis

For any type of analytical modeling, such as link analysis, and hence social network analysis, the understanding about the data available and its contents is quite fundamental. The basic understanding about the data is described in terms of its contents, the range of variable domains, the missing values, the attributes' frequencies, measures of association, and the content distribution.

The UNIVARIATE procedure provides a substantial list of descriptive statistics about the variables within a particular input dataset. These descriptive statistics include moments, skewness, kurtosis, quantiles, percentiles, median, mode, minimum, maximum, frequency tables, and extreme values.

The procedure also provides several graphs describing the variables' distribution in terms of content. These graphs include histograms, quantile-quantile plots, probability plots, probability-probability plots, and, finally, comparative plots that utilize the previous ones.

The UNIVARIATE procedure is quite useful to understand the data available for the analytical modeling, visualizing the quality of this data, its distribution, it outliers' values, and the average content. This understanding allows us to predict the variables to use in model development as well as to gain some business information about the subject.

Descriptive analysis helps to explore the distributions of the variables in a dataset—an important preliminary step in data analysis—for data warehousing and particularly for data mining. Descriptive analysis, by using the UNIVARIATE procedure, helps to find key features of distributions, identify outliers and extreme observations, determine the need for data transformations, and compare distributions. In terms of links analysis and social network analysis, this feature is quite important in order to identify the attributes to be used as nodes, links, types of nodes and links, and the possible weights from them.

Descriptive analysis is often used in order to compare the individual network measures, highlighting the influential nodes for some particular business purpose. Especially considering huge social networks like telecommunications, it is quite difficult to identify the influential nodes directly, graphically, or in other way. After the network measures computation, it is usually useful to compare the values of these measures among the nodes. By doing this, it is possible to identify which nodes have the highest degree, which ones have the highest closeness and betweenness, and so on. By analyzing the network measures in a descriptive approach, the relevant nodes, their links, and also their correlated nodes can be highlighted in a statistical process.

The UNIVARIATE procedure can also be used to perform a descriptive analysis for the entire network measures, calculating the mean of each one and the top percentiles for the distribution, such as 90th, 95th, or 99th. For instance, all nodes with first-order centrality in the top percentiles can be considered to be high connected customers and, hence, the influential ones. Similarly, all nodes with closeness in the top percentiles can be considered to be central customers, and these should be included in a product and service diffusion campaign.

The descriptive analysis of the network measure also makes it possible to understand the network structure, its shape, and the distribution of the nodes and links in terms of social analysis or from the relationships perspective.

The following code shows the UNIVARIATE procedure running over the small dataset **calls**, computing statistics analysis and testing for the variables' **frequency** and **duration**.

```
proc univariate data=calls;
  var frequency duration;
run;
```

The outcome from the UNIVARIATE procedure is presented next, describing the moments for the variables assigned as well as some basic statistics, tests for location, and the respective quantiles.

The UNIVARIATE Procedure
Variable: frequency

Moments

N	11	Sum Weights	11
Mean	5.09090909	Sum Observations	56
Std Deviation	3.1130225	Variance	9.69090909
Skewness	0.99081448	Kurtosis	1.25105161
Uncorrected SS	382	Corrected SS	96.9090909
Coeff Variation	61.1486563	Std Error Mean	0.9386116

```
                    Basic Statistical Measures
            Location                    Variability
   Mean        5.090909    Std Deviation          3.11302
   Median      5.000000    Variance               9.69091
   Mode        3.000000    Range                 11.00000
                           Interquartile Range    4.00000


                  Tests for Location: Mu0=0

         Test        -Statistic        ---p Value---
   Student's t    t   5.423872    Pr > |t|    0.0003
   Sign           M   5.5         Pr >= |M|   0.0010
   Signed Rank    S   33          Pr >= |S|   0.0010


                  Quantiles (Definition 5)

                  Quantile          Estimate

                  100% Max              12
                  99%                   12
                  95%                   12
                  90%                    8
                  75% Q3                 7
                  50% Median             5
                  25% Q1                 3
                  10%                    2
                  5%                     1
                  1%                     1
                  0% Min                 1
```

The UNIVARIATE procedure allows useful statistical analyses over the social network of the outcomes, particularly over the network measures computed based on the distribution of nodes and links within the social structure. This sort of statistics analysis makes it possible to recognize the behaviors of average nodes inside the social network, how they relate to one another, and, mostly, which are the outlier nodes in terms of network metrics (which ultimately means those customers who hold more relevance or importance within the social structure according to the network measures).

GROUPING BASED ON RELATIONSHIP SIMILARITIES

Cluster analysis is most often deployed in order to draw useful information about groups of observations and to consider their similarities in some way. From a set of observations, with no premise or previous assumption, it is possible to group them according to their main characteristics and put them into distinct clusters, based on their average values.

In terms of business, Cluster analysis is quite important to segment customers according to their similarities or types of behavior. By putting customers into distinct clusters, it is possible to understand all different types of behaviors within the customer base and the distinctive characteristics, and, therefore, to establish more focused and appropriate campaigns, offerings, and relationship programs. Business actions can be more effective because of improved accuracy of targeting customers.

Most often clustering takes into consideration the demographic attributes of the customers and their usage in terms of products and services. In this way distinct groups of customers can be defined based on their characteristics and behavior. However, a different approach for clustering could use group segmentation based on customers' relationships. From the perspective of social network analysis, this is more intuitive than correlating customers based on their isolated demographic attributes. In social network analysis, the links among the customers—that is, what ties customers into groups of similarities are the relationships among them. Therefore, it is natural and appropriate to create groups of related customers—those who have connections—rather than creating clusters of customers based on similar demographic characteristics.

This type of cluster method creates groups of customers according to their relations within the social structure they belong to. By putting related customers into connected groups, it is possible to create a sense of community inside the social network. This concept can be quite useful when a target subset of customers needs to be created for particular campaigns, especially for campaigns involving diffusion or cascade effects, such as purchasing and churn processes. A community can hold few customers who are leaders and other customers who are followers. Based on the internal relationships among the customers in that particular community, it might not be necessary to contact all of them. Once they are connected, a small subset of influential customers may be contacted, and they can spread the message throughout the entire community.

In order to create the clusters based on the customers' relationships, it is important to identify not just those customers who are connected but also how strongly they are connected. What makes a customer stay closer to another is the strength of their relationship. Thus, by identifying the customers who are connected to one another and calculating the strength of those connections, clusters based on relationship similarity can be created. The clustering process will gather the closest customers into groups of similarities. The similarity in this particular case is the strength of the links.

The customers' positions in the social network and the thickness of their links can be calculated by using the multidimensional scaling approach, thereby establishing close coordinates for the close customers in terms of relationships. Those customers' coordinates can be used in a clustering model, such as MODECLUS, to produce the customers' segmentation based on the strength of the relationships among them.

By clustering the nodes inside a telecommunications network, specific groups of customers with similar behavior in terms of relationships can be recognized. Very often, the clustering technique is applied to group observations based on isolated attributes or characteristics. This means that the clustering process is grouping the customers based on who they are. The clustering process based on network measures allows the cluster to be based on how customers act or behave inside the social structure. It is a completely distinct way to analyze similarities of customers. This means that this particular clustering process groups customers based on how they behave. In terms of marketing, especially in designing sales campaigns, creating bundles and packages of products and services based on similar behaviors and preferences is a new perspective. Some attributes, especially demographics, are sometimes collected and made part of the customer profile, even though customers do not behave according to those attributes. However, the way the customers relate to one another tells a lot about their behavior and can lead to a more realistic Cluster analysis based on social interactions and structure.

Multidimensional Scaling

Multidimensional scaling (MDS) is a method of estimating coordinates for a set of objects in a space of specified dimensionality. These coordinates are estimated based on a set of variables according to their similarities or dissimilarities. The information used as input for MDS should represent a sort of distance among the observations.

Some additional models are able to compute distances among observations in a space of specified dimensionality, such as the DISTANCE procedure.

The input data for MDS are represented in a square matrix of similarities between a particular pair of observations. As a matter of fact, this is one of the most relevant constraints on the use of MDS. Even though the set of observations provided to compute the distances is not large, the square matrix required to serve as input dataset for MDS could be huge.

In telecommunications, for instance, it is not possible to calculate coordinates for an entire network. The square matrix would be an unfeasible table of distances between pairs of customers in the network structure. However, suppose, for example, that a very small community, or connected components, consists of just five customers: John, Karl, Eamonn, Kielty, and Eoin. Regardless of whether these friends call each other, a square matrix with 25 cells can be produced as input data for MDS. The missing values about the calls can be presented in that square matrix. If John calls Karl and Eamonn; Karl calls only Eamonn; Eamonn calls John, Karl, Kielty, and Eoin; Eoin calls John; and Karl and Kielty call only Eamonn, theoretically there are just 12 relations among them. However, in the square matrix, all these 12 relations can be presented, as well as the 5 auto-relations that do not exist (the diagonal) and all other 8 missing relations among those friends.

The square matrix assigned to this example is shown next. When a relation exists, the number of calls is presented in the square matrix. When there is no relation, a zero is included in the respective cell.

	John	Karl	Eamonn	Kielty	Eoin
John	—	9	3	0	7
Karl	9	—	6	0	0
Eamonn	3	6	—	8	5
Kielty	0	0	8	—	0
Eoin	7	0	5	0	—

This matrix of relations among those friends can be shown in a dataset as indicated by the following piece of code.

```
data calls;
input (John Karl Eamonn Kielty Eoin) (2.) @10 name
$6.;
datalines;
0         John
9 0         Karl
3 6 0       Eamonn
0 0 8 0   Kielty
7 0 5 0 0 Eoin
;
```

The MDS, therefore, can be called by this code:

```
proc mds data=calls level=absolute similar out=
outmds;
   id name;
run;
```

This code will produce the coordinates in relation to the friends' connections within this particular social structure. These coordinates can be used to plot the friends in a graph based on two dimensions.

The next code plots the friends in a spatial graph with two dimensions, which are the coordinates generated by MDS.

```
%plotit(data=outmds, datatype=mds, labelvar=name);
run;
```

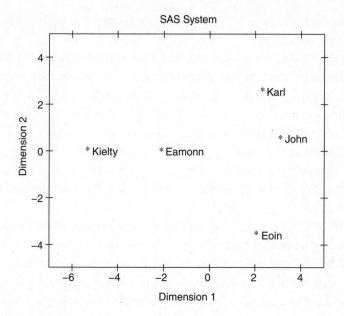

Figure 10.1 MDS Procedure Outcomes

Figure 10.1 shows the result of the MDS procedure by plotting the coordinates in a graph.

The option SIMILAR is used to compute the coordinates based on similarities rather than dissimilarities, which is the default. For this particular social structure, John and Karl talk to each other nine times, which is the greatest connection among the pair of friends. By using the option SIMILAR, John and Karl will be close in the graph. By omitting this option, the coordinates will be computed by dissimilarities and, therefore, John and Karl will be far away from each other.

Clustering

A clustering process is very often applied to gain some useful information about a particular set of observations. From the business perspective, using the telecommunications scenarios, the clustering procedure is suitable to group together customers with similar attributes in terms of characteristics and related usage behavior. In relation to the social network analysis methodology, a distinct type of clustering could be very useful. A set of clusters based on the strength of the relationships among the customers can show a different aspect of the network and how the customers are related to one another over the social structure.

The MODECLUS groups together a set of observations in a dataset by using different types of algorithms, most often based on nonparametric density estimates. The data provided as input can be numeric coordinates or distances. As described earlier, MDS is aimed at computing coordinates for a set of observations according to a particular attribute of similarity or dissimilarity. Using this approach, MDS should be performed first to compute the coordinates, and MODECLUS should be performed later to cluster the original set of observations.

MODECLUS produces as output a dataset containing some statistics and estimates for each observation that fit into the clusters established by the procedure. MODECLUS has several algorithms to find the best number of clusters according to the data available. One particularly useful approach is the *k-means* technique, a method based on least squares criterion. This method tends to fit roughly the same number of observations into the clusters established. The *k* factor in the *k-means* technique defines the number of clusters to be established in order to include all observations in the population.

The following code describes the use of MODECLUS based on the previous example, in relation to the social network about a particular group of friends.

```
proc modeclus data=outmds method=3 k=2 out=
outmodclu;
  var dim1 dim2;
  id name;
run;
```

The **outmds** dataset is the output of the MDS, containing the coordinates for John, Karl, Eamonn, Eoin, and Kielty. The dataset **outmodclu** is the output for the MODECLUS, containing the cluster in which each one of those friends was fitted in. MODECLUS has six methods to cluster the observations provided by the input dataset. The method most often used is method 1, which is based on the nearest neighborhood technique. However, for discrete coordinate data with only a few space values, method 3 is more suitable. Method 3 is also

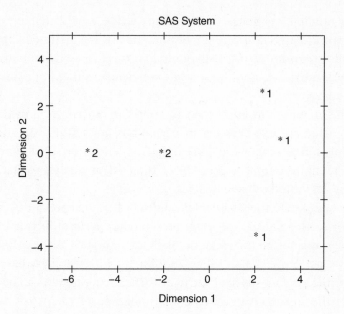

Figure 10.2 MODECLUS Procedure Outcomes

based on nearest neighborhood technique, with some details from method 1.

The following code plots the friends in a spatial graph with two dimensions, which are the coordinates generated by MDS but labeled with the cluster established by the MODECLUS.

```
%plotit(data=outmodclu, datatype=mds, labelvar=
cluster);
run;
```

Figure 10.2 shows the result of MODECLUS by plotting the friends in a graph. By the MODECLUS, John, Karl, and Eoin were fitted into cluster 1 whereas Kielty and Eamonn were fitted into cluster 2.

SUMMARY

The third part of this book describes the SAS capabilities to develop models in relation to social network analysis and analyzes the network outcomes. The first step is crucial, and it is the method for understanding customers' relationships inside a particular network. The second step is also very important, and it is the method of analyzing the network outcomes. In summary, the first step computes the network measures, and the second one evaluates them in a business perspective.

This chapter introduces the basic statistics procedures provided by SAS, including ones directed to simple but important tasks such as creating sorted datasets and creating frequencies of some subset of data, to more complex procedures directed at analyzing statically unique and multivariate variables.

In addition to the statistical procedures described previously, some further mathematical tasks were presented to perform further evaluations in relation to the social network analysis such as the MDS. The MDS is performed to calculate coordinates for customers based on similarities on some specific attributes. These coordinates can be used to plot the customers in a two-dimensional space.

Finally, the clustering methodology was briefly covered in order to present a technique to group customers according to a set of individual attributes. The difference here is the attributes that are used to cluster customers. Usually the attributes are personal and individual for each customer, describing characteristics of customers. In this case, the attributes used to cluster customers were network measures, grouping customers according to their relationship behaviors in the telecommunications network. In this approach, customers are clustered according to the way they relate to other customers instead of according to their isolated and individual attributes.

The statistical and mathematical procedures are useful to depict the network outcomes; they are quite fundamental to associate network results with business issues. As stated earlier, the first step of this process is very important—the social network analysis itself—but the second step is crucial—evaluation of network outcomes from the business perspective.

NOTE

1. *Base SAS Procedures Guide: Statistics Procedures* and *SAS/STAT User's Guide*.

CHAPTER 11

Overview of the Link Analysis Node

P art I of this book covered the theoretical foundation of social network analysis. Part II presented a case study in which most of this foundation was applied. Part III aims to describe how SAS® addresses this theory, including macros, procedures, and graphical tools used to deliver network analysis capabilities.

Part III starts by presenting the basic statistical capabilities provided by SAS. These procedures are used to prepare input datasets in order to compute the relevant network measures. Further analysis of the network measures can be performed by using the basic statistical procedures presented in Chapter 10. In summary, Chapter 10 presented the tools needed to prepare the input dataset for calculation of social network measures and the tools to analyze the outcomes of the network measures.

This chapter covers the main goal of this book in terms of the capability to perform social network analysis. SAS provides the link analysis node inside SAS® Enterprise Miner™, which contains the link analysis macros used in the case study presented in this book, such as **%_rawnodes**, **%_rawlinks**, **%_rawmerge**, **%_rawstats**, **%_centrality**, **%_prefix** and **%_final**.

This chapter is important in terms of practical tasks, describing SAS features in relation to social network analysis. These features allow analysts and data miners to study large amounts of data associated with telecommunications networks.

The case study presented in Part II used most of the link analysis macros contained in the link analysis node. By using the macros, the case study covers the most common social network analysis used to study telecommunications networks, computing the basic network measures and gathering useful information about customer relationship behavior.

As stated before, the first step is to perform a preliminary data analysis, an exploratory analysis of the available data in relation to a particular problem. In this step, the data should be prepared and changed as needed in order to calculate the network measures. In terms of social network analysis, this step is also related to the identification of data that will represent nodes and links that make up the social structure being studied. The second step consists of the calculation of the network measures, where all metrics about the nodes and links of the social structure are computed. These network measures are usually in relation to the distances between the nodes and the strength of the links, as well as detection of connected groups within communities. The third step consists of analysis of the outcomes. After computing the network measures, it is crucial to analyze the results in terms of the social structure, recognize which nodes and links have more value within the network, and identify how connected the network is.

The link analysis node belongs to the Explore category of the SAS SEMMA (Sample, Explore, Modify, Model, and Assess) data mining process. Link analysis consists of, among other procedures, the examination of linkages between effects in a complex system. Exploratory analysis typically employs a variety of techniques including OLAP (On-Line Analytical Processing), associations, sequences, clustering, and, most important graphics to examine the relationships between entities in a complex system. This sort of analysis aims to discover patterns of activity that can be used to derive useful conclusions and business information about a subject. Some applications include fraud detection, discovery of criminal networks, credit risk assessment, investigating insurance exaggeration, studying telephone traffic patterns, Web site structure and usage, database visualization, tracking product and service usage, and certainly social network analysis.

In this particular case, the telecommunications industry is the focus of this technique. Link analysis, as a part of the methodology of social network analysis, can be applied to traffic data in order to gather relevant information about customer behavior, especially in terms of customer relationships inside the network.

DEFINING NODES AND LINKS

SAS Enterprise Miner provides the link analysis node,[1] intended to recognize correlations among relationship's data. Also, information about relationships, or a particular social structure, can be provided through different formats of the link analysis node. This node recognizes the pattern of relationships within a network and highlights relevant characteristics in relation to them. In addition, the link analysis node is able to graphically plot the social structure in study, providing a useful method of visualization analysis. Finally, the link analysis node performs a clustering process, grouping all observations within a particular social structure into distinct groups according to a set of similarities.

There are a few different types of training methods provided by the link analysis node, usually based on two types of data, nodes and links. As in any social network analysis method, nodes are the observations within the data that represent an entity. Links are events that connect the entities within a network. For the links analysis node, each node should have a unique identification, and each link should contain two unique identifications, related to the identity of the node.

The link analysis node within Enterprise Miner can handle input data in three distinct ways: as raw data, matrix, and transactional data. Raw data are used when the input data are in a coordinate format. Matrix data are used when the input data are in a distance format, as in the MDS example presented in the previous chapter. Finally, transactional data are used when the input data are in a sequence format.

In order to use the raw data in a transactional format, the original data, such as those presented in Table 10.1, should be transformed into a transactional sequence by splitting the rows containing the columns **anumber** and **bnumber** into two distinct rows with the same identification **id**.

```
data cdrstrans;
  input id number frequency duration;
datalines;
1  84011853  12  166
1  84251406  12  166
2  84223809  3   34
2  75053478  3   34
3  23893455  5   57
3  23346789  5   57
4  87659384  6   52
4  45678769  6   52
5  34768900  3   23
5  34452311  3   23
6  98675723  4   43
6  45867399  4   43
7  34897599  2   9
7  37563544  2   9
8  23548766  1   34
8  45738239  1   34
9  88970403  5   59
9  87605767  5   59
10 45647867  7   26
10 99877659  7   26
11 26216897  8   64
11 26223099  8   64;
```

Figure 11.1 displays the graph plotting the network among phone numbers and the calls that connect them.

In this example, by using transactional data, the column **id** in the input dataset should be set to have a role as ID, and the column **name** should be set to have a role as TARGET.

It is also possible to configure which interaction terms will be used to include and exclude the link analysis. If a large number of input variables are presented, the list of variable interactions can be so huge

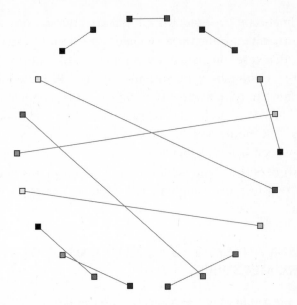

Figure 11.1 Graph Representing Calls among Phone Numbers by Using the Link Analysis Node

that the outcome of the link analysis graphs could be difficult to understand, especially when all of the nodes are included in the visualization.

When the input data are transactional, it is possible to configure the association or sequence data for the link analysis. If the transactional data have no sequence variable or timestamp, it is possible to define the minimum support threshold for association and the maximum number of items that are allowed in an association.

The "level of support" refers to how frequently a particular combination occurs within the transaction' database. Combinations that occur less frequently than a minimum support cannot be included as valid associations. The maximum number of items in a particular association defines how strong it can be in terms of correlation among the items. Few items can indicate a stronger association than a large number of items.

If the input data are transactional with sequence or timestamp variables, it is possible to configure how sequences are defined and used in the link analysis procedure.

It is important to note that in telecommunications scenarios, transactional data are the most suitable to be used in the Enterprise Miner. In that case, one single call should be split into two records. A call from customer A to customer B can be represented in a telecommunications network as a single CDR (call-detail record). However, in order to fit the original data into the link analysis node, this CDR should be split into two distinct records with the same ID, as explained before. When the size of a regular telecommunications network is usually large, for each original call it is necessary to split into two records, computational effort and storage could be a constraint.

USING LINK ANALYSIS MACROS TO CALCULATE THE NETWORK MEASURES

The issue presented in the previous section can be overcome by using the macros of the link analysis node in the Enterprise Miner. By using these macros, it is possible to define call by call, without needing to split the original records into two distinct ones.

Users of Enterprise Miner can also define the minimum item count that must be met in order to become a sequence. Set the permissible time range for a sequence to occur by using the time period setting. The length setting defines the permissible numerical range of items within a sequence.

In some cases, transaction data can contain very long sequences, which make it more difficult to analyze the original data by using the link analysis node. If these very long sequences are necessary, it is possible to configure how to create them and make the link analysis output easily understandable.

For example, imagine A, B, and C as elements in a long sequence. If the sequence is A, A, A, B, C, B, and so on, link analysis node allows the application of filters in order to reduce the logical sequence, such as A, B, C, B.

Users can define which sequences should appear in the link analysis sequence. Choices are sorted by processing order. Users can sort by reverse processing order or in descending count, sort the first *N* items, sort by using the first item in a sequence, or sort by using the last item in a sequence.

Finally, Enterprise Miner saves the output data in a matrix for further processing. This is important for the further analysis that should be performed over the outcomes dataset. The link analysis macros only calculate the network measures, describing the structure of the social network being studied and the main characteristics of the social relations. However, to understand what those measures mean, especially in terms of business, it is necessary to analyze the outcomes from the perspective of a particular business. The outcomes dataset should be analyzed according to a particular business event or corporate problem, such as customer churn, product diffusion, service acquisition, risk, fraud, and so on. The business objective should dictate the direction of the analysis, looking for average behavior, outliers, leaders, and followers, among other characteristics.

The outcome dataset, consisting of the network measures, can be understood as information about the network; regarding the telecommunications network, it can be the pattern of customer relationships. Analysis of the network measures based on a particular business perspective can be understood as business intelligence, applying the information gathered from the previous analysis to create a competitive advantage in terms of business.

Telecommunications networks are probably the simplest format used by the link analysis node in the Enterprise Miner. For regular purposes, a record containing the originating phone number and the destination phone number is enough to establish a social network. Additional information, such as frequency and total duration, can be included as a way to assign value to the links. The date of a call can also be included in the raw record. Telecommunications data seem to be the easiest information to use to build social networks.

CENTRALITY MEASURES

As stated in the first part of this book, the most important measures of a network are in relation to centrality. Distinct types of centralities can explain and depict the main characteristics of a network, according to its nodes and, mostly, its links. Centrality explains how influential, or important, the nodes that flow information through the network are. It can define the ones that affect other nodes, the nodes that follow the leaders, and so on. Centrality describes, based on a business perspective, the structure of the network from a customer behavior point of view.

The link analysis node automatically calculates centrality measures. Centrality measures format the weighting of the nodes and links inside a particular network. Centrality measures use social network concepts to measure the importance of a node within a network. The link analysis node in the Enterprise Miner can compute two types of centrality measures:

1. **First-order centrality:** Determines the importance of a node in a social network. This measure describes the number of other nodes directly connected to a specific node.

2. **Second-order centrality:** Determines not the direct importance of a particular node but the cumulative importance of the nodes that are connected to the specified one. This measure describes the number of nodes connected to the nodes directly related to the original node.

In the majority of social network studies, nodes that have more connections are considered more important. Depending on the business objective, the relevance of nodes can be measured in different ways. Considering the telecommunications industry, for instance, perhaps first-order centrality can determine the important nodes for a retention campaign or in any business action which relies on direct and strong relationships. Second-order centrality can determine the relevant nodes to participate in a bundle diffusion campaign or in any business action that relies on wide influence. Similarly, links with the highest traffic in a social network are considered the most important.

First- and second-order centrality can be measured with or without the use of weights:

■ **Weighted:** Nodes and connections are each ranked by importance in the diagram. The important weights (which are continuous and in the range of [0,1]) for nodes and connections are used in calculating centrality measures.

- **Unweighted:** All nodes are assumed to be equal in importance to all other nodes, and all connections are assumed to be equal in importance to all other connections. All nodes and connections are assigned weights of 1.

Weight measures compensate for the relative importance of nodes and links in a social network. The weighted first-order centrality value in undirected graphs uses relevance calculations by ranking the intermediate links among the nodes and assigning numeric values to them. The weighted first-order centrality value in undirected graphs is the C1 variable of the NODES dataset. The second-order centrality value in undirected graphs, when weighted, is the C2 variable of the NODES dataset. The unweighted first- and second-order centrality values are the C1u and C2u variables in the NODES dataset, respectively.

The case study presented in the earlier chapters used both social network concepts presented earlier, either in terms of centrality or of weights. First- and second-order centralities were used in conjunction to consider the directly correlated nodes, suitable for the business event in relation to churn, for instance; and the undirected correlated nodes (or correlated in a second order, with one or more nodes among the particular pair of nodes considered) suitable for the business event in relation to the bundle diffusion, for example.

Both nodes and links had their weights defined. The customers, or nodes, used customer segmentation as weight, and the calls, or links, used total duration and frequency weight. Different attributes can be used as a way to establish weights for nodes and links. Customer segment, average billing, customer score, and so on can be used as a method of distinguishing customers from one another. Similarly, number of calls, total duration, type of call, rate of call, or any combination of these attributes can be used to establish weight for links as a way to distinguish the relationships among the customers.

Enterprise Miner has been enhanced to handle variables with a large number of class variables. Analyzing datasets with class variables that have many levels can reach a limit of resources to overcome a time-consuming threshold. In order to properly handle datasets with many levels within class variables, Enterprise Miner uses a macro variable called DM_MAX_TRAIN_LEVELS.

When the link analysis node processes a dataset containing variables with a very large number of classes or levels, it compares the number of levels of class variables to two values, the link analysis node class variable threshold value of 100,000 and the value stored in the macro variable DM_MAX_TRAIN_LEVELS. If the number of levels in a class variable exceeds the higher of these two values, Enterprise Miner generates an error and halts the process flow.

To use the DM_MAX_TRAIN_LEVELS macro variable to control variable levels in transaction data with the link analysis node, the variable must be set to some value greater than 100,000. Users can set the macro variable to a new value of 120,000, for example, by entering the following line of code.

```
%let DM_MAX_TRAIN_LEVELS = 120000
```

Once again, centrality measures describe the main features of a social network. Considering a predefined business event, it is possible to understand the role of each node inside the network and how nodes connect to each other. The analysis of social networks, from a business point of view, can gather information not just about the customers but also about their relationships.

RESULT ANALYSIS

The link analysis node provides statistical procedures that allow network measures to be analyzed in terms of individual values, comparisons, distributions, and visualizations.

A relevant stage of network analysis is graph analysis, which enables one to understand the distribution of centrality measures in terms of the entire network. This sort of analysis defines a lot of relevant information about the network structure, its behavior, and how the nodes relate to each other by considering their small communities inside the network. Figure 11.2 is a histogram showing the distribution of links according to the nodes. This histogram is based on the network of relationships presented earlier. In that particular case, all

Link Distribution

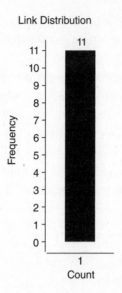

Figure 11.2 Histogram for the Result Analysis

phone numbers have just one call to another phone, meaning that all nodes have a frequency link of 1. The link distribution is not a distribution at all, because all points in the distribution have the same value.

In addition to link distribution, the link analysis node provides graphs in relation to link count, node distribution, node count, node distribution for C1/C1U/C2/C2U, node first-order weighted/unweighted centrality by count, node first-order weighted/unweighted centrality, node second-order weighted/unweighted centrality by count, and node second-order weighted/unweighted centrality.

The link analysis node also provides the code generated by the modeling process. By checking the code, you notice the set of SAS macros that perform the link analysis task behind the scenes. These macros can be run outside Enterprise Miner, but users need to completely understand the functionality, parameters, and results expected by running macros outside their environment.

Information about the log is also available in the Enterprise Miner for further analysis. The log information explains how the process works, how long it takes, the different stages of computing and analysis, and so on. Even a brief look at the log information can help you understand not just the link analysis process but also tasks, steps, and the results produced.

The output from the link analysis node also produces a summary of information in relation to the running process. This output is basically in database format, which can be used for further analysis inside or outside Enterprise Miner. The output summary contains information about the link and node datasets.

Additional content regarding the output results varies according to the type of data that were provided as the input dataset to the link analysis node.

- Transaction data for association
    - Associations by product
    - Link analysis nodes
    - Link analysis links
- Transaction data for sequences
    - Product sequences
    - Combined products
    - Link analysis nodes
- Link analysis links
- Raw data for interactions
    - Link analysis nodes
    - Link analysis links

All features used to analyze social networks provided by the link analysis nodes are useful and allow users to understand the shape and structure of the network as well as the influential nodes and strong links inside the network. The histograms and the metrics used to analyze the network outcomes should be used to identify which nodes are relevant to a particular business aspect and which links are important in terms of the relationships that make up telecommunications networks.

It is important to bear in mind the additional statistical analyses that should be performed on the network outcomes, such as those presented in the previous chapter. Unique and multiple variable analyses are very useful in understanding the individual network measures assigned to nodes and links and to recognize groups behavior. The distribution analysis can highlight the outlying nodes and links within the network and identify the nodes with high connections to average values, with the strongest links compared to regular connections. Outliers are also indicative of high usage and, in terms of telecommunications networks, are good indicators of influential customers.

SUMMARY

The link analysis node in the Enterprise Miner is a powerful tool to analyze data containing observations and the relationships among them. It is possible to define different types of input datasets, such as transaction, association, and sequence. These produce different results and hence distinct information and understanding about the network being studied.

The set of SAS macros used to perform the link analysis can also be used outside Enterprise Miner. However, by doing so, the user can miss a lot of useful functions used to configure the network and analyze the outcomes.

The case study presented in Part II was developed by using the link analysis macros, specifically because it needs to consider both directions of links. In telecommunications, both outgoing and incoming calls are very important and should be taken into consideration for network analysis. Also, because distinct types of calls, or links in terms of social network analysis, represent different values for the company, either according to their revenue or profit, it is necessary to examine those two types of links by using different weights.

When using the link analysis node inside the Enterprise Miner, the user is not allowed or, at least, not easily allowed to consider both directions of the links in a single network analysis. In order to establish distinct values for different types of links in the same network analysis, some additional data preparation must be performed.

The important message here is that, for most applications, or for general purposes, the link analysis node can deliver a great set of network analysis capabilities and also calculation of measures. For particular problems, the macros available in the link analysis node can address distinct business issues.

NOTE

1. *Data Mining Using SAS Enterprise Miner: A Case Study Approach*, 2nd ed. SAS Publishing, 2003.

CHAPTER **12**

Visualization Capabilities for Social Network Analysis

Probably the most important stage of the social network analysis process is the data analysis, particular the results analysis, which comes from computing the network measures. One of the final stages of analysis is data visualization of the network structure and, therefore, getting some insights from the way the network behaves and mostly from the relations among the nodes.

There are several different approaches to analyzing the outcomes from a social network, which, in practice, becomes analyzing the outcome data. According to the business issue, such as churn, sales, marketing, risk, fraud, and others, different sets of steps can take place. In order to analyze the social network measures for churn, it is important to consider the most influential customers and how they relate to the other customers. Are they influencers? If they decide to leave, what is their likelihood to lead their pairs on this same path? Some particular centrality measures can direct the analysis toward to this main goal. First- and second-order centralities as well as

255

eigenvector and some measures like influence based on page rank, authority, or hub can be deployed to define the best set of measures to identify central customers to be retained. However, if the subject is marketing and sales, a different set of network measures can be used to understand who the best customers are when those particular business issues are considered. Network measures, such as closeness and betweenness, can point to the most likely customers to better diffuse the information through the network, because those measures are about how central the customers are and how frequently they appear in the shortest path inside the network. For risk and fraud, an outlier analysis over the network measures can be applied in order to identify unusual occurrences in the entire set of observations.

In summary, despite the different types of approaches for analyzing network outcomes, one approach in particular can be very straightforward and intuitive: data visualization.

SAS® provides distinct methods to analyze data visually among tools, macros, and procedures. This chapter presents two methods that can be quite effective in terms of data visualization analysis. The first one is a tool called the SAS/GRAPH® Network Visualization Workshop, and the second one is a macro in the SAS/GRAPH® called %DS2CONST.

NETWORK VISUALIZATION WORKSHOP

SAS/GRAPH NV Workshop is a wonderful tool to analyze the social network structure, particularly in terms of the relationships among the nodes. Several different types of algorithms can be used to plot the social structure, which allows users to recognize the best shape of the network in the specific study.

NV Workshop is also good for medium to large networks, making it possible to analyze some particular subgraphs within the entire network. These subgraphs can be understood as small communities with the same interests, groups of customers with similar behavior, or circles of families and friends. By using the graphs provided by NV Workshop, it is possible to understand quickly the network structure and the relevant subnetworks within the social structure according to the nodes and links distribution.

NV Workshop handles two distinct types of datasets, one to load the nodes and another to load the links. It is also possible to create the nodes dataset from the links dataset by creating a unique intersection between the originating and destination nodes within the links dataset. Once the datasets in relation to the nodes and the links are loaded into the tool, it is possible to create different types of graphs, based on distinct algorithms that plot the nodes and their relationships by different shapes.

To create a network graph, NV Workshop manipulates the two datasets that constitute the network data. Each link connects two nodes, though a node can have multiple connecting links. There can be thousands of links connecting thousands of nodes. In addition to the social structure, NV Workshop provides some statistical graphs that are based on either node data or link data.

A node dataset defines the nodes in a network. In this dataset, each row represents one node in the network. At a minimum, the node dataset must contain a node identifier variable. A name can be specified to reference this variable when a set of data attributes is configured.

A link dataset defines the links in the network. In this dataset, each row represents one link between two nodes in the network. This dataset must contain at least two variables to identify the link. The values of these variables must be node identifiers; that is, the values for these variables must exist in the node identifier column in the corresponding node dataset. The variables perform a *from* and a *to* role, which means they define where the link starts and where it ends. It is also possible to specify the names for these variables when the dataset attributes are configured. Other variables in the link dataset can be used to store attributes related to the links. These variables can be used in several ways, such as to specify the color of the link and its thickness.

NETWORK GRAPHS

NV Workshop provides the following shapes of network structures to be plotted, as discussed in the NV Workshop user's guide.[1]

- **Circular:** The tool assigns all the connected nodes in the network within a circle.

- **Hierarchical:** The tool constructs a treelike depiction of the network and places nodes with more connecting links closer to the center.

- **Hexagonal:** The tool chooses nodes and attempts to distribute them evenly across one or more hexagons.

- **Multilevel force directed:** The tool combines graph partitioning and spring- or force-directed layout heuristics to determine node positions.

- **Fixed position:** The tool arranges nodes according to x and y coordinates that you supply with an SAS dataset.

An initial layout can be chosen to create the network graph. According to the type of input dataset, different layouts can be selected to plot the network structure, allowing distinct kinds of insights about the social relations being studied. However, users are able to manually manipulate the graphs in different perspectives, such as applying zoom over the network structure, selecting a particular portion of the network, and highlighting nodes and links for deeper analyses.

NV Workshop's users can use the tools available to manipulate the graphs in different perspectives. For example, they can zoom in on a portion of a graph or apply a magnifying lens to a network graph. This is useful when a particular investigation process has taken place. NV Workshop's users can also show the labels for particular nodes in a network graph. Once again, this feature is interesting for investigative purposes, highlighting particular nodes to understand their relationships.

DS2CONST MACRO

The Constellation applet provides interactivity for nodes and links graphs. The network assigned to these nodes and links can be shown in associative or hierarchical patterns. In addition, different colors, sizes, shapes, labels, line thicknesses, among others, can be associated to the nodes and links within the social network.[2]

The DS2CONST macro generates and formats an HTML output file and specifies the appearance and behavior of the nodes and the links diagram based on values in the dataset produced. This output file can be loaded in any Internet browser so users can analyze the social structure being studied. The Constellation applet also provides some interactive procedures so users can select some particular subset of nodes and links, change the general appearance of the graph, and zoom pieces of the structure, among other things.

The following code uses the DS2CONST macro to generate the social network based on the call-detail records presented earlier.

```
%ds2const(ndata=cdrstrans,
 ldata=cdrs,
 datatype=assoc,
 layout=auto,
 labels=y,
 linktype=line,
 nodeshap=circle,
 cnode=blue,
 clink=black,
 colormap=y,
 height=640,
 width=480,
 fntsize=10,
 archive=%str(constapp.jar,sas.graph.constapp.jar,
  sas.graph.nld.jar,sas.graph.j2d.jar),
 htmlfile="c:\calls.html",
 lfrom=anumber,
 lto=bnumber,
 lvalue=frequency,
 nid=number,
 nlabel=number,
 nvalue=duration);
```

Figure 12.1 shows the social network in relation to the previous code plotted and visualized by a regular Web browser.

The use of the macro DS2CONST can produce a dynamic graph that can be opened using a regular Web browser. The end user can

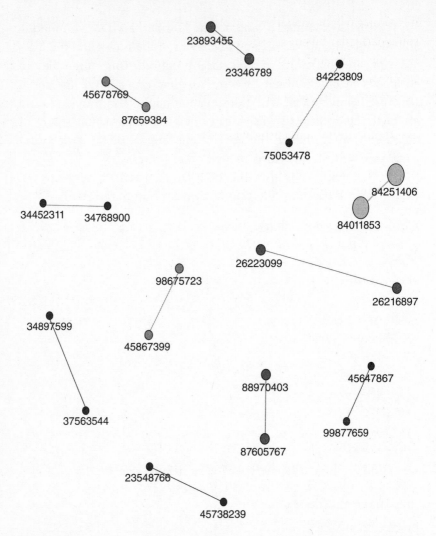

Figure 12.1 Graph Representing the Calls among Phone Numbers by Using the DS2CONST Macro

manipulate the graph over the browser, highlighting some particular nodes and links, fading others, producing a subset of the nodes and their relations, and visualizing the graph into different levels of zoom.

Most graphs in the case study presented in this book were produced by using the DS2CONST. Many subgraphs within the telecommunications network were generated in order to highlight some particular business issue. Once an influential customer is identified, the correlated customers connected to him, by first or second order, can be plotted in a graph to facilitate the visualization analysis. Also, a set of influential customers can be plotted with their correlated customers in order to find similar correlated customers or connections among the influential customers.

Analysis over time can also reveal how the social network is evolving, revealing its growth or reduction in a particular time frame. For instance, the analysis of influence assigned to the top 100 influential customers against a random 100 customers for the bundle diffusion event was produced by using the DS2CONST macro. Several graphs, month by month, for both subsets of customers (influential and random) were built, allowing an easy and simple comparison of the evolution of both small social communities. At the end of the process, after the six-month network analysis, it was easy to see how much larger the subnetwork assigned to the influential customers became in comparison with the subnetwork assigned to the random customers.

SUMMARY

Visualization methods are always quite useful to help statistical analyses. In terms of telecommunications, social networks can reach huge sizes, and preliminary analyses based on graph visualization can lead to future business applications.

Although the process of computing network measures is crucial—in fact, mandatory—and the process of comparing them with one another is important, the visualization process can lead the analyses toward a particular subject of interest.

Analyses of influential customers and their relationships within the telecommunications network can be easily understood by graphic visualization. Also, analyses over the correlated nodes for a subset of influential customers can be easily performed by graphs, allowing the identification of common connections and customers.

The visualization analysis can easily show fraudulent connections, eventually identifying a group or small community. This procedure can reveal the root of the fraud, avoiding useless effort and leakage of funds.

A plot of the entire telecommunications network can tell very little about social relationships. However, small subgraphs within groups of customers can reveal relevant connections in terms of relationships that can lead to some particular business actions.

Finally, a social network analysis over time can be accomplished by using a sequence of subgraphs, showing the evolution of groups of customers in relation to some particular business events. The analysis of sequences of subgraphs over time can reveal the social network evolution and, thereby, trends about some business events of interest.

NOTES

1. *SAS/GRAPH®: Network Visualization Workshop 2.1 User's Guide*, SAS Institute, 2009.

2. *SAS/GRAPH® 9.2 Reference*, 2nd ed., SAS Institute Inc, 2010.

CHAPTER **13**

A Note about
OPTGRAPH

S AS has delivered a very useful program in relation to social network analysis, called OPTGRAPH. This program includes a good range of calculations for network measurement, making it possible to compute metrics for distinct types of connections, such as the one used in the case study in Part II that is based on directed graphs, which are suitable for the telecommunications industry, and undirected graphs, which are suitable for most social network analysis scenarios, such as friendship, authorship, and employment, among others.

Considering both types of graphs, directed and undirected, OPT-GRAPH provides algorithms to calculate degree—including in-degree (input connections) and out-degree (output connections)—eigenvector, closeness, betweenness, influence (first and second order), authority, hub, pagerank, and cluster coefficient. All these network measures can be calculated considering a particular weight or not. The weights can be any business attribute recognized as relevant for the social network analysis. In terms of the telecommunications environment, weights in relation to the nodes can be a customer's value based on any corporate approach, a customer's segmentation, the average customer's billing, and so on. Weights in relation to the links can be the frequency of the calls, the average or total duration of the calls, the rate of the calls, the type of the calls (national, international, or local), and so on. Weights are useful to distinguish relevance and importance, either for nodes or for links, and, therefore, they are indicated to solve business problems by using social network analysis.

Also, OPTGRAPH provides an additional network measure computation, not in relation to the nodes, like the ones described previously, but in relation to the links. Node measures are aimed at depicting the actor's characteristics, such as customers, authors, and so on. However, characteristics in relation to the links are also useful in describing the relationships among the actors. Link betweenness is a network measure calculated to highlight the strength and importance of the connections. As for the nodes, link betweenness can be calculated by using weights to take into consideration any particular business attribute included in the social network analysis.

In addition to the network measure calculation for nodes and links, OPTGRAPH provides a range of further network analyses. These analyses are for the detection of groups of nodes based on distinct techniques; on straight connections, such as connected and biconnected components; or on similarities, such as communities. Communities can be detected by using particular parameters inside the code. Connected components and biconnected components can also be detected by using specific parameters in the OPTGRAPH code. Any type of recognition process for groups of nodes is very expensive in terms of computational effort. The larger the social network considered, the higher the time it takes to calculate these metrics. Communities, connected components, and biconnected components can be computed in parallel by using the OPTGRAPH code. Also, the outcomes from those network analysis techniques can be used in conjunction to gain distinct types of business information. In summary, each network measure, individually or as a group, can be used to interpret a different business perspective.

RECOGNIZING GROUPS INSIDE A NETWORK

Each one of the previously mentioned methods of grouping sets of nodes represents distinct types of analyses, as will be seen later. Connected components identify groups of nodes with strong relationships, where all nodes within the group are able to reach one another via some paths among them. Biconnected components identify groups of nodes with strong relationships, as in the connected components, but additionally, with a particular node, which if excluded from the group, becomes two connected components. The specific node that connects these two connected components is called the articulation point. It is one potential node to be analyzed more deeply in terms of social network analysis. Finally, communities are nodes with medium to strong relationships, in which some nodes within the group could not reach each other. Communities can be recognized by assessing the level of relationship strength, and this level determines how strong the relationships should be among the nodes. By using the maximum level of strength, for instance, the number of nodes within a network is the same as the number of connected components.

Connected Components

When there is a group of nodes in which each node can reach any other, this group of nodes is called connected components. The connected components can be understood as a very close group of nodes, separated from the rest of the network, in which each node is reachable by any other node.

Procedure OPTGRAPH produces an output dataset containing a unique identification for each connected component found in the input data, and it assigns a specific identification to each node within the network.

Biconnected Components

One other important concept in relation to the social network analysis approach is the biconnected component. When there is a connected component that includes a particular node that, if removed, splits this connected component into two distinct connected components, the original connected component can be considered a biconnected component. The specific node that is removed to split the original connected component in two is called the articulation point.

Procedure OPTGRAPH produces an output dataset containing a unique identification for each biconnected component found, assigning this identification to each link in the network. Unlike the connected component, the biconnected component is represented by a node that connects two connected components. Therefore, the biconnected component is identified in the links dataset, and the articulation points—the nodes that connect the connected components—are identified in the nodes output dataset.

Communities

The third relevant concept of the social network analysis approach is about communities. Some techniques are put in place to identify communities inside the entire network. Unlike the connected components, which are isolated from the rest of the network, a community can hold some nodes that have connections outside the community, as branches or arms outside the internal community. In this way, a particular community can be connected with other communities through more than one node. Communities inside networks can be understood as clusters inside populations. The study of the communities can raise some important points in relation to the network's behavior and enables specific analyses in terms of suspicious individuals inside them.

As with the connected components, OPTGRAPH produces an output dataset containing a unique identification for each community found, assigning this identification to each node in the network. The major difference is that OPTGRAPH detects communities at different levels. Then additional output datasets are produced when a community is detected. The new output is delivered, noting each level of community and the number of nodes identified for it. In the nodes output dataset, new columns are included, according to the number of levels of community detected. Each column signifies the unique identification of the community of which the node is part. For instance, in the case of a three-level community, the nodes output dataset has three additional columns, identifying each node, the community identification for level 1, level 2, and finally for level 3.

The higher the level, the weaker the connection required among nodes to establish the communities; therefore, the lower the number of communities, the higher the number of nodes inside communities. For example, level 1 could recognize 1,000 communities, level 2 could recognize 600 communities, and level 3 could recognize 200 communities. The 1,000 communities of level 1 generally include, on average, fewer nodes than the nodes in level 3, which contains 200 communities.

INDIVIDUAL MEASURES FOR THE NETWORK

This section describes the network measures in relation to the nodes provided by OPTGRAPH. The individual network measures assigned to the nodes take into consideration information about the links in addition to some individual attributes.

Degree

Degree represents the number of connections a particular node has. In a directed graph, where the direction of the node is relevant, there is differentiation between the *in-degree*—that is, the number of links a particular node receives—and the *out-degree*—the number of links a particular node sends. The sum of in-degree and out-degree gives the degree measure. The measure of degree is calculated based on directed graphs.

Eigenvector

Eigenvector represents the measure of importance in relation to a particular node inside the network. Relative scores for all nodes are computed based on their connections, considering frequency and strength. Also, the eigenvector also considers the importance of the nodes inside the network. This importance is also based on the number of connections. The eigenvector is a recursive algorithm that calculates the importance of a particular node, considering the importance of all nodes and all connections. The measure of eigenvector is calculated based on undirected graphs.

Closeness

Closeness represents the mean of the geodesic distances (shortest path in the social network perspective) between some particular node and all other nodes connected with it. This measure describes the average distances between one node and all other nodes connected with it. It can be understood as how long a message will take to spread inside the network from a particular node. The measure of closeness is calculated based on undirected graphs.

Betweenness

Betweenness represents how many short paths a particular node makes. Nodes that occur on many short paths between other nodes have higher betweenness than those that do not. Betweenness can be understood as how central a node is, considering the entire network and all connections in it. The measure of betweenness is calculated based on undirected graphs.

Influence 1

Influence 1 represents first-order centrality for a particular node, which indicates how many other nodes it is directly connected to. This measure can be understood as how many "friends" a particular node has. It describes how many other nodes can possibly be directly influenced by a particular node. The measure of influence 1 is calculated based on undirected graphs.

Influence 2

Influence 2 represents second-order centrality for a particular node, which indicates how many other nodes the node to which it is directly connected are directly connected. This measure can be understood as how many "friends" my "friends" have. It describes how many nodes can possibly be influenced by some particular node. The measure of influence 2 is calculated based on undirected graphs.

Authority

Authority is a measure of importance similar to eigenvector, but it is calculated based on directed graphs. It assigns relative scores to all nodes according to the nodes' absolute scores inside the network. The concept here is that connections with important nodes are also important and increase the score of the relative nodes. Authority is basically represented considering the income connections and could be understood as a node which many other nodes are pointed to. The measure of authority is calculated based on directed graphs.

Hub

Hub is very similar to the measure of authority. It assigns relative scores to all nodes according to the nodes' scores inside the network. The concept here is that connections with important nodes are also important and increase the nodes' scores relatively. Hub is represented using the outgoing connections, and it can be understood as a node that points to a relatively large number of authorities. The measure of authority is calculated based on directed graphs.

Pagerank

Pagerank is based on the Google's PageRank algorithm. It is a variant of the eigenvector measure of importance, and, although both types of graphs could be applied to it, it is more effectively represented with directed graphs. Pagerank calculates the importance of a particular node based on the relevance of its interactions. Hub and authority measures consider the importance of the nodes that are connected, and Pagerank considers the importance of the connections themselves.

Cluster Coefficient

The cluster coefficient represents the number of existing connections that a particular node can have from all possible connections in its neighborhood. This measure describes the relative strength of connectivity for a particular node, presenting the total number of possible connections a node can have in relation to the number of relationships that the node currently has. The measure of cluster is calculated based on undirected graphs.

The description about the network measure in relation to the links provided by OPTGRAPH is presented next. Like the network nodes measures, the links measure takes into consideration the information within the links to compute its own metric.

Link Betweenness

Link betweenness represents how many short paths a particular link has within the network. Links that have a short path between nodes have higher link betweenness than those links that do not have a short path between nodes. Link betweenness can be understood as how central a link is considered in the entire network and to all possible connections. It also can be understood as how a particular link makes a node central within the network.

The measure of link betweenness is calculated based on undirected graphs.

SUMMARY

Procedure OPTGRAPH was released in early January 2010, and some update patches were provided by the time this book went to press. This procedure remained closed to regular SAS® users for a while. At the time of this writing, it is delivered as part of the SNA Server.

The overall network analysis capabilities delivered by procedure OPTGRAPH can be applied to different circumstances, different industries, and distinct types of business problems. The set of network measures that can be computed by OPTGRAPH allows several different approaches to social network analysis, making it possible to understand a wide range of social networks. Companies in industries like telecommunications, insurance, banking, and retail, among others, can use social network analysis to understand more than just their customers but their customers' relations. Relationships are probably one of the best attributes by which to understand customers' behavior, no matter the type of network. Relationships tell more about how customers behave inside a social network than do any other individual attribute.

Finally, social network analysis is a very good approach to understand customer behavior, and should be used as a score, flag, or attribute to highlight some set of customers tied by a particular interest, to target a subset of customers for a specific campaign, or even to gain some business information about a certain topic. Social network analysis is not a surrogate analytical model for companies but instead a complementary analytical mode. As a matter of fact, in an analytical process, several different scores should be mixed in order to better analyze a particular point of interest.

Bibliography

Backstrom, L., D. Huttenlocher, J. Kleinberg, et al. *Group Formation in Large Social Networks: Membership, Growth, and Evolution.* Philadelphia: KDD '06, 2006.

Barabási, A. L. *Linked: The New Science of Networks.* New York: Basic Books, 2002.

Baxter, N., D. Collings, and I. Adjali. "Agent-Based Modeling—Intelligent Customer Relationship Management." *BT Technology Journal* 21(2) (2003): 126–132.

Borgatti, S. P., A. Mehra, D. J. Brass, and G. Labianca. "Network Analysis in the Social Sciences." *Science* 323(5916) (2009): 892–895.

Breiger, R. L. "The Analysis of Social Networks." In *Handbook of Data Analysis,* edited by Melissa Hardy and Alan Bryman, 505–526. London: Sage Publications, 2004.

Carrington, P. J., J. Scott, and S. Wasserman. *Models and Methods in Social Network Analysis.* Cambridge: Cambridge University Press, 2005.

Culotta, A. *Maximizing Cascades in Social Networks: An Overview.* Amherst, MA: University of Massachusetts, 2003.

Dasgupta, K., R. Singh, B. Viswanathan, et al. "Social Ties and Their Relevance to Churn in Mobile Telecom Networks." EDBT '08. Nantes, France, ACM, 2008.

Degenne, A., and M. Forse. *Introducing Social Networks.* Thousand Oaks, CA: Sage Publications, 1999.

Emir Bayer, M., and J. Goodwin. "Network Analysis, Culture and the Problem of Agency." *American Journal of Sociology* 99(6) (1994): 1411–1454.

Fleming, L., A. Marin, J. McPhie, et al. "Why the Valley Went First: Aggregation and Emergence in Regional Collaboration Networks." In *Market Emergence and Transformation,* edited by John Padgett and Walter Powell. Cambridge, MA: MIT Press, forthcoming.

Hanneman, R. A., and M. Riddle. *Introduction to Social Network Methods.* Riverside, CA: University of California, 2005. Available at http://faculty.ucr.edu/~hanneman/nettext/Introduction_to_Social_Network_ Methods.pdf (accessed November 3, 2010).

Hill, S., F. Provost, and C. Volinsky. "Network-Based Marketing: Identifying Likely Adopters via Consumer Networks." *Statistical Science* 21(2) (2006): 256–276.

Katz, J., Martin Sylvan, and R. Ben. "What Is Research Collaboration?" *Research Policy* 26 (1997): 1–18.

Kempel, D., and J. Kleinberg. "Maximizing the Spread of Influence through a Social Network." SIGKDD '03. Washington, DC, 2003.

Kempe, D., J. Kleinberg, and E. Tardos. *Influential Nodes in a Diffusion Model for Social Networks*, edited by L. Caires et al. 1127–1138. Berlin: Springer-Verlag, 2005.

Knoke, D., and S. Yank. *Social Network Analysis*. Thousand Oaks, CA: Sage Publications, 2007.

Kretschmer, H. "Author Productivity and Geodesic Distance in Bibliographic Co-authorship Networks, and Visibility on the Web," *Scientometrics* 60(3) (2004): 409–420.

Laumann, E. O., P. V. Marsden, and D. Prensky. *The Boundary Specification Problem in Network Analysis, Research Methods in Social Network Analysis*. New Brunswick, NJ: Transaction Publishers, 1992.

Leskovec, J., L. A. Adamic, and B. A. Huberman. "The Dynamics of Viral Marketing." ACM Transactions on the Web, May 2007.

Mahlck, P., and O. Persson. "Socio-Bibliometric Mapping of Intradepartamental Networks." *Scientometrics* 49(1) (2000): 81–91.

Marin, A., and B. Wellman. *Social Network Analysis: An Introduction*, June 2009. Available at http://www.hsph.harvard.edu/massconect/files/social_ network_analysis._an_introduction.pdf (accessed October 26, 2010).

Nanavati, A., R. Singh, D. Chakraborty, et al. "Analyzing the Structure and Evolution of Massive Telecom Graphs." *IEEE Transactions on Knowledge and Data Engineering*, 2008.

Newman, M. E. J. "From the Cover: The Structure of Scientific Collaboration Networks." *Proceedings of the National Academy of Sciences of the United States of America* 98 (2001): 404–409.

Onnela, J.-P., J. Saramäki, J. Hyvönen, et al. "Structure and Tie Strengths in Mobile Communication Networks." *Proceedings of the National Academy of Sciences of the United Sates of America* 104(2007): 7332–7336.

Otte, E., and R. Rousseau. "Social Network Analysis: A Powerful Strategy, also for Information Sciences." *Journal of Information Science* 28(6) (2002): 441–453.

Pandit, V., N. Modani, and S. Mukherjea. "Extracting Dense Communities from Telecom Call Graphs." *Proceedings of the Third International Conference on Communication Systems Software and Middleware* (2008): 82–89.Pinheiro, C. A. R.. "Social Network Analysis Evaluating the Customers Influence Factor Over Business Events in Telco." In *International Journal of Artificial Intelligence & Applications* (2010): Vol. 1, No. 4, 122–131.

Pinheiro, C. A. R., and M. Helfert. "Creating a Customer Influence Factor to Decrease the Impact of Churn and to Enhance the Bundle Diffusion in Telecommunications Based on Social Network Analysis." SAS Global Forum, 2010.

Pinheiro, C. A. R.. "Highlighting Unusual Behavior in Insurance Based on Social Network Analysis" SAS Global Forum, 2011.

Pinheiro, C. A. R., and M. Helfert. "Customer's Relationship Segmentation Driving the Predict Modeling for Bad Debt Events." In User Modeling, Adaptation and Personalization, Lectures Notes in Computer Science (2009): Vol. 5535 319–324 Springer.

Pinheiro, C. A. R., and M. Helfert. "Mixing Scores from Artificial Neural Network and Social Network Analysis to Improve the Customer Loyalty Process." *Second International Workshop on Data Management for Wireless and Pervasive Communications* (2009).

Pinheiro, C. A. R., and M. Helfert. "Neural Networks and Social Network to Enhance the Customer Loyalty Process." In *Innovations and Advances in Computer Sciences and Engineering* (2010): 91–96, edited by Tarek Sobh. New York: Springer, 2010.

Saito, K., R. Nakano, and M. Kimura. "Prediction of Information Diffusion Probabilities for Independent Cascade Model." In *KES 2008, Part III*, edited by I. Lovrek, R. J. Howlett, and L. C. Jain, 67–75. Berlin: Springer-Verlag, 2008.

SAS Institute Inc. *Base SAS 9.2 Procedures Guide: Statistics Procedures*, Third Edition. SAS Publishing, 2010.

SAS Institute Inc. *SAS/STAT 9.2 User's Guide*. SAS Publishing, 2008.

SAS Institute Inc. *Data Mining Using SAS Enterprise Miner: A Case Study Approach*, Second Edition. SAS Publishing, 2003.

SAS Institute Inc. *SAS/GRAPH: Network Visualization Workshop 2.1 User's Guide*. SAS Publishing, 2009.

SAS Institute Inc. *SAS/GRAPH 9.2 Reference*, Second Edition. SAS Publishing, 2010.

Seshadri, M., S. Machiraju, and S. Ashwin. "Mobile Call Graphs: Beyond Power-Law and Lognormal Distributions." KDD '08, ACM SIGKDD (2008): 596–604.

Simmel, G. *The Sociology of Georg Simmel*. Glencoe, IL: Free Press, 1950.

Simmel, G. "The Web of Group Affiliations." In *Conflict and the Web of Group Affiliations*, edited by Kurt Wolff, 125–195. Glencoe, IL: Free Press, 1955.

Simmel, G., D. N. Levine, M. Janowitz, and Georg Simmel. *On Individuality and Social Forms: Selected Writings*. Chicago: University of Chicago Press, 1972.

Travers, J., and S. Milgram. "An Experiment Study of the Small World Problem." *Sociometry* 32(4) (Dec. 1969): 425–443.

Wasserman, S., and K. Faust. *Social Network Analysis*. Cambridge: Cambridge University Press, 1994.

Watts, D. *Small Worlds*. Princeton, NJ: Princeton University Press, 1999.

Watts, D. *Six Degrees*. New York: Norton, 2003.

Watts, D., P. Dodds, and M. Newman. "Identity and Search in Social Networks." *Science* 296 (2002): 1302–1305.

Wellman, Barry. "Structural Analysis." In *Social Structures*, edited by Barry Wellman and S. D. Berkowitz, 19–61. Cambridge: Cambridge University Press, 1988.

Wellman, B., and S. Wortley. "Different Strokes from Different Folks." *American Journal of Sociology* 96(3) (1990): 558–588.

Wellman, B. "The Community Question." *American Journal of Sociology* 84 (1979): 1201–1231.

Wellman, B., and K. Frank. "Network Capital in a Multi-level World." In *Social Capital*, edited by Nan Lin, Karen Cook, and Ronald Burt, 233–273. Chicago: Aldine DeGruyter, 2001.

Wellman, B., B. Hogan, K. Berg. "Connected Lives: The Project." In *Networked Neighborhoods*, edited by Patrick Purcell, 157–211. Guilford, UK: Springer, 2006.

Wellman, B., and A. Marin. "Social Network Analysis: An Introduction," Forthcoming in *Handbook of Social Network Analysis*, edited by Peter Carrington and John Scott. London: Sage, 2011.

Wortman, J. "Viral Marketing and the Diffusion of Trends on Social Networks." University of Pennsylvania Department of Computer and Information Science, Technical Report No. MS-CIS-08-19, 2008.

Yoshikane, F., and K. Kageura. "Comparative Analysis of Co-authorship Networks of Different Domains: The Growth and Change of Networks." *Scientometrics* 60(3) (2004): 435–446.